FOURTH EDITION

Weight Training

STEPS TO SUCCESS

Thomas R. Baechle

Roger W. Earle

HUMAN KINETICS

Library of Congress Cataloging-in-Publication Data

Baechle, Thomas R., 1943-
  Weight training : steps to success / Thomas R. Baechle, Roger W. Earle. -- 4th ed.
    p. cm.
  Includes bibliographical references.
  ISBN-13: 978-1-4504-1168-4 (soft cover)
  ISBN-10: 1-4504-1168-1 (soft cover)
  1. Weight training. I. Earle, Roger W., 1967- II. Title.
  GV546.3.B34 2012
  613.713--dc23

                        2011026944

ISBN-10: 1-4504-1168-1 (print)
ISBN-13: 978-1-4504-1168-4 (print)

Copyright © 2012, 2006, 1998 by Human Kinetics, Inc.
        © 1992 by Leisure Press

The web addresses cited in this text were current as of August 2011, unless otherwise noted.

Acquisitions Editor: Justin Klug; **Managing Editor:** Coree Clark; **Assistant Editor:** Elizabeth Evans; **Copyeditor:** Mary Rivers; **Permissions Manager:** Martha Gullo; **Graphic Designer:** Keri Evans; **Cover Designer:** Keith Blomberg; **Photographer (cover):** © Human Kinetics; **Photographs (interior):** © Human Kinetics; figures 1.1*b* and 1.7*a-b* courtesy of Roger Earle; **Visual Production Assistant:** Joyce Brumfield; **Photo Production Manager:** Jason Allen; **Art Manager:** Kelly Hendren; **Associate Art Manager:** Alan L. Wilborn; **Illustrations:** © Human Kinetics; **Printer:** United Graphics

Human Kinetics books are available at special discounts for bulk purchase. Special editions or book excerpts can also be created to specification. For details, contact the Special Sales Manager at Human Kinetics.

Printed in the United States of America   10 9 8 7 6 5 4 3 2 1

The paper in this book is certified under a sustainable forestry program.

Human Kinetics
Website: www.HumanKinetics.com

United States: Human Kinetics
P.O. Box 5076
Champaign, IL 61825-5076
800-747-4457
e-mail: humank@hkusa.com

Canada: Human Kinetics
475 Devonshire Road Unit 100
Windsor, ON N8Y 2L5
800-465-7301 (in Canada only)
e-mail: info@hkcanada.com

Europe: Human Kinetics
107 Bradford Road
Stanningley
Leeds LS28 6AT, United Kingdom
+44 (0) 113 255 5665
e-mail: hk@hkeurope.com

Australia: Human Kinetics
57A Price Avenue
Lower Mitcham, South Australia 5062
08 8372 0999
e-mail: info@hkaustralia.com

New Zealand: Human Kinetics
P.O. Box 80
Torrens Park, South Australia 5062
0800 222 062
e-mail: info@hknewzealand.com

FOURTH EDITION

Weight Training

STEPS TO SUCCESS

Contents

Climbing the Steps to Weight Training Success

Get ready to climb a staircase—one that will lead you to become stronger, more fit, and more knowledgeable about weight training. You cannot leap to the top, but you can reach it by climbing one step at a time.

Research by sporting goods manufacturers acknowledges that weight training, with over 50 million participants, is the single most popular type of fitness training activity in the United States. The reason for this popularity is quite simple. The results are quick, and they dramatically contribute to improved strength, muscle tone, body reproportioning, appearance, and health. Unfortunately, not many books on the subject are written so that an inexperienced person can easily understand the information and use it with confidence. Terminology is often confusing, explanations are unclear, and readers are expected to understand too much information at one time. The approach taken in this book does not assume that one explanation or illustration is enough to allow readers to become knowledgeable about and skilled at weight training concepts and exercises. Instead, carefully developed procedures and drills accompany each step and provide you with ample practice and self-assessment opportunities.

This book focuses on two primary areas. First, it helps you learn common weight training exercises that are used in a well-balanced training program. Second, it provides the knowledge you need to design your own weight training program. We begin by describing how your body will respond to weight training and the importance of good nutrition. These discussions are followed by important information regarding how to prepare to start training and how to safely use various types of weight training equipment. Building on this foundation of information, we introduce basic lifting and spotting techniques and exercises and follow them with descriptions of techniques specific to the exercises recommended in this book. Great care has been taken to introduce new information and higher training intensities gradually. For instance, you will start out lifting lighter training loads (weight) while you are learning proper exercise technique. Later, after you have mastered the exercises, you will progress to heavier loads. Organizing and sequencing exercises and loads in this manner offers you the best opportunity to learn how to perform the exercises without fear of injury, and it provides an excellent opportunity to realize dramatic improvements in muscular endurance, strength, body composition, and your overall fitness level. Exercises designed to develop a specific muscle area are described in steps 4 to 9 and include additional exercises that can be added if you desire more challenging workouts. These additional exercises are noted with an asterisk(*) in the text and tables and a ✳ in the figure captions. If you have previous experience in weight training, the total-body exercises presented in step 10 will complement those described in steps 4 to 9. Completing all of the steps leading up to step 14 prepares you for the exciting challenge of designing your own weight training program.

You will find that the practice procedures and drills included in this text are unique and provide an effective approach to explaining and understanding the content and skills of weight training. The step-by-step explanations and self-assessment activities make this book the easiest guide to weight training.

In addition, this new edition includes an expanded discussion of the physiological effects of training, more exercises, a new section on core training, updated references, and exciting variations of the previous practice and learning activities by making them more streamlined and easier to use. Also, new exercises have been added, and they will challenge you to develop a higher level of skill, making this text appropriate for those new to weight training as well as those who are more experienced and better trained.

Each of the 14 steps you will take is an easy transition from the one that precedes it. The first 3 steps of the staircase provide a solid foundation of basic skills and concepts. As you progress, you will learn to complete a basic training program in a safe and time-efficient manner. You will also learn when and how to make needed changes in program intensity. As you near the top of the staircase, you will find that you have developed a sense of confidence in your weight training skills and knowledge of how to design programs that meet your specific needs. Perhaps most important, you will be pleased with your improved fitness and energy levels and how your body's appearance has changed.

To understand how to build your training around steps 1 to 3, familiarize yourself with the concepts and information presented in the sections that lead up to step 1. They provide information that will help you become aware of how your body reacts and adapts to weight training, will teach you the importance of proper nutrition, and will provide the keys to making every minute that you invest in training pay off.

The *Steps to Success* method provides a systematic approach to executing and teaching weight training techniques and designing programs. Approach each of the steps in this way:

1. Read the explanation of what is covered in the step, why the step is important, and how to execute or perform the tasks described in each step; these may be a basic skill, a concept, an approach, or combination of all three.

2. Follow the technique photos that show and explain exactly how to position your body so that you will perform each exercise correctly. The photos show each phase of the exercise. For each exercise in the basic program, you typically will be instructed to select one exercise from three choices: one free-weight and two machine exercises. In step 9, you will select from body-weight and machine exercises and in step 10, from free-weight exercises only.

3. Look over the missteps section after each exercise description and use this information to make needed corrections for how you perform exercises before moving to the practice procedures and drills at the end of each step.

4. The practice procedures and drills help you improve your skills through repetition and purposeful practice. Read the directions and the success checks for each drill and quiz. Practice accordingly and record your scores.

The drills progress from easy to difficult, so be sure to achieve a satisfactory level of performance before moving on to the next drill. This sequence is designed specifically to help you achieve continual success. At the end of each step, total your success check scores and determine your mastery of the material before moving on to the next one.

After you have selected an exercise for each body area and have mastered the necessary skills in steps 4 to 9, you are ready to start training in step 11. Advanced lifters should consider adding one or more exercises presented in step 10 before moving to step 11.

In step 11, the real fun begins. You don't have to determine which exercises to include or the number of sets and repetitions to perform; those decisions have already been made. All you need to do is follow the program as it is described.

Steps 12 and 13 introduce you to the logic—the whys and hows—behind the program in step 11. These steps include formulas and guidelines to assist you in the difficult task of determining warm-up and initial training loads and making needed adjustments to them. The helpful instructions, as well as examples and self-assessment opportunities (answers included), will prepare you for the challenge of designing your own program.

Step 14 takes you through the process of designing a program based on all of the previous steps. It is especially valuable if you are helping students design their own programs or if you are a personal trainer who designs programs for clients.

Good luck on your step-by-step journey toward developing a strong, healthy, attractive body, a journey that will be confidence building, rich in successes, and fun!

Acknowledgments

We would like to thank several people at Human Kinetics who influenced the development and completion of this book. Jason Muzinic, the director of the consumer division, who simply *trusted* us to get this edition done and selected it to be one of the first full-color versions of the Steps to Success series; Justin Klug, the acquisitions editor, who inherited this edition and then stayed true to the original scope of the book; and Coree Clark, the managing editor, who accepted the manuscript just about "as is" and always had good news about the book's progress along the way.

Most important have been our families—Susie, Todd, and Clark Baechle and Tonya, Kelsey, Allison, Natalia, and Cassandra Earle—who have provided us with the support and time we needed to complete this edition.

Fundamentals of Weight Training

When weight training occurs on a regular basis and is accompanied by sensible eating choices, the systems of the body change in positive ways. Muscles become stronger, better toned, and less susceptible to fatigue with each additional session of training. The neuromuscular (nerve–muscle) system learns to work in better harmony. That is, the brain learns to selectively recruit specific muscles, and the types of muscle fibers within them, to handle the loads used for the weight training exercises. The neuromuscular system also improves its ability to control the speed of movement and follow the correct movement patterns that are required in each exercise.

This section will help you understand how your body responds physiologically to weight training. You will learn more about your nutrition needs, issues surrounding weight gain and weight loss, the importance of rest, and concerns about equipment and safety.

UNDERSTANDING MUSCLES

Muscle tissue is categorized into three types: smooth, skeletal, and cardiac (figure 1). In an activity like weight training, the development of skeletal muscles is of paramount importance. As shown in figure 2, skeletal muscles (sometimes referred to as *striated* muscles) are attached to the bone via tendons. Skeletal muscles respond to voluntary stimulation from the brain.

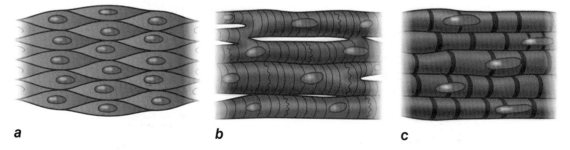

a   b   c

Figure 1   Three types of muscle tissue: *(a)* smooth; *(b)* skeletal; *(c)* cardiac.

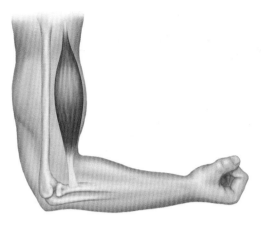

Figure 2 The biceps muscle converges into a tendon and attaches to the radius bone in the forearm.

Although many of the more than 400 skeletal muscles are grouped together, they function either separately or in concert with others. Which and how many skeletal muscles become involved when someone performs an exercise depend on the exercise selected and the techniques used for the exercise. The width of the grip, stance of the feet, and the path through which the bar moves determine which muscles are recruited and to what extent they are stressed. Located throughout this text are photos and explanations of the muscle groups that are trained during a workout.

Isometric, concentric, and eccentric are the three different types of muscle actions that can occur during weight training. The term *isometric,* or static, refers to situations in which tension develops in a muscle but no observable shortening or lengthening occurs. Sometimes during a repetition a *sticking point* is reached and a momentary pause in movement occurs. The action of the muscle(s) at this point would be described as being static.

Concentric muscle action occurs when tension develops in a muscle and the muscle shortens. For example, when the biceps muscle moves the barbell toward the shoulders in the dumbbell curl exercise shown in figure 3*a*, the muscle's action is described as concentric. The action of a muscle during concentric activity is also referred to as *positive work.*

The term *eccentric* is used to describe muscle action in which tension is present, but the muscle lengthens instead of shortens. Using the biceps curl as an example again, once the dumbbell begins the lowering phase (figure 3*b*), the eccentric action of the biceps controls the descent of the dumbbell. There is still tension in the biceps muscle; the difference (as compared to the concentric action) is that the muscle fibers

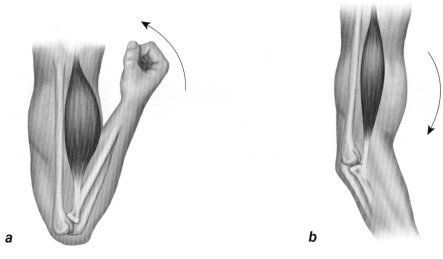

a   *b*

Figure 3 *(a)* During the concentric (upward) phase of the biceps curl, the muscle shortens; *(b)* during the eccentric (downward) phase, the muscle lengthens.

slowly lengthen to control the rate at which the dumbbell is lowered. This is referred to as *negative work* because it is performed in the direction opposite to the concentric (positive) action. The eccentric (lengthening) action, not the concentric (shortening) action, is primarily responsible for muscle soreness associated with weight training.

IMPROVEMENTS IN MUSCULAR STRENGTH

The strength you develop from weight training is influenced by neuromuscular changes (or simply neural changes) that occur through the process of learning the exercises and increasing muscle mass and by your fiber type composition and genetic potential.

The term *muscular strength* refers to the ability to exert maximum force during a single effort. It can be measured by determining a *one-repetition maximum effort*—referred to as a 1RM—in one or more exercises. For example, if you loaded a bar to 100 pounds (45.5 kg) and were able to complete only one repetition using maximum effort, your 1RM would equal 100 pounds (45.5 kg). Strength is specific to a muscle or muscle area. This *specificity concept* will be discussed later.

The strength increases that occur in response to weight training have two explanations. One is associated with neural changes, and the other involves increases in muscle mass. In the first case, the term *neural* refers to the nervous system working with the muscular system to increase strength. In doing so, the nerves that are attached to specific muscle fibers are taught when to stimulate those muscle fibers. Thus, an improvement in exercise technique occurs that permits the person to lift heavier loads more efficiently and with less effort.

In the second case, through consistent training your body becomes able to recruit more fibers and select those that are most effective to lift a load or perform an exercise. Thus a *neural-learning factor* contributes to strength changes, some of which may be quite dramatic. This factor explains the strength improvements seen in previously sedentary people during the first four to eight weeks of weight training.

After the first few weeks, although the neural-learning factor continues to play a role, continued gains in strength are mostly associated with increases in muscle mass. As the cross-sectional area of a muscle becomes greater because the individual fibers become thicker and stronger, so does the muscle's ability to exert force. Therefore, the neural factor accounts for early increases in strength, whereas muscle mass increases are responsible for the changes seen later.

Strength Expectations

Reported strength increases typically range from 8 to 50 percent, depending on a person's training habits and level of strength at the time of initial testing, the muscle group being evaluated, the intensity of the training program (loads, repetitions, sets, rest periods), the length of the training program (weeks, months, years), and genetic potential. The greatest improvements are seen among those who have not weight trained before and whose programs involve large-muscle exercises, heavier loads, multiple sets, and more training sessions. Unique characteristics, such as the lengths of muscles and the angles at which their tendons connect to the bone, provide mechanical advantages and disadvantages and can increase or limit an individual's strength potential.

Hearing that men are typically stronger than women should not be surprising. However, this disparity has nothing to do with the quality of muscle tissue or its ability to produce force because these are almost identical in both sexes. The quantity of muscle tissue in the average male (40 percent of total body weight) versus a female (23 percent of total body weight) is largely responsible for men's strength advantage. This difference also helps to explain why women are normally 43 to 63 percent weaker than men in upper-body strength and 25 to 30 percent weaker in lower-body strength.

However, to conclude that women do not have the same potential as men to gain strength is incorrect. A female can develop strength relative to her own potential, but it will not be at the same absolute strength levels achieved by males. Furthermore, weight training research studies repeatedly show that women can make dramatic improvements in strength and muscle tone without fear of developing unwanted muscle bulk. At the same time, they can decrease body fat, which results in a healthier and more attractive appearance.

Research shows that prepubescent children who participate in a well-designed, supervised weight training program can increase muscular strength above what they would experience by merely growing up. Muscular strength can increase as much as 40 percent, and children as young as age six have benefited from weight training. Other benefits include stronger bones, improved body composition, and an increased ability to generate power and speed.

As researchers undertake studies that involve older populations, it becomes apparent that people who follow regular exercise programs maintain their fitness levels, while those who become inactive lose about a half-pound (or about a quarter-kilogram) of muscle per year during their 30s and 40s and as much as 1 pound (0.45 kg) per year after age 50. Herbert deVries, a well-respected researcher, contends that much of the strength loss observed in older individuals is a function of sedentary living as much as it is an outcome of the aging process.

The benefits of weight training for older people can be dramatic and positive. It can create a stronger musculoskeletal system that resists osteoporosis by enhancing bone mineral density. Plus, increased body strength reduces the incidence of degenerative diseases and improves quality of life.

In both men and women, old and young, the strength improvements that occur in response to weight training are not typically noticeable until the third or fourth week of training. The first week is usually characterized by losses in strength, perhaps due to the *microtrauma* (tearing down) of muscle tissue. Fatigue may also be a contributing factor. Decreases in strength performance are especially apparent during the final training session of the first week, so do not be surprised if you feel weaker toward the end of a week. Of course, you will be impressed with and excited about your strength gains, which may be as great as 6 percent per week.

Muscle Size Increases

Exactly what accounts for muscle size increases is not fully understood; however, factors that are often discussed are hypertrophy, hyperplasia, and genetic potential.

Muscle size increases are most often attributed to an enlargement of existing fibers, the same fibers that were present at birth. Very thin protein strands (actin and myosin) within the fiber increase in size, creating a larger fiber. The collective effect of increases in many individual fibers is responsible for the overall muscle size changes observed. This increase in existing fibers is referred to as *hypertrophy* (figure 4).

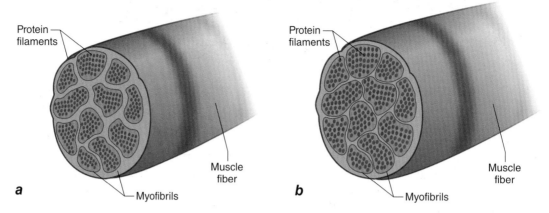

a

b

Figure 4 Muscle hypertrophy: *(a)* the muscle before training; *(b)* the muscle after training. Note the changes in the diameters of the protein filaments that constitute the myofibrils.

Although hypertrophy is the most commonly accepted explanation of why a muscle becomes larger, some studies suggest that fibers split lengthwise and form separate fibers, a theory referred to as *hyperplasia.* The splitting is thought to contribute to an increase in the size of the muscle.

If one accepts hypertrophy as the process whereby existing fibers increase in size, then one must also accept that genetic limitations exist regarding the extent to which a muscle will increase in size. This is because increases are due to the thickening of fibers that already exist. Just as we know that some people are born with muscle-tendon attachments that favor force development, the same is true about the number of muscle fibers. Some people are born with a greater number of muscle fibers than others; therefore their genetic potential for hypertrophy is greater. Regardless of your genetic inheritance, your challenge is to design an effective training program and to train diligently so that you develop to your full potential.

The skeletal muscle tissue mentioned earlier can be categorized into two basic types, each with unique capabilities and characteristics. A *fast-twitch muscle fiber* has the capacity to produce a great deal of force but fatigues quickly. Typically, its size will also increase more rapidly. Fast-twitch fibers, because of their high force capability, are recruited during weight training exercises and in athletic events that require high levels of explosive strength, such as the shot put, discus, and javelin in track and field, or American football.

A *slow-twitch muscle fiber* is not able to exert as much force or develop force as quickly, but it is more enduring—that is, the fiber can continue contracting for longer periods of time before fatigue sets in. Slow-twitch fibers are recruited for aerobic-oriented events, such as distance running, swimming, and biking, which require less strength but greater muscular endurance.

Not everyone possesses the same ratio of fast-twitch to slow-twitch muscle fibers. Those who possess a greater proportion of fast-twitch fibers have a greater genetic potential to be stronger and, therefore, to be more successful in certain strength-dependent sports or in activities like weight training. Conversely, individuals with a higher percentage of slow-twitch fibers have a greater genetic potential to be successful in activities that require lower levels of strength and greater levels of muscular endurance, such as long-distance swimming or marathon events.

IMPROVEMENTS IN MUSCULAR ENDURANCE

Muscular endurance refers to the muscle's ability to perform repeatedly with moderate loads for an extended period of time. Improvement in muscular endurance is demonstrated by an ability to extend the period of time before muscular fatigue occurs, allowing you to perform more repetitions of an exercise. It is different from muscular strength, which is the measure of a single, all-out muscular effort. But like strength, muscular endurance is specific to the muscle or muscles involved. For instance, regularly performing a high number of repetitions in the biceps curl will increase muscular endurance in the muscles in the front of the upper arm, but not in the leg muscles.

Weight training produces muscular endurance improvements by reducing the number of muscle fibers involved during earlier periods of an activity, thereby leaving some in reserve if the activity continues. The reduction in the number of fibers involved is related to strength improvements that permit a task to be undertaken using a lower percentage of effort. For example, if you had to perform a 25-pound (11.3 kg) biceps curl and had 50 pounds (22.7 kg) of strength in your biceps, this exercise would require 50 percent of your strength. If, however, your biceps strength increased to 100 pounds (45.5 kg), the task would require only 25 percent of your strength—a lower percentage of effort.

IMPROVEMENTS IN CARDIOVASCULAR FITNESS

The effects of weight training on cardiovascular fitness, usually expressed as changes in *oxygen uptake* (the ability to transport and utilize oxygen by the muscles), have been studied by numerous researchers. It is safe to say that weight training programs that involve heavier loads, fewer repetitions, and longer rest periods between sets have a minimal effect on cardiovascular fitness. However, when they include light to moderate loads (40 to 60 percent of 1RM), a greater number of repetitions (15 or more), and very short rest periods between sets (30 to 60 seconds), a small (5%) improvement in oxygen uptake may be expected. The extent of such changes is also influenced by the intensity and length of the overall training period (weeks, months, years) as well as fitness and strength levels at the start of the program. Despite that, disregarding these considerations when evaluating the merits of reported cardiovascular fitness improvements attributed to weight training programs is an oversight.

The most effective way to develop cardiovascular fitness is to engage in *aerobic* training activities such as walking, running, swimming, cycling, or cross-country skiing. Such activities involve continuous, rhythmic movements that can be sustained for longer periods of time than anaerobic activities such as weight training. Guidelines for developing an aerobic exercise program can be found in books by Baechle and Westcott (2010), Baechle and Earle (2005), and Westcott and Baechle (2007) which are listed in the reference section at the end of this book. A well-designed overall fitness program includes both weight training and aerobic activities.

IMPROVEMENTS IN MUSCULAR COORDINATION AND FLEXIBILITY

Despite evidence to the contrary, some people still believe that weight training will negatively affect muscular coordination and reduce flexibility. However, the numbness (loss of touch) and the feelings of heaviness in the arms and legs that occur immediately after a set of repetitions are only temporary and will not reduce coordination levels. Weight training sessions most likely will have the opposite effect. Handling and moving bars from the floor to overhead (push press), balancing the bar on your back (back squat), and evenly lifting two dumbbells (dumbbell chest fly) all contribute to improved muscular coordination.

Weight training exercises that are performed using good technique and a controlled manner can improve strength throughout all ranges of joint motion. They will also improve flexibility, provide a better stimulus for strength development, and reduce the likelihood of injury. No evidence supports the contention that properly performed weight training exercises reduce flexibility or motor coordination.

DELAYED-ONSET MUSCLE SORENESS AND OVERTRAINING

You should not be surprised or discouraged to find that the first week or two of weight training is accompanied by some degree of muscle soreness. Although no definitive explanation exists for why we experience *delayed-onset muscle soreness*, we do know that it is associated with the eccentric phase of an exercise. For example, the lowering (eccentric) phases of the biceps curl and bench press exercises can result in muscle soreness, but their upward (concentric) phases typically do not. Usually the discomfort of muscle soreness subsides after two or three days, especially if you stretch before and after training. Surprisingly, the very thing that stimulates the soreness—exercise—helps to alleviate it. Light exercise combined with stretching is ideal for speeding the recovery from muscle soreness.

Delayed-onset muscle soreness is not the same as overtraining. *Overtraining* is a condition in which there is a plateau or drop in performance over time. This occurs when your body does not have time to adequately recuperate from training before the next workout. Often the overtrained state is a result of overlooking the need to rest between sessions, working out too aggressively (by returning to training too soon after an illness or including too many training sessions per week), or not following recommended program guidelines.

The physical warning signs of overtraining are

- extreme muscular soreness and stiffness the day after a training session;

- a gradual increase in muscular soreness from one training session to the next;

- a decrease in body weight, especially when no effort to lose weight is made;

- an inability to complete a training session that, based on your present physical condition, is reasonable; and

- a decrease in appetite.

If you develop two or more of these symptoms, reduce the intensity, frequency, or duration of training until these warning signs subside. Preventing overtraining is more desirable than trying to recover from it.

Do the following to help prevent overtraining:

- Increase training intensity gradually.

- Alternate aggressive training weeks with less aggressive training weeks to allow for sufficient recovery between training sessions (discussed in step 13).

- Get adequate amounts of sleep.

- Eat properly.

- Make adjustments in training intensity as needed.

EATING SMART

Nutrition is the study of how carbohydrate, protein, fat, vitamins, minerals, and water provide the energy, substances, and nutrients required to maintain bodily functions during rest and exercise conditions. When a sound nutrition program is combined with regular training sessions, success is a natural outcome.

The general guidelines for a healthy diet—55 percent carbohydrate, 30 percent fat, and 15 percent protein—are appropriate for those who are weight training. Try to select foods that are high in complex carbohydrate instead of simple sugar and that contain unsaturated, not saturated, fat. A diet that includes appropriate amounts of fluids (six to eight glasses per day) and follows these guidelines will provide the necessary energy and nutrients to promote positive changes in strength, muscular endurance, and muscularity.

The discussion that follows is an overview of the nutrition and dietary factors that affect your body. For more information on this topic, refer to *Nancy Clark's Sports Nutrition Guidebook* (2008).

Nutrition Needs

Carbohydrate is the body's primary source of energy. It provides four calories per gram and is categorized as either complex or simple. For those who train intensely, an increased intake of complex carbohydrate is very important. Preferred sources of carbohydrate are cereal, bread, flour, grains, fruit, pasta, and vegetables (complex carbohydrate). Other sources are candy, sweetened cereals, sugary beverages, pastries, and honey (simple sugar).

Fat provides a concentrated form of energy—nine calories per gram, more than twice that of carbohydrate or protein. Fat is involved in maintaining healthy skin, insulating against heat and cold, and protecting vital organs. Fat can be found in both plant and animal sources and is usually classified as saturated or unsaturated. Unsaturated types of fat (mono- and poly-), such as those found in olive, canola, and corn oil, are preferred because they are associated with a lower risk of developing heart disease. Common sources of saturated fat are meats (such as beef, lamb, chicken, and pork), dairy products (such as cream, milk, cheese, and butter), and eggs.

Protein is the building block of all body cells. It is responsible for repairing, rebuilding, and replacing cells, regulating all bodily processes, and, under certain conditions, serving as a source of energy. Protein, which provides four calories per gram, is made up of basic units called *amino acids,* which are in turn further described as essential or nonessential. Of the 20 amino acids, 8 (or 9, depending on which reference is consulted) are termed essential and must be supplied through the diet. The other 12 (or 11), the nonessential amino acids, can be produced by the body. Foods that contain all of the essential amino acids are called complete proteins. Meat, fish, poultry, eggs, milk, and cheese are sources of complete proteins. Suggested protein sources that are low in fat are milk products, lean meats, and fish. Incomplete sources of protein are breads, cereals, nuts, dried peas, and beans.

Vitamins are essential nutrients needed for many body processes. They are divided into two types, *fat soluble* and *water soluble.* Regardless of the type, vitamins do not contain energy or calories, and vitamin supplementation will not provide more energy.

Minerals function as builders, activators, regulators, transmitters, and controllers of the body's metabolic processes. Like vitamins, they do not provide calories.

Water, although it does not provide energy for activity, provides the medium for and is one of the end products of metabolism. Water makes up about 72 percent of the weight of muscle tissue and represents 40 to 60 percent of a person's total body weight. Through the regulation of thirst and urine output, the body is able to keep a delicate water balance.

The nutrient guide, My Plate, developed by the United States Department of Agriculture and the Center for Nutrition Policy and Promotion can help you choose the best foods for a healthy diet. Eating a variety of foods, increasing the amount of bread, fruit, and vegetables in your diet, and reducing the amount of fat and added sugar are recommended. Go to the USDA website (www.choosemyplate.gov) to learn which foods and amounts are right for you based on your age, sex, and activity level.

Dieting and Weight Loss

Body composition refers to the ratio of fat weight to fat-free weight (muscles, bones, organs) that composes your body. In contrast to judging physical makeup solely on your bathroom scale weight, body composition is a more accurate way to describe your health and fitness status. Two factors that have a profound effect on body composition are food intake and activity level.

Unfortunately, more than 66% of Americans are on some type of diet at any given time. Millions more are going on diets every day. Some are losing weight, but many are gaining it back. All hope to somehow lose weight and keep it off. The truth is that the diets designed to create fast weight loss usually are not effective in helping people stay healthy and trim. In fact, many of those diets are harmful.

There are good reasons why diets typically don't work, and better reasons why wise food choices plus regular exercise do work. Crash diets, in particular, are not effective because the body quickly adapts to a lower food intake by reducing its metabolic rate (the rate at which food is burned for energy). This compensatory action by the body resists the burning of fat. When a dietary restriction results in a loss of 10 pounds (4.5 kg), for example, the body adjusts to the restricted diet. Later, when increased food intake occurs, even though daily consumption is still less than it was before dieting, the body treats the increase as excess and stores it as fat. This yo-yo cycle of losing weight and quickly gaining it back is not only ineffective in creating a positive body appearance, but it's also unhealthy.

The weight loss experienced during the early part of a strict diet program is usually a loss of water, not fat. Many diets restrict carbohydrate intake. This reduces the water content of the body because much of the water stored in our bodies is accumulated in the process of storing carbohydrate. Weight loss due to the reduction of water stores is only temporary. Once the fluid balance is restored, a scale will not reflect the loss of body fat that was assumed to have occurred.

Also, if a female dieter consumes (on average) fewer than 1,200 calories a day (1,500 for a male), muscle tissue as well as fat is usually lost. The further the caloric intake dips below this amount, the more muscle tissue is lost compared to fat. So even though the dieters lose weight, they are actually fatter because the amount of body fat compared to lean body weight has increased.

The goal of a sound diet should be to reduce total body weight without losing muscle tissue. People who are on the roller coaster of dieting, gaining weight, and dieting again may be weakening their bodies every time they diet.

It appears that many overweight people justify overeating by thinking that they need more food to nourish their bodies because they are heavy. Actually, the opposite is true in many cases. Too much of their body weight is fat, which, unlike muscle, is not as metabolically active. In contrast, muscles that are exercising burn calories. The more muscle people have, the more energy they expend, and the faster stored fat is lost. Compare two individuals who are the same height, one of whom weighs more and is in worse physical condition than the other. The lighter person has more muscle and less stored fat due to a good fitness level and requires a greater caloric intake than the less active, heavier, fatter, and less muscular person.

For many people, the most effective way to decrease excess body fat is to moderately reduce caloric intake while participating in an aerobic and weight training program. These exercise programs will burn calories and maintain or build muscle tissue, encouraging an improvement in the fat-to-muscle ratio. Aerobic activities involve the large muscles in continuous, repetitive motions such as those in cycling, swimming, walking, jogging, cross-country skiing, and rope skipping. These activities promote the greatest caloric expenditure. Golf, by comparison, is an example of an activity that is not continuous or rhythmic and, therefore, expends only half the calories that swimming the backstroke does for a person with the same body weight.

Weight training sessions do not normally burn as many calories as aerobic exercise sessions, but they do maintain or increase muscle mass. This is important because by adding more muscle, more calories are expended.

If you want to lose body fat, attempt to lose it at a rate of 1 to 2 pounds (0.45-0.91 kg) per week. Losses greater than this typically result in losses of muscle tissue. A pound of fat has approximately 3,500 calories, so a daily dietary reduction of 250 to 500 calories will total 1,750 to 3,500 calories a week. Combined with regular exercise, this decrease will promote the recommended rate of fat loss per week and help keep it off.

Gaining Weight

Most people who exercise have no interest in gaining body weight; however, some do participate in weight training programs specifically to gain muscle. To accomplish this, an increase in caloric intake is necessary, in combination with regular training. Weight training stimulates muscle growth and increases body weight. The consumption of additional calories beyond one's daily needs provides the basis for an increase in muscle tissue. The addition of one pound (0.45 kg) of muscle requires 2,500 extra calories. An equal increase in protein and carbohydrate (with an emphasis on complex carbohydrate) with no change in fat intake should help promote lean tissue growth and an increase in muscle size.

Note that a woman typically does not become as muscular as a man, so gaining significant body weight in response to weight training is unlikely unless she makes an effort to do so by increasing food intake and following a program designed to develop hypertrophy. Even with those efforts made, the amount of muscle tissue gained is less than a man would gain.

Protein Needs, Supplements, and Steroids

Although many people endorse protein, mineral, and vitamin supplementation, little research substantiates claims that it improves muscular endurance, hypertrophy, or muscular strength in people who have nutritionally sound diets. Again and again, dietitians, exercise physiologists, and sports medicine physicians conclude that a normal diet will meet the protein dietary needs of the average person. The exception may be that an increase in carbohydrate and protein intake is appropriate for those who participate in aggressive weight training programs.

Conversations regarding supplementation are all too often accompanied by questions concerning steroids. It is human nature, especially among people who desire to make their bodies stronger, healthier, and more attractive, to look for shortcuts. But there are no safe shortcuts. Anabolic-androgenic steroids, in the presence of adequate diet and training, can contribute to an increase in lean body mass; however, the harmful side effects can greatly outweigh any positive effect.

There are two forms of steroids: oral (pills) and injected (a water- or oil-based liquid that is injected using a hypodermic needle). Their potency is gauged by comparing the *anabolic effects* (muscle building and strength inducing) versus the *androgenic effects* (increased male or female secondary sex characteristics such as increased body-hair length or density, voice lowering, and breast enlargement). This ratio is termed the *therapeutic index.*

Studies included in a position paper by the National Strength and Conditioning Association (Hoffman et al. 2009) on steroid use have cited increases in muscle size and strength, but not all outcomes from their use are positive. Prolonged high dosages of steroids can lead to a long-lasting impairment of normal testosterone endocrine (natural steroid) function, a decrease in natural testosterone levels, and a potential reduction in future physical development. With a decrease in testosterone, the body cannot make gains or retain what has already been developed.

The negative health consequences of steroid use are chronic illnesses such as heart disease, liver trouble, urinary tract abnormalities, and sexual dysfunction. The immediate short-term effects include increased blood pressure, acne, testicular atrophy, *gynecomastia* (male breast enlargement), sore nipples, decreased sperm count, prostatic enlargement, and increased aggression. Other side effects have been well publicized, including hair loss, fever, nausea, diarrhea, nosebleeds, lymph node swelling, increased appetite, and a burning sensation during urination. Extreme psychological symptoms have also been reported, including paranoia, delusions of grandeur, and auditory hallucinations.

When steroid use is discontinued after short-term use, most side effects disappear. However, females who take steroids experience permanent deepening of the voice, facial hair, baldness, and a decrease in breast size.

One of the most serious concerns associated with taking anabolic steroids is the development of coronary artery disease. Some researchers have reported high levels of total cholesterol, low levels of the desirable high-density lipoproteins (HDLs), and elevated blood pressure as a consequence of taking steroids, all of which are significant risk factors for heart disease. However, others suggest that the cholesterol levels reported may have been present before the use of steroids began.

KEYS TO SUCCESSFUL TRAINING

Before you learn proper lifting technique, let's review some fundamentals of training that you need to know in order to train safely, efficiently, and effectively. The essentials of productive training that are outlined here are reiterated and discussed as needed in the rest of the steps of this book.

- **Obtain medical clearance.** Weight training may be an inappropriate activity if you have (or have a history of) joint problems such as arthritis, respiratory conditions such as asthma, or cardiovascular problems such as hypertension, heart arrhythmias, or heart murmurs. The implications of such conditions must be addressed before you develop an exercise program and certainly before exercise begins. Carefully consider the questions presented below. If you answer yes to any of them, talk with your doctor before beginning a weight training program.

Talk with your doctor before beginning a weight training program if you answer yes to any of the following questions.

Yes No

___ ___ Have you had surgery or experienced bone, muscle, tendon, or ligament problems (especially back or knee problems) that might be aggravated by an exercise program?

___ ___ Are you over age 50 (female) or 45 (male) and unaccustomed to exercise?

___ ___ Do you have a history of heart disease?

___ ___ Has a doctor ever told you that your blood pressure was too high?

___ ___ Are you taking any prescription medications, such as those for heart problems or high blood pressure?

___ ___ Have you ever experienced chest pain, spells of severe dizziness, or fainting?

___ ___ Do you have a history of respiratory problems such as asthma?

___ ___ Is there a physical or health reason not already mentioned to suggest that you should not begin a weight training program?

Adapted, by permission, from T. R. Baechle and R.W. Earle, 1995, *Fitness weight training* (Champaign, IL: Human Kinetics), 24.

- **Always warm up and cool down.** Workouts should always begin with some warm-up exercises so that the muscles are better prepared to meet the challenges presented by the exercises. A cool-down period allows your muscles to recover and offers an excellent opportunity to work on flexibility. Guidelines for appropriate warm-up and cool-down exercises are presented in step 2.

- **Train on a regular basis.** The old adage "use it or lose it" is unfortunately true when it comes to maintaining cardiovascular efficiency, muscular strength and endurance, flexibility, and lean muscle mass. The body is unlike any machine yet to be developed. Its efficiency improves with use, in contrast to machines, and it deteriorates with disuse. Sporadic training will slow down your progress and be the downfall of many beginning lifters who started out with good intentions.

  All too often, the demise of a regular training program begins with one missed workout and ends with missing many more. Each time a training session is missed, goals for improving fitness, strength, and appearance move further out of reach. Working out regularly is important because decreases in training status begin to occur after 72 hours of no training.

- **Gradually increase training intensity.** The body adapts to the stresses of weight training when training occurs on a regular basis and when its intensity increases progressively over a reasonable period of time. Conversely, when the intensity of training is haphazard, the body's ability to adapt and become stronger and more enduring is compromised. The dramatic improvements observed in response to training do not happen under these conditions, and the excitement that prompts you to continue training is no longer present. As excitement dwindles, working out becomes more difficult, and improvements become nonexistent. Infrequent training often results in muscle soreness that does not go away, further reducing your enthusiasm for training.

- **Strive for quality repetitions.** Many people seem to believe that doing more repetitions in an exercise is synonymous with improvement, regardless of the technique used. The speed with which repetitions are performed is a very important factor in your ability to perform quality repetitions.

  In an advanced weight training exercise program designed to develop power, explosive exercise movements are required. However, in a beginning program, slow, controlled movements are desired. Exercises must be performed slowly enough to permit full extension and flexion at a joint. In the biceps curl, for example, the elbow should be fully extended and then fully flexed. Jerking, slinging, and using momentum are not recommended ways to complete a repetition. Other recommendations concerning proper exercise technique are provided in steps 4 through 10.

- **Use proper etiquette.** Just as participants in tennis, bowling, golf, and other sports recognize certain rules and courtesies, you should understand the rules that apply to weight training. Some are related to safety; others are matters of courtesy. When everyone abides by the following rules and courtesies, training experiences for all will be safer and more enjoyable.
  - Return equipment to its proper location.
  - Wipe off the equipment after using it (especially the upholstery).

- Do not perform overhead exercises near someone who is performing exercises in a supine position, such as the bench press, dumbbell chest fly, or abdominal crunch.
- Do not monopolize equipment; offer to let others *work in* (use the same piece of equipment) between your sets.
- Offer to spot others if you have the skill and strength to do so.
- Set barbells and dumbbells down on the floor instead of just dropping them.

- **Eat smart.** Nutrition is a key factor. It makes no sense to train hard if you are not eating nutritionally sound meals. Poor nutrition in itself can reduce strength, muscular endurance, and hypertrophy. Because training puts great demands on your body, you need nutrients to encourage adaptation and promote gains. To neglect this aspect of your training is an oversight if you are serious about improving.

- **Build days of rest into your program.** The intervening days of rest in your training program are important for improving your muscular fitness. Training on consecutive days without allowing the rest that your body needs to recuperate may result in a drop in performance, a training plateau, or an injury. Properly timed rest is as important as training on a regular basis.

- **Be willing to persevere.** To maximize the time spent in training, you must learn to push yourself to the uncomfortable point of muscle failure during many of your sets (after you know how to properly perform the exercise, of course). You must be willing to persevere through the discomfort (not pain) that accompanies reaching this point.

Believing that weight training can make dramatic changes in your health and physique—which it can—is essential to making the commitment to train hard and regularly. Typically, you will feel the difference in muscle tone (firmness) immediately. Strength and muscular endurance changes become noticeable after the second or third week. Be prepared, however, for variations in performance during the early stages of training and do not become discouraged if one workout does not produce the same outcome as a previous one.

Your brain is going through a learning curve as it tries to figure out which muscles to *recruit* (call into action) for specific movements in each exercise. Your neuromuscular system (brain, nerves, and muscles) is learning to adapt to the stimulus of training. Be patient! This period is soon followed by significant gains in muscle tone and strength and decreased muscle soreness. This is an exciting time in your program! At this point your attitude dictates the magnitude of the future gains you will experience.

RESOURCES

Little doubt remains that weight training has gained universal acceptance as an expedient and effective method of improving the health, performance, and appearance of millions of people. The mythology surrounding weight training's "dark ages" has given way to mounting scientific evidence that encourages its use and an enlightened understanding of its benefits.

There are many resources that focus on weight training. They range from large-scale professional membership-based organizations to print and electronic books and online courses for college students taking a class, preparing to pass a certification exam for a job, or following a personal exercise program. There are two comprehensive publications that provide the greatest breadth and depth regarding weight training concepts and recommendations: *Essentials of Strength Training and Conditioning* and *NSCA's Essentials of Personal Training*. To learn more about these two foundational resources, go to www.HumanKinetics.com.

Learning About Equipment and Its Proper Use

Thus far you have learned how the body responds to weight training and the importance of sound nutrition. Now is an ideal time for you to learn about the different types of equipment that are commonly used in weight training programs. This step will present and discuss the characteristics of the different types of equipment and how to use them correctly and safely.

EQUIPMENT USE AND SAFETY

Walking into a well-equipped weight room for the first time can be confusing and somewhat intimidating. You will see machines of various sizes and shapes, short and long bars, and weight plates of varying sizes with holes of different sizes. There may also be large and small balls and elastic tubing of various colors, thicknesses, and length. Understanding equipment terminology better, learning what each type of equipment is designed to do, and learning how to use each one properly will increase your confidence and make your training safer.

The equipment available will also dictate which exercises you can include in your workouts. For example, if you do not have access to a high-pulley cable machine for step 5 (back exercises), you will not be able to select the lat pulldown exercise to strengthen the back muscles. Therefore, becoming familiar with the equipment and its proper use is a logical first step in starting a weight training program. This step includes information about the types, characteristics, and safe use of machine and free-weight training equipment. Step 9 includes a discussion of equipment that may be used when performing core exercises.

Machines

Most machines in a workout facility are designed to accommodate what is referred to as a *dynamic* form of exercise—that is, exercise that involves movement. In contrast are *isometric* (static) exercises, such as pulling or pushing against a fixed bar, in which no observable movement occurs. Dynamic exercises performed on weight machines challenge muscles to shorten against resistance and lengthen in a controlled manner.

Figure 1.1 shows single- and multi-unit machines. They are referred to as *selectorized* machines because they allow you to choose or "select" the load on the weight stack to use, typically using an inserted pin or key. The single-unit pulley machine (figure 1.1*a*) is designed to isolate muscular stress on one muscle area. Multi-unit machines (figure 1.1*b*) have two or more stations attached to their frame and allow many muscle areas to be trained by simply moving from one station to another.

Figure 1.1   Weight training machines: *(a)* single-unit pulley machine; *(b)* multi-unit machine.

Fixed-Resistance Equipment

A machine that features a pre-set pulley design is commonly referred to as a *fixed-resistance machine*. A closer look at the structure of these machines is seen in figure 1.2. In that example, the weight stack of the machine is lifted up by pulling on a handle attached to a cable–pulley arrangement. Sometimes a chain or flat belt is used in place of the cable.

You will notice when using fixed-resistance equipment that some movement phases require more effort than others, as though someone were changing the weight during the exercise. The limitation of this type of equipment is that the muscles are not taxed in a consistent manner throughout the range of movement in the exercise.

Figure 1.2   Fixed-resistance, pulley-type seated row machine.

Variable-Resistance Equipment

To create a more consistent stress on the muscles, *variable-resistance machines* may feature a kidney-shaped wheel or cam (figure 1.3). The effect of a cam shape on the relative position of the weight stack is shown in figure 1.4. As the chain, cable, or belt tracks over the peaks and valleys of the cam, notice that the distance between the *pivot point* (the axle on which the cam rotates) and the weight stack changes. This variation

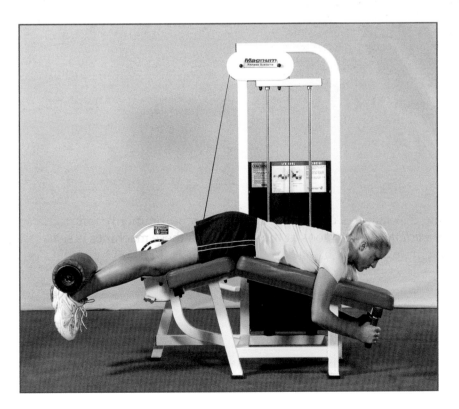

Figure 1.3   Variable-resistance, cam-type knee curl machine.

3

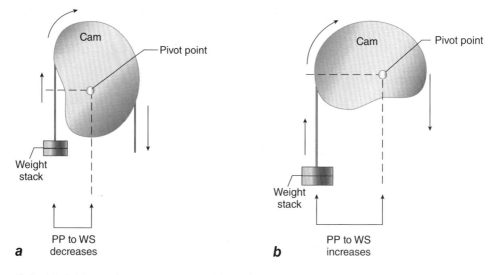

a   PP to WS decreases   *b*   PP to WS increases

Figure 1.4 Variable-resistance cam machines function by varying the distance between the pivot point (PP) and the weight stack (WS) to create a more even stress on the muscles: *(a)* when the distance between the PP and the WS decreases, the weight is easier to lift; *(b)* when the distance between the PP and the WS increases, the weight is harder to lift.

in distance is what creates a more even stress on the muscles. That is, at the point when the exercise becomes most difficult to perform, the design of the machine causes the distance from the weight stack to the pivot point to decrease, making the weight easier to lift (figure 1.4*a*). Conversely, at the easiest point in the exercise, the distance between the stack and pivot point increases (figure 1.4*b*). If you want a better understanding of the principles involved in the equipment described here, consider reading Baechle and Earle (2008), Baechle and Earle (2005), and Earle and Baechle (2004).

Isokinetic Equipment

An *isokinetic machine* (figure 1.5) is found in some fitness facilities, but predominately it is used for injury rehabilitation in a physical therapy clinic. These machines are designed so that exercises are performed at a constant speed. Unlike variable-resistance machines that involve concentric and eccentric muscle actions, isokinetic equipment involves only concentric activity. Instead of using weight stacks, these machines create resistance by using hydraulic, pneumatic (air), or frictional features. Control settings on these machines allow you to select movement speeds that relate to the level of resistance desired, ranging

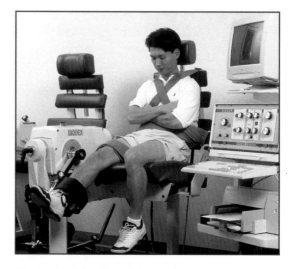

Figure 1.5 Isokinetic machine.

from slower speeds that require greater effort to faster speeds that require less effort as you move through the range of the exercise movement.

Isokinetic machines provide a resistance to movement that is equivalent to the force you exert. The harder you push or pull, the greater the resistance you experience; the weaker the effort, the less the resistance. The primary difference between variable-resistance and isokinetic machines is that with variable-resistance machines, the shape of the cam or the position of the roller dictates the effort you must exert. With isokinetic machines, how hard you push or pull determines the effort throughout the exercise movement.

Training Precautions When Using Machines

You might hear that weight training machines are safer than free weights. It's true they are inherently safer because the weight stacks are located away from the lifter, and the bars are suspended or stationary. The stationary nature of machines also permits safer travel to and from exercise stations (verses carrying a barbell or dumbbell). Another advantage is that if you intend to train on your own, you will not need a spotter.

Even though machines offer advantages over free weights, injuries can still occur (probably because many people who train on machines have limited experience in the weight room). A lack of experience, overconfidence when using machines, and inadequate instruction contribute to many of the muscle, tendon, and joint injuries that occur frequently in training facilities.

Before using a machine, check for frayed cables and belts, worn pulleys and chains, broken welds, loose pads, and uneven or rough movement. If any of these exist, do not use that machine until it is repaired. Adjust the levers and pads to accommodate your body size. Never place your fingers or hands between weight stacks to dislodge a selector key or adjust the load, and always keep your fingers and hands away from the chains, belts, pulleys, and cams.

When preparing to use a machine, get into (or *assume*) a stable position on the seats, pads, and rollers. Fasten any seat belt securely. When choosing the appropriate load, be sure to insert the selector key all the way into the weight stack. Perform exercises through the full range of motion in a slow, controlled manner. Do not allow the weight stacks to bounce during the lowering phase of the exercise or to hit the top pulley during the upward phase.

Free Weights

Free-weight equipment is different in design and slightly different in function than its machine counterpart. The term *free* refers to its nonrestrictive effect on joint movement, in contrast to machines that create a predetermined movement pattern. It is this characteristic that enables a lifter to perform many exercises with only one barbell or a pair of dumbbells.

Barbells

The *standard barbell* (figure 1.6*a*) is about 1 inch (2.5 cm) in diameter and has a pair of *collars* that stop the weight plates from sliding in toward the hands. After the lifter adds the weight plates to the bar, a *lock* is added to each end of the bar to keep the weight plates from sliding off the bar. A typical standard bar with collars and locks weighs approximately 5 pounds per foot (about 7.5 kg per meter), so a 5-foot (1.5 m) bar weighs about 25 pounds (11.4 kg).

The longest barbell in a weight room, an *Olympic bar* (figure 1.6*b*), is about 7 feet (2.1 m) long and weighs about 45 pounds (20.5 kg) without locks. It has both smooth and rough (called *knurling*) areas and permanent, fixed-position collars. Olympic locks vary in shape, and their individual weight can range from less than 1 pound (0.5 kg) (figure 1.7*a*) to 5 pounds (2.3 kg) (figure 1.7*b*). Therefore, an Olympic bar with locks can weigh as much as 55 pounds (25 kg). They have the same diameter as most bars in the weight room; however, the section between the collar and the end of the bar (where the weight plates are placed) has a diameter of approximately 2 inches (5 cm). This is an important distinction to recognize when loading an Olympic bar; only Olympic weight plates that have a larger diameter hole will fit on an Olympic bar. The standard weight plates have holes that are too small to fit on an Olympic bar (see figure 1.8).

CAUTION: Only use standard weight plates on a standard bar; do not use Olympic weight plates on a standard bar because they will slide in toward your hands or off the end of the bar.

Another type of bar is a *cambered* bar (figure 1.6*c*), also called an *EZ-curl* bar. It has the same characteristics as a standard or an Olympic barbell (depending on the diameter) except that its curves create natural places to grasp the bar to place an isolated training stress on certain muscle groups during an exercise (e.g., the EZ-bar biceps curl).

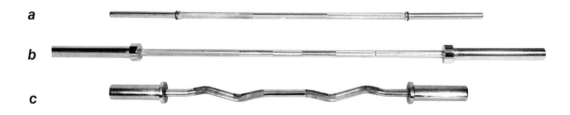

Figure 1.6 Types of bars: *(a)* standard; *(b)* Olympic; *(c)* cambered (also called EZ-curl).

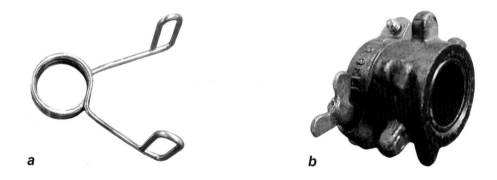

Figure 1.7 Locks for Olympic barbells: *(a)* spring lock that weighs less than one pound (0.5 kg) and is usually not included in the total weight of the bar; *(b)* Olympic lock that weighs up to five pounds (2.3 kg).

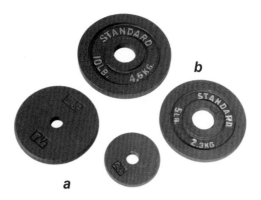

Figure 1.8 Weight plates: *(a)* standard; *(b)* Olympic.

Dumbbells

Dumbbells (figure 1.9) are similar to barbells, but they are shorter, and the entire middle section of the bar between the weight plates is usually knurled. If the dumbbell is the type with a short bar and added weight plates, the weight of bar, collars, and locks, approximately 3 pounds (1.4 kg), is not usually added to the total weight of the dumbbell. For example, a dumbbell with a 10-pound (4.5 kg) plate on each side is described as weighing 20 pounds (9.1 kg), not 23 pounds (10.5 kg). The dumbbells shown in figure 1.9 are only three of many dumbbell designs that you see in a well-equipped weight room.

Figure 1.9 Dumbbells: *(a)* plate-loaded; *(b)* premolded chrome; *(c)* premolded hex.

Training Precautions When Using Free Weights

Using free-weight barbells and dumbbells requires higher levels of motor coordination than using machines. The freedom of movement allowed by free weights easily translates to potential injury when correct loading, lifting, and spotting techniques are not used. However, free-weight training is not dangerous; when reasonable precautions are taken, it is very safe and can be more effective than machines in strengthening the body.

As you become more familiar with the free-weight equipment, you will realize that barbells and dumbbells offer tremendous versatility—your choice of exercises is virtually unlimited. If you plan to train at home, versatility and lower cost make free weights the preferred type of equipment.

Certain precautions are advisable when using either free weights or machines. The following actions will help you avoid potentially dangerous situations and make training safer.

- **Load bars properly.** If the ends of a free-weight bar are not loaded evenly, serious injury can occur to you and those nearby. Learning the weight of the weight plates and staying alert when loading each end of a bar will help prevent these errors.

- **Lock barbells and dumbbells.** Lifting with unlocked barbells and dumbbells is dangerous. Weight plates that are not secured with locks can easily slide off the bar and land on feet or other body parts. Locks should be checked for tightness before each set of exercises. Do not assume that the last person who used the barbell or dumbbell tightened the locks. Also, if the collars or locks are welded to the bar, always check that the weld is intact.

- **Avoid backing into others.** Because of a sudden loss of balance or being unaware that anyone is near you, you may back into someone. Take care to avoid this; an untimely bump may cause an accident resulting in injury to you, the lifter, people nearby, or any combination of these.

- **Be aware of extended bars.** Extended bars are those that overhang or extend outward from machines (like the bar for the lat pulldown exercise), barbells supported on racks (on the squat rack, for example) or uprights (like in the bench press), or bars held in the hands for any exercise. Of special concern is a bar positioned at or above shoulder height, which is not as easily noticed and can cause serious facial injuries if a person walks or leans into it. Be especially cautious around people who are performing overhead exercises or are backing out of racks with a barbell on their shoulders.

- **Store equipment properly.** Each piece of equipment in a training facility should have a particular storage location. Barbells, dumbbells, and weight plates that are not returned to their proper locations or are left unattended are often tripped over or slipped on. Always place the equipment you use in appropriate racks and locations, whether at home or in a training facility. Care should be taken to secure weight training equipment so that children do not have access to it without proper supervision; it is dangerous for them to climb on equipment and lift plates and bars that are too heavy for them.

- **Wear a weight belt in the appropriate situations.** Another safety consideration is using a weight (or weightlifting) belt (figure 1.10). Its use may contribute to injury-free training, but it alone will not protect you

Figure 1.10 Weight (or weightlifting) belt.

from back injuries—only good technique will. The decision to wear one depends on the exercise being performed and the relative amount of the load being used: You should wear a weight belt for the exercises that stress the back *and* involve maximum or near-maximum loads. Pull it snugly into position around your waist and be sure to breathe properly during the exercise. Performing exercises while wearing a belt that is too tight or while not breathing properly can contribute to dizziness, blackouts, and cardiovascular complications. See step 2 for more guidelines about breathing.

EQUIPMENT DRILLS

A logical starting point for novice lifters is to become familiar with the types of weight training equipment and their proper use. This includes being able to identify what the equipment is designed to do, knowing how to use it, and determining whether it is in good working order. It is unwise to train on any piece of equipment until these details are known. The following drills test your understanding of the concepts covered; modify them as needed to fit your specific facility.

Equipment Drill 1.
What Equipment Is Available?

Survey the equipment in your facility. Which types do you recognize? Place a check mark next to the equipment you see.

Machine Equipment

1. Fixed ___

2. Variable (cam) ___

3. Isokinetic ___

Free-Weight Equipment

1. Standard bar ___

2. Standard weight plate ___

3. Olympic bar ___

4. Olympic weight plate ___

5. Cambered curl bar ___

6. Dumbbell ___

7. Lock ___

8. Collar ___

9. Weight belt ___

Equipment Drill 2. Equipment Safety Review

Safety is so important that you need to get in the habit of checking the equipment each time you train. Walk through the facility and check the status of the equipment using the checklists shown below. Repeat this process each time you work out. A common cause of litigation involves equipment that was not in good working order when the person was injured.

Machine Equipment Safety Checklist

Mark each item as it is checked or completed.

Before each training session:

___ Check for frayed cables and belts, broken pulleys and hooks, worn chains, and loose pads.

___ Check for proper lever and seat adjustments.

During each training session:

___ Insert the selector key or pin properly.

___ Get into a stable position on the seats and pads.

___ Fasten belts securely (if applicable).

___ Perform all exercises in a slow, controlled manner.

Free-Weight Equipment Safety Checklist

Mark each item as it is checked or completed.

Before performing each set:

___ Check for integrity of collar welds.

___ Check for tightness of collars and locks.

___ Check for correct load on both ends of the bar.

During each training session:

___ Avoid walking into bars that extend outward.

___ Avoid walking near people who are performing overhead exercises.

___ Avoid backing into others.

___ Perform all exercises in a slow, controlled manner.

After each training session:

___ Return equipment to its proper location.

SUCCESS SUMMARY FOR WEIGHT TRAINING EQUIPMENT

There is a variety of equipment commonly used in a weight training program. It is important that you understand the characteristics of the different types of equipment and how to use them correctly and safely.

After you have learned about weight training equipment and its proper use, you are ready to move on to step 2. In this step you will learn fundamental weight training skills, including how to warm up and cool down from a workout, how to breathe correctly while weight training, and how to be a spotter for free-weight exercises.

Before Taking the Next Step

Honestly answer each of the following questions. If you answer yes to all of them, you are ready to move on to step 2.

1. Can you identify the three types of weight training machines?

2. Can you identify and differentiate between standard free-weight equipment and Olympic free-weight equipment?

3. Have you successfully completed the two drills in this step?

Mastering Stretching, Lifting, and Spotting Skills

So far you have learned about the physiology behind weight training and the equipment you will use. Now is an ideal time to master the fundamental lifting skills that you will use in every workout. The lifting techniques described in this step can be applied to everyday physical tasks at home and work, thus decreasing the likelihood of injury to your low back. You will also learn how to warm up and cool down appropriately, how to breathe correctly while weight training, and how to use and be a spotter for free-weight exercises.

Correctly performing basic lifting skills avoids placing excessive stress on muscles, tendons, ligaments, bones, and joints. One of the most common debilitating conditions is low back pain, a condition that affects at least 80 percent of adults at some point in their lives. Americans spend at least $50 billion each year on care of low back pain and miss an average of more than seven days of work a year. The total economic cost in the United States when health care, loss-of-work time, and reduced productivity are considered has been estimated to be over $200 billion each year. In addition to preventing injury, proper lifting skills produce quicker training results because muscles can be properly stressed and stimulated more effectively. Effective training sessions should start and end with warm-up and cool-down exercises that are explained in this step.

The fundamentals learned in this step can be applied to all exercises and spotting procedures described in this text. When you are learning and practicing basic lifting and spotting skills, consider using a dowel stick (like a broom handle), a very light bar, the lightest weight plate on a machine, or only your body weight.

WARM-UP AND COOL-DOWN EXERCISES

Because of the demands that training places on muscles and joints, warming up and cooling down properly before and after each training session is important. Warm-up activities such as brisk walking or jogging in place for about five minutes followed by an appropriate stretching routine help to increase blood and muscle temperature, thereby enabling muscles to contract and relax with greater ease. Stretching also improves *flexibility* (the ability to move joints through a full range of motion) and helps prevent injury.

Go through a warm-up activity and then follow the series of static stretching exercises described and shown in this step. Be sure to move slowly into the stretched positions; do not bounce. The stretches presented involve major joints and muscle groups, especially the less flexible muscles of the backs of the legs, the upper and low back, and the neck.

Also perform these stretching exercises immediately after each training session to help speed recovery from muscle soreness. Hold each of the stretching positions for at least 10 seconds and repeat two or three times.

Chest and Shoulders

Grasp your hands together behind your back and slowly lift them upward (figure 2.1), or simply reach back as far as possible if you are not able to grasp your hands. For an additional stretch, bend at the waist and raise your arms higher.

Figure 2.1 Chest and shoulder stretch.

Upper Back, Shoulder, and Arm

With your left hand, grasp your right elbow and pull it slowly across your chest toward your left shoulder. You will feel tension along the outside of your right shoulder and arm (figure 2.2). Repeat with the other arm. You can vary this stretch by pulling the arm across and down over your chest and upper abdomen.

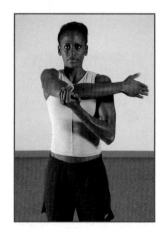

Figure 2.2 Upper back, shoulder, and arm stretch.

Shoulder and Triceps (Back of Upper Arm)

Bring both arms overhead and hold your right elbow with your left hand. Allow your right arm to bend at the elbow, and let your right hand rest against the back of your upper back. Slowly pull with your left hand to move your right elbow behind your head until you feel a stretch (figure 2.3). Repeat with the other arm.

Figure 2.3 Shoulder and triceps stretch.

Back and Hip

Sit with your left leg straight. Bend your right leg and cross your right foot over your left leg, placing it next to the outside of your left knee with the sole of your foot flat on the floor. Then twist your body to the right and use your left elbow to push against the outside of your upper right thigh, just above the knee. Next, place your right hand on the floor behind you, slowly turn your head to look over your right shoulder, and rotate your upper body toward your right hand and arm (figure 2.4). You should feel tension in your low back and your right hip and buttocks. Repeat with the other leg.

Figure 2.4 Back and hip stretch.

Back, Hamstring, and Inner Thigh

While seated on the floor, straighten your left leg. Bend your right leg and place the sole of your right foot so that it is slightly touching the inside of your left knee. Slowly bend forward at the hips and reach toward your left ankle until you feel tension in the back of your left thigh (figure 2.5). Be sure to keep the toes of your left foot pointing up, with your ankle and toes relaxed. Perform the same stretch with the right leg.

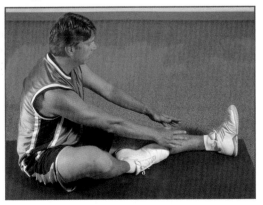

Figure 2.5 Back, hamstring, and inner thigh stretch.

Quadriceps

This stretch is performed in the standing position. Using a wall or stationary object for balance, grasp your right foot with your right hand and pull so that your heel moves back toward your buttocks (figure 2.6). You should feel tension along the front of your right thigh. Repeat with your left leg and left hand.

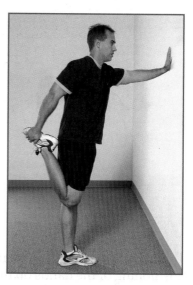

Figure 2.6 Quadriceps stretch.

Calves

Stand facing a wall about two feet (0.6 m) away. Place your left foot halfway between your right foot and the wall with your left knee slightly flexed. With the heel of your right foot flat on the floor and your right knee straight, lean forward and place your hands on the wall. Apply a stretch on your right calf by slowly moving your hips toward the wall. Be sure to keep your right heel on the floor and your back straight (figure 2.7). Perform the same stretch with the left leg. You can stretch another muscle area of the calf by allowing your right knee to flex slightly while in this same position.

Figure 2.7 Calf stretch.

Warm-Up and Cool-Down Drill.   Review

Before performing any of the exercises in steps 4 through 10, take time to review and practice the warm-up and cool-down exercises described here. Start with a brisk walk or jog in place for five minutes, then perform the appropriate stretching exercises for the major joints and muscle groups: the chest and shoulders; upper back, shoulder, and arm; shoulder and triceps; back and hip; back, hamstring, and inner thigh; quadriceps; and calves.

Hold each stretch for at least 10 seconds and repeat two to three times. Avoid bouncing! Once you start training, remember to repeat two to three sets of each stretch after your workout as well. For additional information on stretching, consider reading the book, *Facilitated Stretching* by McAtee and Charland (2007).

Success Check

- Always warm up before stretching and after training.
- Move slowly into the stretches.
- Use static (not ballistic) stretches.

CORRECT LIFTING TECHNIQUE

Now with your warm-up completed, you are ready to learn proper lifting techniques that focus on

1. acquiring a good grip,

2. having a stable position from which to lift,

3. keeping the object being lifted close to your body, and

4. using your legs, not your back, when lifting a weight or bar off the floor.

Gripping the Bar

Two things to consider when establishing a grip are the type of grip used and the positioning of the hands on the bar (where on the bar and how far apart they are from each other). The grips that may be used to lift a bar off the floor are the *overhand*, or *pronated*, grip; the *underhand*, or *supinated*, grip; and the *alternated* grip. The palms are facing down or facing away from you in the overhand grip (figure 2.8*a*). In the underhand grip (figure 2.8*b*), the palms are facing upward or toward you with the thumbs pointing away from each other. The alternated grip (figure 2.8*c*), sometimes referred to as a *mixed grip*, involves having one hand in an underhand grip and the other in an overhand grip. In the alternated grip, the thumbs point in the same direction. (It does not matter which hand is positioned overhand or underhand in the alternated grip.) All of these are called *closed grips*, meaning that the fingers and thumbs are wrapped (closed) around the bar.

Figure 2.8 Closed bar grips: *(a)* overhand; *(b)* underhand; *(c)* alternated.

An *open grip* (figure 2.9), sometimes referred to as a *false grip,* is one in which the thumbs do not wrap around the bar. This grip type is very dangerous because the bar can easily roll out of your hands onto your head, face, or foot, causing severe injury. Always use a closed grip!

Figure 2.10 shows several grip widths used in weight training. In some exercises, the width of the grip places the hands approximately at shoulder-width and equidistant from the weight plates. This is referred to as the *common grip.*

Some exercises require a narrow grip and others use a wider grip. Learn the proper width for each exercise, as well as where to place the hands, so that the bar is held in a balanced position. Improperly gripped bars with weight plates that are not locked can result in the weights falling or being catapulted off the ends of the bar, causing serious injury. Becoming familiar with the smooth and knurled areas of the bar and where the hands should be placed will help you establish a balanced grip. Note that the common grip is used later in explaining proper lifting techniques.

Figure 2.9 An open, or false, grip on the bar increases the risk of injury because the bar can roll out of the lifter's hands.

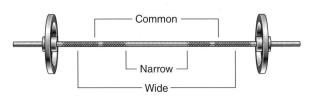

Figure 2.10 Grip widths: common, narrow, and wide.

Lifting the Bar off the Floor

Several phases must be followed to safely lift a bar off the floor. Some exercises require you to lift the bar from the floor just to the front of your thighs (see figure 2.13, page 20). Other exercises require you to lift the bar from the floor up to your shoulders in two distinct movements (figures 2.13 and 2.14, pages 20 and 22). This approach is typically used to get into the initial or preparatory body position to perform an exercise (for example, see the standing press exercise in step 6, page 70). Some exercises consist entirely of lifting the bar off the floor (see step 10 for descriptions of total-body exercises).

The next section describes the four phases for safely lifting a bar: a beginning or starting phase, two movement phases, and a final phase. The beginning phase has no movement; you just get into the correct initial body position for the exercise. Then, during the final phase, you safely return the bar to the floor.

Preparatory Lifting Position

Take hold of the bar using an overhand grip and position the hands outside of the legs. Now move into the correct preparatory position shown in figure 2.11. Shuffle your feet toward the bar so that your shins are almost touching it. Positioning the bar close to the shins keeps the weight being lifted closer to the body during the lifting/pulling action, enabling you to exert a more effective force with your legs (and avoiding straining your low back). A key concept to remember is that a stable lifting position strategically positions the leg muscles to effectively contribute to lifting the barbell.

Figure 2.11 PREPARATORY LIFTING POSITION

Side View

1. Grip slightly wider than shoulder width
2. Feet are shoulder-width apart
3. Feet are flat on floor, toes pointed slightly outward
4. Hips are low—in a "gorilla" position
5. Arms are straight, shoulders are over or slightly forward of bar
6. Head is up and eyes are focused straight ahead throughout exercise
7. Back is flat and tensed
8. Shoulder blades are pulled toward each other

Establish a stable position by placing your feet flat on the floor, shoulder-width apart or slightly wider, with the toes pointing slightly outward. A wide stance, or base of support, provides greater stability and a more balanced lifting position. Establishing a stable position is especially important when performing overhead exercises with dumbbells or a barbell. It is also important when performing machine exercises that require the positioning of the feet on the floor, or the head, torso, hips, and legs on or against equipment.

Think of the body position of a gorilla! Believe it or not, this is an ideal position for lifting a barbell off the floor. To get into this position, grasp the bar as previously described and simultaneously straighten your elbows as you lower your hips. Now position your shoulders over or slightly ahead of the bar while keeping the head up. Focus your eyes straight ahead. Your back should be in a flat or slightly arched position. Establish a chest-out-and-shoulders-back position by pulling the scapulae (shoulder blades) toward each other. Avoid the rounded back position shown in figure 2.12.

In addition, a proper head position, with the eyes looking straight ahead, is critical to maintaining proper body positioning. If there is a mirror available, watch yourself as you move into the low preparatory position. Does your back stay in a flat position, and do your heels

Figure 2.12 Do not round the back when lifting the bar from the floor. This puts unnecessary stress on the low back.

stay in contact with the floor? Often one or both heels will lift up when you move into the low position shown in figure 2.11, causing you to step forward to catch your balance.

Get a mental picture of the head, shoulder, back, and hip positions. The most important things to remember are to keep the barbell, dumbbell, or weight plate as close to you as possible and to use your leg muscles, not your back! In preparation for standing up to pull the bar off the floor, breathe in to stabilize your upper torso.

From the Floor to the Thighs

During the floor-to-thigh phase shown in figure 2.13, pull the bar upward in a slow, controlled manner. Do not jerk the bar off the floor. Once it reaches the mid-thigh level, exhale. At this height, the barbell may be placed in a rack or handed to a partner. Bringing the bar to this height is also the first phase of a movement that takes the bar to a position at the shoulders in preparation for the standing press exercise described in step 6 on page 70.

Figure 2.13 FLOOR-TO-THIGH PHASE

Preparation

1. Inhale before pulling
2. Pull in a slow, controlled manner
3. Keep the back flat

Lift

1. Begin to straighten knees while hips stay low
2. Keep elbows straight
3. Keep bar close to shins, knees, and thighs

Straighten

1. Keep shoulders over the bar as knees straighten
2. Exhale when bar reaches mid-thigh level

MISSTEP

Your upward pull is not smooth.

CORRECTION

Straighten your elbows before pulling and pull slowly.

MISSTEP

Your hips rise first when pulling.

CORRECTION

This movement puts stress on your back rather than on your legs. Your knees are straightening too soon. Think: *I lead my upward movement with my shoulders, not my hips.* This will enable you to use your legs instead of your back to do the lifting.

MISSTEP

Your heels lift up or you have too much weight shifted onto the balls of your feet (or both).

CORRECTION

Sit back into the low position and concentrate on evenly distributing the weight onto both feet.

From the Thighs to the Shoulders

If you need to lift the barbell to your shoulders, continue the upward movement initiated by the previous two phases. Do not allow the bar to slow down or rest on your thighs and do not exhale yet. Instead, continue pulling the bar so that it brushes against your thighs as you pull upward. This keeps the bar close and reduces stress on the low back. As your knees straighten, your hips should move forward quickly.

Follow this movement phase with a rapid shoulder shrug using the trapezius muscles between the neck and shoulders. Exhale immediately after the shrug. At the end of the shrugging motion, flex your elbows and move them upward and out to the sides to continue pulling the bar as high as possible (figure 2.14*a*).

Once the bar reaches its highest point, rack (catch) the bar on the front of your shoulders by rotating your elbows down under and then up in front of the bar as it touches down on your shoulders and clavicles (figure 2.14*b*). While catching the bar, flex the knees and hips partially to help absorb the force of the bar's impact on your shoulders. After reaching a balanced position with your upper arms parallel to the floor, finish the phase by standing up straight.

Figure 2.14 THIGH-TO-SHOULDER PHASE

From Thighs to Highest Bar Position

1. Continue pulling bar upward
2. Bar brushes middle or tops of thighs
3. Keep bar close to body as hips drive forward
4. Keep elbows straight
5. Straighten legs and hips completely then rapidly shrug the shoulders
6. Keep elbows straight and shrug as high as possible
7. Immediately flex elbows and move them upward and sideways
8. Continue pulling bar upward until it reaches its highest point

Figure 2.14 **THIGH-TO-SHOULDER PHASE** *(CONTINUED)*

Catch

1. Immediately rotate elbows down under, then up in front of bar
2. Catch (rack) bar on the front shoulders
3. Flex knees and hips to absorb bar's impact
4. Move upper arms to be parallel to floor
5. Gain balance and stand up

MISSTEP

The bar stops on your thighs.

CORRECTION

The pull from the floor to your shoulders should be continuous. Do not allow yourself to pause or stop the bar at your thighs.

MISSTEP

The bar swings away from your thighs and hips.

CORRECTION

Concentrate on pulling the bar up straight and keeping it in close to your thighs and hips.

MISSTEP

Your elbows flex too soon.

CORRECTION

Wait until your shrug is at its highest point before flexing your elbows.

From the Shoulders to the Floor

When lowering the bar (or any other heavy object) to the floor, use what you have learned about establishing a stable position, keeping the bar close and the back flat, and using your legs instead of your back to lower the bar. Also remember to lower it to the floor in a slow, controlled manner.

With the bar at shoulder height as shown (figure 2.15*a*), allow its weight to slowly pull your arms to a straightened position (figure 2.15*b*), which should briefly place the bar in a resting position on your thighs. Your hips and knees should be flexed so that as the bar touches your thighs, its weight is absorbed momentarily before you lower it to the floor. Remember to keep your head up and your back flat throughout the bar's return to the floor (figure 2.15*c*).

Figure 2.15 **SHOULDER-TO-FLOOR PHASE**

a   b   c

Lower

1. Unrack the bar
2. Lower bar to thighs first
3. Flex hips and knees to absorb weight

Pause

1. Keep back flat or slightly arched
2. Keep shoulders back
3. Keep bar close to thighs, knees, shins

Return

1. Lower bar to floor, under control

MISSTEP

The bar does not pause at your thighs.

CORRECTION

Visualize the downward phase as a two-count movement, "one" to the thighs, "two" to the floor.

MISSTEP

Your hips remain high as you lower the bar from the thighs to the floor.

CORRECTION

This position is stressful on the back! Once the bar reaches the thighs, squat down to lower it while keeping an upright, flat back position.

BREATHING

The best time to exhale in most exercises is during the *sticking point*, or the most difficult point in a repetition. Inhalation should occur during the relaxation phase or easiest point in a repetition. For example, in the upward movement of the biceps curl, exhalation should occur when the forearms are parallel with the floor (the most difficult point). Inhalation should occur as the bar is being lowered (the easiest point). In exercises in which upper-torso stabilization is needed to help maintain a correct lifting position, such as in the back squat (step 8) or hang clean (step 10), breathing should occur at the end of the sticking point. For most of the exercises and drills shown in steps 4 through 10, remember to breathe out through the sticking point!

Be aware that in most exercises you will have a tendency to hold your breath too long. This should be avoided because it is dangerous! By not exhaling, you reduce the return of blood to your heart, which in turn reduces the blood flow to the brain. If the brain is deprived of oxygen-rich blood, you will become dizzy and may faint. Holding your breath too long is especially dangerous if you are performing overhead free-weight exercises or if you have high blood pressure. Learning to exhale at the correct time can be confusing, but the technique sections in this book will tell you when to exhale for each exercise.

CAUTION: Do not hold your breath. Exhale through the sticking point of an exercise.

SPOTTING

A spotter assists and protects the person lifting from injury. Spotters play a crucial role in making weight training a safe activity.

If you are asked to be a spotter, realize that being inattentive can cause serious injuries (muscle or tendon tears, facial and other bone fractures, and broken teeth). Not all exercises require a spotter, but the free-weight bench press and the back squat, and those exercises involving over-the-head or over-the-face movements definitely require one. Specific spotting instructions are provided for the applicable exercises in steps 4 through 9.

Just as you may need to rely on a spotter, the person you spot is relying on you. Do not underestimate the significance of your responsibilities as a spotter. Read and adhere to the following guidelines for spotting free-weight exercises. You should also understand the guidelines about your responsibility to the spotter when you are lifting. Remember: Spotters with poor technique can be injured, too!

1. Remove all loose plates, barbells, and dumbbells from the area to avoid slipping or tripping on them.

2. Learn and practice the spotting techniques and procedures for exercises that involve a spotter.

3. Place your body in a good lifting position in case you have to catch the bar. Keep your knees flexed and your back flat.

4. Effectively communicate with the person you are spotting. For example, before your partner begins a set, ask how many repetitions will be attempted.

5. Use the appropriate grip—a closed grip is a must! Use the proper hand location on the bar if you need to grip it.

6. Check that the bar is properly and evenly loaded.

7. Be knowledgeable about potentially dangerous situations associated with each exercise. These are identified throughout this book.

8. Be alert and quick to respond to the needs of the person you are spotting.

9. Know when and how to guide the bar in the desired path.

10. Know when and how much lifting assistance is needed to complete an exercise.

11. As a last resort, handle all of the weight of the bar, but only if your partner might be injured if you do not take action.

As the person performing a weight training exercise, your actions are important to your spotter's safety as well as yours. Following these suggestions will help make training safer for both of you.

1. Tell the spotter the number of repetitions you intend to complete before you begin the exercise.

2. Be vocal about when you need assistance.

3. Always stay with the bar. That is, once the spotter needs to assist, remember not to let go of the bar or stop trying to complete the exercise. If you do, the spotter must handle the entire weight of the bar and might be injured.

4. Know your strength and technique limitations and select an appropriate load for each set. (This is a common problem for those who are new to training.)

Lifting Fundamentals Drill 1.
Grip Selection and Location

This drill involves lifting an empty bar or a dowel stick from the floor using the three types of grips in the three grip-width positions described on pages 17-18. When completing this drill, you should position your hands so that the bar is balanced when being pulled to the thighs.

. Using the wide grip width (see figure 2.10, page 18) and an overhand grip (see figure 2.8a, page 17), lift the bar to the thighs and then lower it back to the floor using correct lifting techniques. Lift the bar twice more to your thighs, using first the underhand grip (see figure 2.8b, page 17) and then the alternated grip (see figure 2.8c, page 17).

Now move your hands to the common grip width, and use the three different types of grips. Next move your hands to the narrow grip, and do the same. Perform all grips with your thumbs around the bar. Check off each correctly performed grip and grip width.

Success Check

- Establish the proper hand spacing.
- Keep your thumbs around the bar.
- Remember the names of the grips.

Score Your Success

Complete three overhand grips with correct technique = 3 points

Complete three underhand grips with correct technique = 3 points

Complete three alternated grips with correct technique = 3 points

Your score ___

Lifting Fundamentals Drill 2.
Preparation Position

This drill will help you develop a better sense of balance and a greater awareness of proper body positioning.

Without falling forward or allowing either or both heels to rise, squat down into the gorilla position with your hands clasped behind your head. Move into this position 10 times. Performing this drill in front of a mirror is a great way to critique and perfect your technique.

Success Check

- Keep heels on floor and back flat.
- Keep head upright.
- Keep eyes focused straight ahead.

Score Your Success

Give yourself 1 point for each repetition performed with good balance, for a maximum total of 10 points.

Your score ___

Lifting Fundamentals Drill 3. Floor-to-Thigh

This drill is designed to help you learn to keep the bar close to your shins, knees, and thighs in order to avoid low back injury when lifting and returning the bar to the floor.

From a standing position, move into the preparatory (gorilla) lifting position. Using the overhand grip, pull the bar to the middle of your thighs. Remember good lifting techniques: Keep your head up and back flat and let your legs do the lifting. Lower the bar to the floor in the same manner. Repeat this drill 10 times. Have a qualified professional check your technique.

Success Check

- Maintain a flat back with your head up.
- Feel the shoulders-back position.
- Keep your hips low.

Score Your Success

Give yourself 1 point for each repetition performed with good lifting technique, based on the evaluation of a qualified professional, for a maximum total of 10 points.

Your score ___

Lifting Fundamentals Drill 4. **Shrug**

Most beginners have a tendency to flex the elbows too soon during what is commonly referred to as the second pull—that is, the pull from the thighs that brings the bar to the shoulders. This drill will help you avoid this common technique flaw.

Using an overhand grip, pick up the bar and hold it at your thighs with your elbows fully extended. With your knees and hips slightly flexed, perform a quick shoulder shrug, then immediately extend your hips and knees while keeping your elbows straight. You may want to think of the movement as jumping with a bar while keeping your elbows straight. After each jump, return the bar to your thighs, not to the floor. Repeat this drill 10 times.

Success Check

- Feel the stretch in the trapezius muscles.
- Keep elbows fully extended.

Score Your Success

Give yourself 1 point for each repetition you complete with straight elbows, for a maximum total of 10 points.

Your score ___

Lifting Fundamentals Drill 5. **Racking the Bar**

This drill will help you develop the timing you need to flex your hips and knees when racking the bar on your shoulders.

Follow the same procedures used in the previous drill but pull the bar to your shoulders after the jump. Work on timing the catch of the bar at your shoulders by flexing your hips and knees and moving your feet to a stance that is somewhat wider than the initial position. Repeat 10 times.

Success Check

- Cushion the catch on the shoulders by flexing the knees.
- Remember to keep your elbows straight until your hips are fully extended.

Score Your Success

Give yourself 1 point for each repetition you successfully complete—hips, knees, and feet properly positioned—for a maximum total of 10 points.

Your score ___

SUCCESS SUMMARY FOR BASICS OF LIFTING AND SPOTTING

Weight training should begin with determining if medical clearance is warranted (see checklist on page xxi); if so, obtain it before you start a program. Sound training technique requires a proper grip and a stable position from which to lift. You must keep the object being lifted close to your body and use your legs rather than your back. Remember that hips stay low as the legs straighten. This is true whether you are lifting a barbell or a box off the floor or spotting an exercise. Developing good fundamental techniques will help you avoid injury and train your muscles in ways that produce optimal results.

After you have learned about and practiced fundamental lifting skills and proper breathing and spotting techniques, you are ready to move on to step 3. In this step you will go through five practice activities, called *practice procedures,* to learn how to perform and use the weight training exercises that will make up your new program.

Before Taking the Next Step

Honestly answer each of the following questions. If you answer yes to all of them, you are ready to move on to step 3.

1. Have you completed the medical clearance checklist (see page xxi) and, if necessary, obtained permission from your doctor to begin a weight training program?

2. Can you identify and perform the three types of grips? Have a qualified professional observe your technique.

3. Can you identify and perform the four phases of lifting a bar off the floor to the shoulders? Have a qualified professional observe your technique.

4. Do you know how to breathe properly during a repetition?

5. Have you identified an appropriate spotter to assist you in exercises that require one?

6. Have you successfully completed the five drills in this step?

Learning How to Select Exercises and Training Loads

Acquiring the ability to perform weight training exercises correctly creates a sense of accomplishment and enables you to make each training session more satisfying and productive. As you learn the exercises in steps 4 through 10, you will apply the basic techniques you mastered in step 2 and the practice procedures you will learn in this step.

"Practice makes perfect" is the underlying theme for this step. It consists of a series of five practice activities called *practice procedures.* Insight gained from these procedures will help you learn exercises quickly and safely, while increasing your confidence, enjoyment, and weight training success. The procedures are as follows:

1. Choose one exercise for each muscle area.

2. Determine the warm-up and trial loads for each exercise.

3. Practice proper exercise technique.

4. Perform repetitions with the trial load to determine the training load.

5. Make needed adjustments to the training load.

1. CHOOSE ONE EXERCISE

Steps 4 through 8 include a choice of one free-weight and two machine exercises that have been selected for those new to weight training because they are easy to learn and perform correctly. In step 9 you will select from body weight and machine exercises and in step 10 from only free-weight exercises. If you are new to weight training, you will choose one exercise from steps 4-9 for each of the muscle groups shown in figure 3.1. If you are an experienced lifter, consider adding exercises to emphasize muscular size, strength, or muscular endurance. Such exercises are presented after the basic ones in steps 4 through 9 and are identified by an asterisk (*) in the text and a ✳ in the captions. If you consider yourself an advanced lifter, you may want to add one or more of the total-body exercises presented in step 10 to your workout.

For all of the exercises in steps 4 through 10, you should read the technique explanations and then study the photos and main technique points. Consider the equipment and spotting requirements of each exercise. Step 11 will explain how to record the exercises you have selected on a workout chart.

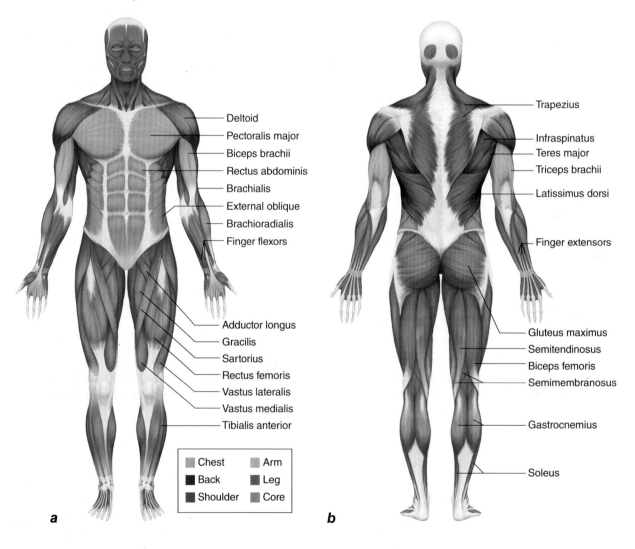

Figure 3.1 Muscle groups: *(a)* anterior, or front, view; *(b)* posterior, or back, view. Exercises for each of these muscle groups are included in the basic program.

2. DETERMINE WARM-UP AND TRIAL LOADS

Using light loads in the early stages of learning weight training exercises enables you to concentrate more on the techniques required and less on how hard to push or pull. Out of enthusiasm or curiosity, you may be tempted to use loads that are too heavy. Selecting loads that are too heavy, even if your technique is perfect, increases the chance of injury. Avoid this temptation!

Provided next are two safe methods for determining warm-up and trial loads. If you are new to weight training, use the first method to determine loads for basic exercises. If you are an experienced lifter, use the second method to determine loads for *additional exercises.

Basic Exercises

This practice procedure explains how to use the formulas shown in figure 3.2 to determine the warm-up and trial loads for the basic exercises. If you select one of the first three exercises listed in steps 4 through 9, you will need to identify the *coefficient* (a number that represents a certain percent of the person's body weight) associated with that exercise to determine warm-up and trial loads. Each step includes exercises and coefficients that are specific to a certain muscle group. The example provided in figure 3.2 is associated with the chest muscle area from step 4. Realize that using the coefficients results in an *estimated* warm-up or trial load. Individual differences, combined with the variation in equipment design, make it difficult, if not impossible, to derive coefficients that are without error. Those presented in this text are starting points for determining appropriate loads. If there is a need to convert pounds to kilograms or kilograms to pounds, refer to the conversion chart in the back of the book.

You will notice that for the first three exercises, the letters FW (for free weight), C (for cam), and M (for multi-unit machine—but it can apply to a single-unit machine too) identify the type of equipment that is used when performing them.

After you've located the name of the exercise you've selected, write your body weight in the appropriate space and multiply it by the number to the right of it (the coefficient). The coefficient is a number that has been derived from studies of males and females who, for the most part, do not have experience in weight training. When multiplied by your body weight, the coefficient can be used to estimate training loads, and using one-half of it provides an appropriate warm-up load. The use of body weight in determining appropriate loads is based on its relationship to strength. This is the same logic used for creating weight divisions in sports such as wrestling, boxing, and weightlifting.

Note that if you are a male who weighs more than 175 pounds (79.5 kg), you should record your body weight as 175 pounds (79.5 kg). If you are a female who weighs more than 140 pounds (63.6 kg), record your body weight as 140 pounds (63.6 kg).

To complete this procedure, round the number to the nearest 5-pound (2.3 kg) increment or to the closest weight-stack plate. This becomes your trial load. The example seen in figure 3.2 is of a female who weighs 120 pounds (54.5 kg) and has selected the free-weight bench press from the three chest exercises available. In this example, the rounded-off trial load equals 40 pounds (18.2 kg) and one-half of that equals a warm-up load of 20 pounds (9.1 kg).

Figure 3.2   Sample Calculation of Warm-Up and Trial Loads for Basic Exercises.

Female

Exercise	Body weight		Coefficient		Trial load	Warm-up load (Trial load ÷ 2)
FW–bench press	120	X	0.35	=	42 lbs. (round off to 40)	20 lbs. (40 ÷ 2)
C–pec deck		X	0.14	=		
M–chest press		X	0.27	=		

Male

Exercise	Body weight		Coefficient		Trial load	Warm-up load (Trial load ÷ 2)
FW–bench press		X	0.60	=		
C–pec deck		X	0.30	=		
M–chest press		X	0.55	=		

FW = free weight, C = cam, M = multi- or single-unit machine exercise.

Note: If you are a male who weighs more than 175 pounds (79.5 kg), record your body weight as 175 (79.5). If you are a female who weighs more than 140 pounds (63.6 kg), record your body weight as 140 (63.6).

Using this method sometimes results in a warm-up load that is lighter than the lightest weight stack plate on a machine. If this occurs, select the lightest weight plate and recruit a qualified professional to safely assist (by pushing or pulling) in accomplishing the movement patterns involved in the exercise. The bars available for free-weight exercises may pose the same problems. If so, very light dumbbells, a stripped-down dumbbell bar, a single weight plate, or even a wooden dowel stick (less than 1 pound [0.5 kg] in weight) may be used during warm-up sets.

The warm-up load is used in learning the exercise techniques in practice procedure 3, while the trial load is used in practice procedure 4 to determine the training load. Note that the term *trial load* is used because you will be *trying it out* in practice procedure 4 to see if it is an appropriate load to use later for training. Trial loads that are too heavy or light can be adjusted using practice procedure 5.

*Additional Exercises

If you are an experienced lifter, you should consider supplementing the basic workout with one or more of the *additional exercises presented in steps 4-9 and, possibly, one or more exercises from step 10. Additional exercises with an asterisk (*) or an ✳. If you do, you will need to follow the approach described next to determine training loads for each *additional exercise. (If you chose an exercise from step 10, follow the directions in that step for determining loads.)

Based on your previous experience and awareness of the weight that you can handle, select a weight that will allow you to perform 12 to 15 repetitions and write it in the "Estimated trial load for 12 to 15 repetitions" column. Then determine an effective warm-up load by multiplying the trial load by 0.6 (or use about two-thirds of the trial load if that calculation is easier), and round the number to the nearest 5-pound (2.3 kg) increment or to the closest weight-stack plate.

The example seen in figure 3.3 is from step 4. An experienced male lifter wants to add the *dumbbell chest fly exercise to his basic program. He estimates that he can lift 35 pounds for 12 to 15 repetitions, which makes his rounded-off warm-up load 20 pounds (35 × 0.6 = 21, rounded down to 20).

Figure 3.3 Sample Calculation of a Warm-Up Load for an *Additional Exercise.

Exercise	Estimated trial load for 12-15 repetitions				Warm-up load
*Dumbbell chest fly	35 lbs.	x	0.6	=	20 lbs.

The warm-up load is used in learning the exercise techniques in practice procedure 3, while the trial load is used in practice procedure 4 to determine the training load. Trial loads that are too heavy or light can be adjusted using practice procedure 5.

3. PRACTICE PROPER TECHNIQUE

In this practice procedure, you will use warm-up loads while learning the grip, body positioning, movement pattern, bar velocity, and breathing pattern for each exercise. Carefully read the information and directions that follow concerning each of these technique considerations and try to apply them in steps 4 through 10.

- **Grip.** As you learned in step 2, a variety of weight training grip styles and grip widths can be used. For each exercise, learn which type of grip is appropriate and where to place your hands when using that grip.

- **Body positioning.** Body positioning refers to the initial posture of the body, not arm or leg movements. Proper positioning provides a balanced and stable position from which to pull or push. Improper positioning can reduce the benefits of an exercise or result in serious injury.

- **Movement pattern.** The movement pattern refers to how the arms, legs, and trunk move during an exercise. It is important to complete the full range of movement. Performing exercises through the movement ranges and in the patterns shown enables you to get your arms, legs, and trunk more active during each repetition and, therefore, become better trained. Learning and practicing correct movement patterns and ranges also contribute to safer training sessions.

- **Bar velocity.** Velocity refers to the speed of the barbell, dumbbell, or handle as it moves through the range of motion in an exercise. During this practice procedure, getting into the habit of performing slow, controlled movement patterns is especially important. Try to allow about two seconds for the concentric phase (usually the more difficult, upward movement) and two-four seconds for the eccentric phase (usually the easier, downward movement) of the exercise. Doing so will avoid the buildup of momentum that is commonly associated with weight training injuries.

- **Breathing pattern.** Trying to remember when to exhale and inhale can be confusing, especially when there are other skills to remember at the same time. As you practice performing exercises with warm-up loads, learn to identify where in each exercise the sticking point occurs and breathe out as described in step 2. Remember that the sticking point in a repetition is the position at which the exercise becomes most difficult. Inhale during the recovery movement phase.

Visualization is an excellent method to help perform correct exercise and spotting techniques. Use all of your senses while visualizing the correct way to perform an exercise. Try to find a quiet location in the weight room or develop the ability to concentrate even under noisy conditions. Clearly visualize the proper grip, body positioning, movement pattern, velocity, and breathing for each exercise. Concentrate on feedback from your muscles and joints as you mentally rehearse exercises. This will help you learn how the exercise feels when you are performing it correctly.

You may also want to mimic the correct movement patterns of exercises in front of a mirror, making note of the feedback you sense from your muscles, tendons, and joints. Attempt to do this for 1 or 2 minutes immediately before you begin each exercise in practice procedure 2 or 3. Try to find time before each training session to visualize the proper techniques for each exercise until you have mastered them.

4. DETERMINE TRAINING LOAD

The correct load will result in muscular failure on the 12th to 15th repetition when maximum effort is given. Simply use the trial load determined in practice procedure 2 to load the bar or to select the right place to insert the pin or key in the machine weight stack; then perform as many repetitions as possible with proper and safe exercise technique. If the number of repetitions you can complete is 12 to 15, you have found an appropriate training load. Record this number in the "Training load" column on the workout chart located in step 11 (see figure 11.1 on page 146). If you performed fewer than 12 or more than 15 repetitions in any of steps 4 through 9, you have one more practice procedure to complete before moving on to the next exercise.

5. MAKE NEEDED LOAD ADJUSTMENTS

Because individuals differ in physical characteristics and experience, and because weight training equipment differs in design, the trial loads may not produce the desired range of 12 to 15 repetitions. If you performed fewer than 12 repetitions, the trial load is too heavy. On the other hand, if you performed more than 15 repetitions, the load is too light.

In this practice procedure, you will use a load adjustment chart to make necessary corrections. Once you begin training, you may need to use the chart several times before an accurate training load is determined.

Figure 3.4 shows how the load adjustment chart is used to make needed adjustments to the trial load for the basic and *additional exercises in steps 4 through 9. The example shown is taken from step 4 for someone who performed 9 repetitions with 100 pounds (45.5 kg) in the free-weight bench press exercise. Because only 9 repetitions (instead of 12 to 15) were performed, the weight was too heavy, and so the load needs to be reduced.

Reading across the load adjustment chart, you can see that a 10-pound (4.5 kg) reduction is recommended when only 9 repetitions are performed. The result is a more appropriate training load of 90 pounds (40.9 kg). Follow these same procedures to adjust the trial load in each exercise, if necessary.

Write in the name of the muscle group and the name of the exercise you selected for the chest, followed by those selected for the back, shoulders, arms (both biceps and triceps), and legs, in that order, as shown in figure 3.5. If you want to include one or more *additional exercises, write it on the workout chart immediately after the basic exercise that you selected for that muscle group from steps 4 through 9. If you chose one or more total-body exercises, you will perform it first regardless of where it appears on the workout chart.

Figure 3.4 Sample Load Adjustment Chart

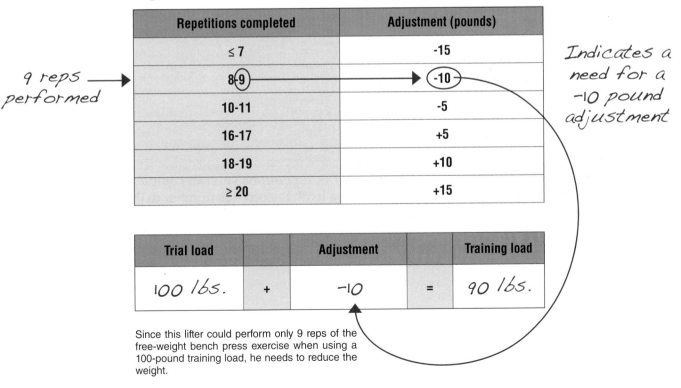

Repetitions completed	Adjustment (pounds)
≤ 7	-15
8-9	-10
10-11	-5
16-17	+5
18-19	+10
≥ 20	+15

9 reps performed

Indicates a need for a -10 pound adjustment

Trial load		Adjustment		Training load
100 lbs.	+	-10	=	90 lbs.

Since this lifter could perform only 9 reps of the free-weight bench press exercise when using a 100-pound training load, he needs to reduce the weight.

Figure 3.5 Example of Recording Exercise Selection and Training Load Information.

Chest Drill 1. CHOOSE ONE EXERCISE

After reading about the characteristics and techniques involved in the exercises and the type of equipment required for each, you are ready to put to use what you have learned. Consider the availability of equipment and access to spotters in your situation; then select one of the following exercises to use in your program:

- Free-weight bench press
- Machine pec deck (seated fly)
- Machine chest press (multi- or single-unit machine)

Write in "Chest" in the "Muscle group" column on the workout chart and fill in the name of the exercise you selected in the "Exercise" column (see figure 11.1 on page 146). If you intend to include the *dumbbell chest fly exercise, record it on the workout chart immediately after the chest exercise selected above.

Success Check

- Consider availability of equipment.
- Consider need for a spotter and the availability of a qualified professional.
- Consider time available.
- Choose a chest exercise and write it on the workout chart.

Trial load		Adjustment		Training load
100 lbs.	+	-10	=	90 lbs.

Weight training workout chart (three days a week)

	Muscle group	Exercise	Training load
1	Chest	Bench press	90
2	Back	Bent-over row	80
3	Shoulders	Standing press	60
4	Biceps	Biceps curl	55
5	Triceps	Triceps pushdown	30
6	Legs	Leg press	165

Practice Procedures Drill.
Practice Procedure Quiz

Select the correct answer for each of the following questions. Answers are on page 201.

1. For how many primary muscle groups will you choose at least one exercise?

   a. one

   b. seven

   c. nine

2. What body weight should be multiplied by a coefficient if a male lifter weighs 220 pounds (100 kg)?

   a. 140 pounds (63.6 kg)

   b. 175 pounds (79.5 kg)

   c. 220 pounds (100 kg)

3. The warm-up load for an *additional exercise represents what percent of the estimated trial load?

   a. 40 percent

   b. 50 percent

   c. 60 percent

4. At what point in the movement of an exercise should you inhale?

   a. before each repetition begins

   b. during the sticking point

   c. during the recovery phase

5. In which practice procedure is the trial load used to determine the training load?

   a. practice procedure 3

   b. practice procedure 4

   c. practice procedure 5

6. If you performed 12 to 15 repetitions with the trial load, should you continue on to practice procedure 5?

   a. yes

   b. no

7. If you performed 17 repetitions with 100 pounds (45.5 kg) in practice procedure 4, what is your adjusted training load?

   a. 105 pounds (47.7 kg)

   b. 115 pounds (52.3 kg)

   c. 120 pounds (54.5 kg)

Score Your Success

Give yourself 1 point for each question you answered correctly, for a maximum total of 7 points.

Your score ___

SUCCESS SUMMARY FOR THE FIVE PRACTICE PROCEDURES

The procedures presented in this step are used in learning the exercises in steps 4 through 10. Begin by selecting one of the exercises shown in each of these steps. Then look up the body weight coefficient for each exercise and determine the warm-up and trial loads as seen in figure 3.2. If an exercise is new, refer to the instructions and photos in steps 4 through 10 to learn the proper technique. Advanced lifters can add any of the *additional exercises and determine warm-up and trial loads using figure 3.3.

If the trial loads are too heavy or too light for the basic or *additional exercises, follow the adjustment guidelines in figure 3.4. Using the procedures in the order presented will make learning weight training exercises very easy, especially if you practice visualizing the correct exercise techniques before practice procedures 4 and 5.

Before performing any of the exercises in steps 4 through 10, take time to review and practice the warm-up and cool-down exercises presented in step 2. Practicing them will serve as a warm-up and provide an opportunity for you to learn how to perform them correctly. Be sure to start and end each training session with the warm-up and cool-down exercises.

Before Taking the Next Step

Honestly answer each of the following questions. If you answer yes to all of them, you are ready to move on to step 4.

1. Can you describe the five practice procedures?

2. Can you determine warm-up and trial loads using an example?

3. Can you determine training loads using an example?

4. Do you understand how to make load adjustments?

5. Have you completed the practice procedure quiz?

In step 4 you will select the first exercises for your program. This step includes four exercises that can be used to develop the chest, each with specific instructions on how they should be performed, from the grip to the lifting movements involved.

Selecting Chest Exercises and Training Loads

Some of the most popular exercises in weight training are those that work the chest muscles, or pectorals (pectoralis major and pectoralis minor). When developed properly, these muscles contribute a great deal to an attractive upper body and to success in many recreational and athletic activities.

The bench press, machine pec deck, machine chest press, and the *dumbbell chest fly (an additional exercise) described in this step provide an added benefit because they also train the muscles of the front shoulder (anterior deltoid). In addition, the bench press and machine chest press train the back of the upper arms (triceps).

If you have access to free weights, you are encouraged to select the bench press or the *dumbbell chest fly to develop your chest. If you prefer working with machines, select the machine pec deck or the machine chest press for your chest exercise.

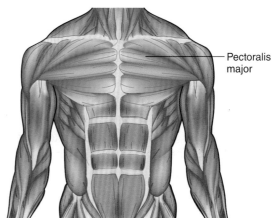

Pectoralis major

FREE-WEIGHT BENCH PRESS

The free-weight bench press involves the use of a barbell and a bench with uprights, called a Begin by sitting on the end of the bench with your back facing the upright supports. Now lie back and position yourself so that your buttocks, shoulders, and head are firmly and squarely positioned on the bench, as shown in figure 4.1*a* on page 44 Your legs should straddle the bench and both feet should be flat on the floor, about shoulder-width apart. This five-point contact (with the bench and the floor) position is important—especially the straddled feet—because it provides stability when you are handling the bar over your chest and face.

From this position, slide toward the upright supports until your eyes are directly below the front edge of the shelf of the uprights. This position helps prevent the bar from hitting the uprights during the upward movement phase but keeps it close enough to be easily placed back on the shelf (racked) after the last repetition is completed. Improper body positioning on the bench is a common error. Make sure your eyes are below the edge of the shelf and check that there are five points of contact.

MISSTEP

Your body does not have five points of contact with the bench and floor.

CORRECTION

Check to be sure that your head, shoulders, and buttocks are squarely on the bench and both feet are flat on the floor.

While the bar is supported on the uprights, grasp it with an evenly spaced overhand grip, hands about shoulder-width apart or wider. An appropriate grip width on the bar positions the forearms perpendicular to the floor as the bar touches the chest. Keep in mind that a wide grip is preferred because it emphasizes a larger area of the chest musculature than a narrow one does.

MISSTEP

Your grip is not evenly spaced.

CORRECTION

Evenly space your hands using the markings on the bar or have your spotter help you locate a balanced position.

From this position, signal "OK" to the spotter and push the bar off the uprights to a straight-elbow position with your wrists directly over your elbows. Pause with the bar in the extended-arm position and then lower it slowly to your chest as shown in figure 4.1*b* The bar should contact your chest approximately 1 inch (1 or 2 cm) above or below the nipples. A common error is touching the bar too high on the chest. Concentrate on having the bar touch or nearly touch at your nipple area. Inhale as you lower the bar to your chest. After the bar touches the chest (do not bounce it off your chest), slowly push it straight upward to an extended-elbow position (figure 4.1*c*). If your elbows extend unevenly, visually focus and concentrate on the arm that is lagging behind. Exhale through the sticking point that occurs when the bar is about halfway up. Do not allow your wrists to hyperextend (roll back); concentrate on keeping them straight.

MISSTEP

The bar bounces off your chest.

CORRECTION

Control the bar's downward momentum and pause briefly at the chest.

Throughout the exercise keep your head, shoulders, and buttocks in contact with the bench and both feet flat on the floor. Signal the completion of the last repetition by saying "OK" to your spotter. Rack the bar and be sure to support the bar until it is racked (figure 4.1*d*).

MISSTEP

Your buttocks lift off the bench, which causes the bar to move backward and over the face.

CORRECTION

Lighten the load and concentrate on keeping your buttocks in contact with the bench.

MISSTEP

When racking, you push the bar into the uprights.

CORRECTION

Visually focus on and maintain control of the bar until it is safely in the rack.

As the spotter, stand 2 to 6 inches (5-15 cm) from the head of the bench and centered between the uprights (figure 4.1*a*). To assist your partner in moving the bar off the supports (called a *handoff*), grasp the bar using the alternated grip. Space your hands evenly between your partner's hands. At the "OK" command, carefully lift the bar from the supports and guide it to a straight-elbow position over your partner's chest. Before releasing the bar, be sure that your partner's elbows are completely straight. Practice making your handoff as smooth as possible. If your handoff is too high, too low, too far forward, or too close to the shelf, it will disturb your partner's stable position on the bench, which may contribute to a poor performance or injury.

Once the downward phase begins, your open hands and eyes should follow the bar's downward path to the chest (figure 4.1*b*) and back up to the starting position (figure 4.1*c*). As your partner's elbows straighten for the last repetition and after you hear the "OK" signal, assist by grasping the bar and moving it back to the supports (figure 4.1*d*). Be sure that the bar is resting on the shelf before releasing it.

Most errors associated with this exercise are a result of lowering and raising the bar too quickly. Any technique error is made worse as the speed of the movement increases; thus, the first step in correcting errors is to make sure that the bar is moving slowly. Then attempt to make the corrective changes for the errors that apply to you.

Figure 4.1 FREE-WEIGHT BENCH PRESS

Preparation

Spotter

1. Place feet hip-width apart, 2 to 6 inches (5-15 cm) from head of bench
2. Slightly flex knees
3. Keep back flat
4. Use alternated grip, inside partner's hands
5. React to "OK" command from partner
6. Assist in lifting bar off supports
7. Guide bar to straight-elbow position
8. Release bar smoothly

Lifter

1. Use an overhand grip at least shoulder-width apart
2. Create five points of contact: head, shoulders, buttocks on bench; both feet on floor
3. Straddle bench
4. Focus eyes below edge of shelf
5. Signal "OK" to spotter
6. Move bar off supports
7. Push to straight-elbow position over chest
8. Keep wrists directly above elbows throughout exercise

Downward Movement

Spotter

1. Closely follow bar movement
2. Assist only when necessary

Lifter

1. Inhale while lowering the bar
2. Keep wrists straight
3. Use slow, controlled movement
4. Touch bar to chest near nipples
5. Pause as bar touches chest

Figure 4.1   FREE-WEIGHT BENCH PRESS *(CONTINUED)*

Upward Movement

Spotter
1. Closely follow bar movement
2. Watch for uneven arm extension
3. Watch for bar stopping or moving toward partner's face
4. Assist only when necessary

Lifter
1. Push upward with elbows extending evenly
2. Exhale during upward movement
3. Pause at straight-elbow position
4. Continue downward and upward movements until set is complete
5. Signal "OK" on last repetition

Racking the Bar

Spotter
1. Grasp bar with alternated grip
2. Keep bar level
3. Guide bar to supports
4. Say "OK" when bar is racked

Lifter
1. Keep elbows straight
2. Move bar to supports
3. Support bar until racked

MACHINE PEC DECK (SEATED FLY)

Get into a sitting position in a pec deck chest machine with your back firmly against the back pad. Adjust the seat until your upper arms are parallel to the floor when you are holding the handles. Sit erect, look straight ahead, and place your forearms on the arm pads with the elbows level with the shoulders. Grip each handle with a closed grip (figure 4.2*a*).

While in this position, squeeze your forearms together until the pads touch in front of your chest (figure 4.2*b*). Exhale as your elbows come together. Pause in this position and then slowly return to the starting position while inhaling (figure 4.2*a*).

MISSTEP

Head and torso lean forward.

CORRECTION

Keep your head and shoulders against the back pad. Lighten the load if necessary.

MISSTEP

You pull with your hands.

CORRECTION

Think: *Press elbows together.*

The machine pec deck is different from the free-weight bench press and the machine chest press in terms of the number of muscle groups exercised. The triceps are involved in the bench press and chest press but not in the pec deck. The free-weight equivalent to the machine pec deck is the *dumbbell chest fly (see page 49).

Figure 4.2   **MACHINE PEC DECK (SEATED FLY)**

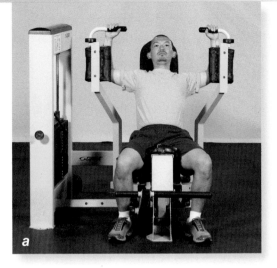 

Preparation

1. Place head, shoulders, and back in contact with back pad
2. Grasp each handle with a closed grip
3. Place forearms on arm pads
4. Check seat height; upper arms should be parallel to floor

Movement

1. Squeeze forearms together; do not pull with hands
2. Keep head and torso on back pad
3. Bring arm pads to front of chest
4. Exhale as elbows come together
5. Pause
6. Return to starting position while inhaling
7. Continue forward and backward movements until set is complete

MACHINE CHEST PRESS

Position your head, shoulders, and buttocks in contact with the bench on a multi- or single-unit machine. Put both feet flat on the floor about shoulder-width apart to complete the five points of contact. Grip the bar handles with your hands slightly more than shoulder-width apart, aligned with your nipples (figure 4.3*a*).

CAUTION: If you are performing this exercise in a supine position, be sure your head is at least 2 inches (5 cm) from the weight stack. If you are too close, the selector key may strike your forehead.

From this position, push to a full elbow extension in a slow, controlled manner (figure 4.3*b*). Exhale through the sticking point. Pause at full extension, then return to the starting position while inhaling (figure 4.3*a*).

Figure 4.3   MACHINE CHEST PRESS (MULTI- OR SINGLE-UNIT MACHINE)

Preparation
1. Head, shoulders, buttocks stay on bench
2. Feet flat on floor
3. Grip slightly wider than shoulders
4. Align grip with nipples

Movement
1. Push to full elbow extension
2. Exhale through the sticking point
3. Pause
4. Return to starting position while inhaling
5. Continue forward and backward movements until set is complete

MISSTEP

During the backward movement phase, the weights stop above the rest of the weight stack.

CORRECTION

Lower the weight stack until it lightly touches the rest of the stack.

✳ DUMBBELL CHEST FLY

If you are an experienced lifter who is ready for a more challenging program, consider adding the *dumbbell chest fly exercise. Often this exercise supplements the bench press, machine pec deck, or machine chest press exercise. Being able to move the dumbbells in unison and in an arcing fashion over the chest requires more coordination than the other chest exercises in the basic program. The *dumbbell chest fly involves the same major muscle area as the other chest exercises—the pectoralis major—and it is a pulling exercise.

Pick up the dumbbells in a neutral grip with the palms turned inward. Lie on the bench with head, shoulders, and buttocks in contact with the bench. Place both feet flat on the floor with legs flexed 90 degrees and straddling the bench (figure 4.4a). Flex your arms slightly at the elbows as you hold the dumbbells over your chest.

Inhale as you slowly lower the dumbbells (figure 4.4b). Keep your arms perpendicular to your torso with your elbows slightly flexed. The dumbbells should move in an arc, not straight up and down like the bench press exercise. Lower the dumbbells to chest height, taking care not to twist or arch your body. Keep your head, shoulders, and buttocks in contact with the bench.

Exhale as you return the dumbbells to the starting position (figure 4.4c). Your feet stay flat on the floor, and your torso remains in contact with the bench at all times.

MISSTEP

You flex your elbows too much.

CORRECTION

Flex the elbows only slightly. Dumbbells should move in an arc.

Like the free-weight bench press, this exercise also requires a spotter. Stand 2 to 6 inches (5-15 cm) from the head of the bench (figure 4.4a). Kneel on both knees or position one knee on the floor with the foot of your other leg forward and flat on the floor. To help move the dumbbells to the correct starting position, grasp your partner's wrists or forearms near the dumbbells. At the "OK" command, help move the dumbbells to a straight-elbow position over your partner's chest. Release the dumbbells smoothly after making sure your partner's elbows are completely straight. When the exercise is performed, your hands should follow close to (without touching) your partner's wrists as the dumbbells are lowered (figure 4.4b) and returned to the starting position (figure 4.4a).

Figure 4.4 ✳ **DUMBBELL CHEST FLY**

Preparation

Spotter

1. Be positioned 2 to 6 inches (5-15 cm) from head of bench
2. Keep back flat
3. React to "OK" command from partner
4. Grasp partner's wrists or forearms near dumbbells
5. Help lifter move dumbbells into position
6. Guide dumbbells up until partner's elbows are fully extended
7. Release wrists smoothly

Lifter

1. Hold dumbbells with neutral grip, palms facing inward
2. Create five points of contact: head, shoulders, buttocks on bench; both feet on floor
3. Signal "OK" to spotter
4. Move dumbbells to straight-elbow position over chest
5. Slightly flex elbows

Movement

Spotter

1. Follow close to (without touching) partner's wrists
2. Assist only when necessary

Lifter

1. Slowly lower dumbbells, keeping arms perpendicular to torso
2. Lower dumbbells to chest height
3. Keep elbows slightly flexed
4. Do not twist or arch body
5. Inhale while lowering dumbbells
6. Pause in lowest position
7. Return to starting position while exhaling
8. Keep feet flat on floor
9. Keep head, shoulders, and buttocks on bench
10. Continue downward and upward movements until set is complete

Chest Drill 1. **Choose One Exercise**

After reading about the characteristics and techniques involved in the exercises and the type of equipment required for each, you are ready to put to use what you have learned. Consider the availability of equipment and access to spotters in your situation; then select one of the following exercises to use in your program:

- Free-weight bench press
- Machine pec deck (seated fly)
- Machine chest press (multi- or single-unit machine)

Write in "Chest" in the "Muscle group" column on the workout chart and fill in the name of the exercise you selected in the "Exercise" column (see figure 11.1 on page 146). If you intend to include the *dumbbell chest fly exercise, record it on the workout chart immediately after the chest exercise selected above.

Success Check

- Consider availability of equipment.
- Consider need for a spotter and the availability of a qualified professional.
- Consider time available.
- Choose a chest exercise and write it on the workout chart.

Chest Drill 2.
Warm-Up and Trial Loads for Basic Exercises

This practice procedure answers the question "How much weight or load should I use?" Using the coefficient associated with the chest exercise you selected and the formula shown in figure 4.5, determine the trial load. (See step 3, pages 33-34 for more information on using this formula.) Round your results down to the nearest 5-pound (2.3 kg) increment or to the closest weight-stack plate. Be sure to use the coefficient assigned to the exercise you selected. Use one-half of the amount determined for the trial load for your warm-up load in the exercise. These loads will be used in drills 4 and 5.

Success Check

- Determine your trial load by multiplying your body weight by the correct coefficient.
- Determine your warm-up load by dividing your trial load by two.
- Round down your trial and warm-up loads to the nearest weight stack or bar weight.
- Write down your warm-up and trial loads.

(continued)

Chest Drill 2. *(continued)*

Figure 4.5 Calculations of the warm-up and trial loads for the chest exercises.

Female

Exercise	Body weight		Coefficient		Trial load	Warm-up load (Trial load ÷ 2)
FW–bench press		x	0.35	=		
C–pec deck		x	0.14	=		
M–chest press		x	0.27	=		

Male

Exercise	Body weight		Coefficient		Trial load	Warm-up load (Trial load ÷ 2)
FW–bench press		x	0.60	=		
C–pec deck		x	0.30	=		
M–chest press		x	0.55	=		

FW = free weight, C = cam, M = multi- or single-unit machine exercise.

Note: If you are a male who weighs more than 175 pounds (79.5 kg), record your body weight as 175 (79.5). If you are a female who weighs more than 140 pounds (63.6 kg), record your body weight as 140 (63.6).

Chest Drill 3.
Determine Trial Load for *Dumbbell Chest Fly

If you are an experienced lifter who decided to add the *dumbbell chest fly, follow the directions to determine your trial load. (See step 3, pages 34-35 for more information.)

Based on your previous experience and knowledge of the weight you can lift, select a weight that will allow you to perform 12 to 15 repetitions. Calculate the warm-up load by multiplying the trial load by 0.6 and round down to the nearest 5-pound (2.3 kg) increment (figure 4.6). These loads will be used in drill 4.

Success Check

- Select a weight that will allow 12 to 15 repetitions.
- Determine the warm-up load by multiplying the trial load by 0.6.
- Round down the warm-up load to the nearest 5-pound (2.3 kg) increment.

Figure 4.6 Calculation of the warm-up load for the *dumbbell chest fly.

Exercise	Estimated trial load for 12-15 repetitions				Warm-up load
*Dumbbell chest fly		x	0.6	=	

Chest Drill 4. **Practice Proper Technique**

In this procedure, you are to perform 15 repetitions with the warm-up load determined in drill 2 (free-weight bench press, machine pec deck, or machine chest press) or drill 3 (*dumbbell chest fly). If you are an experienced lifter who decided to add the *dumbbell chest fly, practice it last.

Review the photos and instructions for the exercise, focusing on proper grip and body positioning. Visualize the movement pattern through the full range of motion. Perform the movement with a slow, controlled velocity, remembering to exhale through the sticking point. Ask a qualified professional to observe and assess your technique.

If you selected the free-weight bench press or the *dumbbell chest fly, you need a spotter. You also need to practice spotting these exercises. Identify a partner with whom you will take turns completing the drill.

Instead of performing 15 repetitions in a continuous manner, rack the bar (free-weight bench press) or return the dumbbells to the floor (*dumbbell chest fly) after each repetition to practice the bench press handoff or the *dumbbell chest fly wrist grasp at the beginning of each repetition. Alternate responsibilities so that you and your partner both have a chance to develop the techniques that are required to correctly perform the spotting techniques. Ask a qualified professional to observe and assess your performance in the basic techniques.

Success Check

- For the free-weight bench press, all handoffs and rackings are performed correctly.

- For the *dumbbell chest fly, all wrist grasps are performed correctly.

- For all exercises, movement pattern, velocity, and breathing are correct.

Chest Drill 5. **Determine Training Load**

This practice procedure will help you determine an appropriate training load designed to produce 12 to 15 repetitions. For basic exercises, perform as many repetitions as possible with the calculated trial load from drill 2. Make sure that the repetitions are performed correctly.

If you performed 12 to 15 repetitions with the trial load, then your trial load is your training load. Record this weight as your training load for this exercise on the workout chart (see page 146). If you did not perform 12 to 15 repetitions, go to drill 6 to make adjustments to the load.

Success Check

- Check that you are using the correct load.

- Maintain proper and safe technique during each repetition.

Chest Drill 6. **Make Needed Load Adjustments**

If you performed fewer than 12 repetitions with your trial load, the load is too heavy, and you need to lighten it. On the other hand, if you performed more than 15 repetitions, the trial load is too light, and you need to increase it. Use figure 4.7 to determine the adjustment you need to make and the formula for making load adjustments.

Success Check

- Check correct use of the load adjustment chart (figure 4.7).

- Write in your training load on the workout chart (see page 146).

Figure 4.7 Making adjustments to the training load for the chest exercises.

Repetitions completed	Adjustment (pounds)
≤ 7	-15
8-9	-10
10-11	-5
16-17	+5
18-19	+10
≥ 20	+15

Trial load		Adjustment		Training load
	+		=	

SUCCESS SUMMARY FOR CHEST EXERCISES

This step involved selecting one chest exercise for which you have the needed equipment and perhaps one more if you have already been training. Using a proper grip, the correct body position, movement, and breathing patterns, and accurate warm-up and training loads will maximize your success.

After you have determined your training load and recorded it on your workout chart, you are ready to move on to step 5. In this step you will select exercises that develop the back muscles. It includes four exercises, each with specific instructions on how they should be performed, from the grip to the lifting movements involved.

Before Taking the Next Step

Honestly answer each of the following questions. If you answer yes to all of the questions relevant to your level and exercise selection, you are ready to move on to step 5.

1. Have you selected a basic chest exercise? If you are an experienced lifter, do you want to add the *dumbbell chest fly?

2. Have you recorded your exercise selection (or selections) on the workout chart?

3. Have you determined a warm-up and training load for the exercise(s) you selected?

4. Have you recorded the training load(s) on the workout chart?

5. Have you learned the proper technique for performing the exercise(s) you selected?

6. If the exercise requires a spotter, have you identified a qualified professional? Have you learned the proper spotting techniques?

Selecting Back Exercises and Training Loads

The bent-over row using free weights, the machine row that uses a cam machine, and the seated row and *lat pulldown (both of which require a multi- or single-unit machine) are excellent exercises to develop the upper back. These muscles—the rhomboids, trapezius, latissimus dorsi, and teres major—work in opposition to the chest muscles. The exercises in this step also develop the back of the shoulder (posterior deltoid, infraspinatus, teres minor), the front of the upper

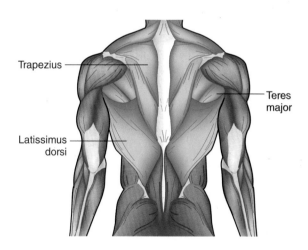

arm (biceps brachii), and the forearm (brachioradialis). Back exercises should be performed as often as chest exercises to keep the anterior and posterior upper-body musculature in balance.

If you have access to free weights, you are encouraged to select the bent-over row to develop your back. If you have access to either a cam or multi- or single-unit machine, select the machine row, the seated row, or the *lat pulldown exercise.

BENT-OVER ROW

Begin with your feet shoulder-width apart and your shoulders slightly higher—10 to 30 degrees—than your hips (figure 5.1*a*). Your back should be flat, abdominal muscles contracted, elbows straight, knees slightly flexed, and eyes looking at the floor about 2 feet (61 cm) ahead of the bar. Grasp the bar in a palms-down overhand grip with thumbs around the bar. Your hands should be evenly spaced 4 to 6 inches (10-15 cm) wider than shoulder width.

Pull the bar upward in a straight line (figure 5.1*b*). Exhale as the bar nears your chest during the upward movement. Pull in a slow, controlled manner until the bar touches your chest near the nipples (or, for women, just below your breasts). Your torso should remain rigid throughout the exercise, with no bouncing or jerking.

MISSTEP

The bar does not touch your chest.

CORRECTION

Reduce the weight on the bar and concentrate on touching your chest with the bar.

When the bar touches your chest, pause momentarily before beginning the downward movement (figure 5.1*a*). Inhale during the downward movement. Slowly lower the bar in a straight line to the starting position without letting the weight touch or bounce off the floor.

Be sure to keep your knees slightly flexed during the upward and downward movements to avoid placing excessive stress on your low back.

MISSTEP

Your upper back is rounded.

CORRECTION

Lift your head, slightly arch your back, and focus on a spot on the floor about 2 feet (61 cm) ahead of the bar.

MISSTEP

Your knees are locked.

CORRECTION

Flex your knees slightly to reduce stress on your low back.

MISSTEP

Your upper torso is not stable and moves up and down.

CORRECTION

Have someone place a hand on your upper back to help remind you of the proper position.

Although the bent-over row is considered to be one of the best exercises for the upper back, it is also frequently performed with bad technique or modified more than usual. Do not be tempted to use a heavier weight, thinking that it will increase your strength faster. Attempting to lift too much weight leads to bad technique and possible injury. Another mistake is to pull upward, simultaneously lifting with your legs and low back, and then quickly leaning forward to make contact with the bar. Too much forward lean combined with nearly or fully extended knees results in a significant amount of stress on the low back and increases your risk of injury.

Figure 5.1   BENT-OVER ROW (FREE WEIGHT)

Preparation

1. Use overhand grip, hands 4 to 6 inches (10-15 cm) wider than shoulder-width apart
2. Keep shoulders higher than hips
3. Keep low back flat
4. Keep elbows straight
5. Slightly flex knees
6. Hold head up, look at floor ahead of bar

Movement

1. Slowly pull bar straight up
2. Pause momentarily as bar touches chest
3. Touch chest near nipples (below breasts for women)
4. Keep torso rigid
5. Exhale as bar nears chest
6. Pause in highest position
7. Return to starting position while inhaling
8. Continue upward and downward movements until set is complete

MACHINE ROW

Equipment designs for the machine row vary. Your exercise facility may not have the type of machine shown in figure 5.2. If not, ask for assistance and learn the proper technique from a qualified professional.

Sit in the cam rowing machine with your chest and abdomen pressed against the chest pad. Sit erect, look straight ahead, and grasp the handles with a closed, neutral, or overhand grip (figure 5.2*a*). Adjust the seat height to position the arms parallel to the floor when they are holding the handles. Both feet should be flat on the floor or on the foot supports if the machine has them.

While maintaining the preparatory body position, pull your arms as far back as possible (figure 5.2*b*) and exhale through the sticking point. Pause and then return slowly to the starting position while inhaling (figure 5.2*a*). Keep your feet flat on the floor at all times.

MISSTEP
You do not complete the full range of motion.

CORRECTION
Bring your elbows back until they form a straight line with each other behind your back.

MISSTEP
Erect posture is not maintained.

CORRECTION
Maintain firm and continuous contact with chest pad. Be sure not to lean backward when you pull on the handles.

MISSTEP
You attempt to "throw" the handles backward.

CORRECTION
Use slow, controlled backward motion.

Figure 5.2   **MACHINE ROW (CAM MACHINE)**

 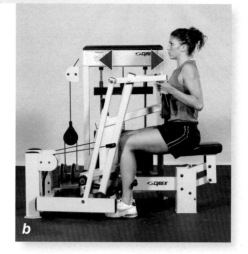

Preparation

1. Sit erect with chest and abdomen pressed against pad
2. Grasp handles with closed grip
3. Position arms parallel to the floor
4. Place feet flat on floor

Movement

1. Pull arms in a rowing movement as far back as possible
2. Keep firm contact with chest pad at all times
3. Exhale while pulling
4. Pause at handles' position nearest to torso
5. Return to starting position while inhaling
6. Continue backward and forward movements until set is complete

SEATED ROW

At the low-pulley station, get into a seated position with your knees slightly flexed and feet on the foot supports (figure 5.3a). Keep your torso erect with your low back and abdominal muscles contracted. Grasp the handles with a closed grip and your palms facing inward (depending on the type of handle that is available). Your elbows should be fully extended with the weight plates you are lifting suspended above the rest of the weight stack.

Maintain this position as you pull the handles slowly and smoothly to your abdomen (figure 5.3b). Exhale as the bar nears your abdomen. Pause, then return to the starting position while inhaling (figure 5.3a). Your upper torso should not move back and forth; keep it rigid and, if necessary, lighten the weight.

MISSTEP

You allow the weight plates to drop quickly and hit the rest of the stack.

CORRECTION

Pause at your chest and then slowly return the handles to the starting position. Maintain control of the weight throughout the exercise.

MISSTEP

Your knees are straight rather than flexed slightly.

CORRECTION

Make sure your knees are slightly flexed to decrease pressure on your low back.

MISSTEP

Your torso and upper back is rounded rather than erect and flat.

CORRECTION

Keep your torso erect by contracting your abdominal and upper and low back muscles.

The most common error committed during the seated row exercise is allowing the upper body to move forward and backward instead of remaining erect and motionless throughout the exercise. When this happens, the low back muscles become involved in extending the back and reduce the pulling action of the upper back muscles. Thus the forward and backward movement compromises the benefit to the upper back muscles for which this exercise was designed.

Figure 5.3 SEATED ROW (MULTI- OR SINGLE-UNIT MACHINE)

Preparation
1. Get into a seated position with feet on supports
2. Slightly flex knees
3. Keep torso erect
4. Fully extend elbows
5. Grasp handles with closed grip

Figure 5.3 **SEATED ROW (MULTI- OR SINGLE-UNIT MACHINE)** *(CONTINUED)*

Movement

1. Pull handles slowly and smoothly toward torso
2. Do not use torso movement to pull weight
3. Exhale as handles near abdomen
4. Pause at handles' position nearest to torso
5. Return to starting position while inhaling
6. Continue backward and forward movements until set is complete

✱ LAT PULLDOWN

A common additional exercise for the upper back is the *lat pulldown. It is similar to the pull-up, but it is performed in a multi- or single-unit machine.

This pulling exercise develops the upper back (latissimus dorsi, rhomboids, trapezius) and involves some anterior upper-arm (biceps) muscles. It can be performed sitting in a machine (as shown in figure 5.4) or kneeling on the floor.

Begin by getting into an upright, seated position facing the weight stack with your legs straddling the thigh support post and your feet flat on the floor. Grasp the bar in an overhand grip, with hands slightly wider than shoulder width (figure 5.4a). Slightly tilt the torso back and fully extend the elbows.

Smoothly pull the bar down in front of your face, past your chin, and then toward the upper chest (figure 5.4b). Keep your elbows out and away from your body. Touch your upper chest with the bar while exhaling.

To return the bar to the starting position, slowly extend the elbows to allow the bar to move upward (figure 5.4a). Control the weight; do not allow the weight plates to hit the rest of the stack. Inhale as you fully extend your elbows.

MISSTEP

You quickly move your torso backward to pull the bar down.

CORRECTION

Keep your torso stationary during the exercise. Use your upper back, arm, and shoulder muscles to pull the bar down.

MISSTEP

You allow the weight plates to fall quickly and hit the rest of the stack.

CORRECTION

Pause when the bar touches your chest and then slowly return the bar to the starting position. Maintain full control of the weight plates.

Figure 5.4 ✳LAT PULLDOWN (MULTI- OR SINGLE-UNIT MACHINE)

Preparation

1. Use an overhand grip slightly wider than shoulder-width apart
2. Get into a kneeling or seated position
3. Lean torso back slightly
4. Fully extend elbows

Movement

1. Pull bar down in front of face
2. Keep elbows out and away from body
3. Keep torso stationary
4. Pull bar past chin and then toward upper chest
5. Exhale as bar touches chest
6. Return to starting position while inhaling
7. Continue downward and upward movements until set is complete

Back Drill 1.   Choose One Exercise

After reading about the characteristics and techniques of the exercises and the type of equipment required for each, you are ready to put to use what you have learned. Consider the availability of equipment in your situation; then select one of the following exercises to use in your program:

- Bent-over row (free weight)
- Machine row (cam machine)
- Seated row (multi- or single-unit machine)

Write in "Back" in the "Muscle group" column on the workout chart and fill in the name of the exercise you selected in the "Exercise" column (see figure 11.1 on page 146). If you intend to include the machine ✳lat pulldown exercise, record it on the workout chart immediately after the previously selected back exercise.

Success Check

- Consider availability of equipment.
- Consider time available.
- Choose a back exercise and write it on the workout chart.

Back Drill 2.
Warm-Up and Trial Loads for Basic Exercises

This practice procedure answers the question "How much weight or load should I use?" Using the coefficient associated with the back exercise you selected and the formula shown in figure 5.5, determine the trial load. (See step 3, pages 33-34, for more information on using this formula.) Round your results down to the nearest 5-pound (2.3 kg) increment or to the closest weight-stack plate. Be sure to use the coefficient assigned to the exercise you selected. Use half of the amount determined for the trial load for your warm-up load in the exercise. These loads will be used in drills 4 and 5.

Success Check

- Determine your trial load by multiplying your body weight by the correct coefficient.
- Determine your warm-up load by dividing your trial load by two.
- Round down your trial and warm-up loads to the nearest 5-pound (2.3 kg) increment or to the closest weight-stack plate.

Figure 5.5   Calculations of the warm-up and trial loads for the back exercises.

Female

Exercise	Body weight		Coefficient		Trial load	Warm-up load (Trial load ÷ 2)
FW–bent-over row		X	0.35	=		
C–machine row		X	0.20	=		
M–seated row		X	0.25	=		

Male

Exercise	Body weight		Coefficient		Trial load	Warm-up load (Trial load ÷ 2)
FW–bent-over row		X	0.45	=		
C–machine row		X	0.40	=		
M–seated row		X	0.45	=		

FW = free weight, C = cam, M = multi- or single-unit machine exercise.

Note: If you are a male who weighs more than 175 pounds (79.5 kg), record your body weight as 175 (79.5). If you are a female who weighs more than 140 pounds (63.6 kg), record your body weight as 140 (63.6).

Back Drill 3.
Determine Trial Load for *Lat Pulldown

If you are an experienced lifter who decided to add the *lat pulldown, follow the directions to determine the trial load. (See step 3, pages 34-35 for more information.)

Based on your previous experience and knowledge of the weight that you can lift, select a weight that will allow you to perform 12 to 15 repetitions. Calculate the warm-up load by multiplying the trial load by 0.6 and round down to the closest weight-stack plate (figure 5.6). These loads will be used in drill 4.

Success Check

- Select a weight that will allow 12 to 15 repetitions.

- Determine the warm-up load by multiplying the trial load by 0.6.

- Round down the warm-up load to the closest weight-stack plate.

Figure 5.6   Calculation of the warm-up load for the *lat pulldown.

Exercise	Estimated trial load for 12-15 repetitions				Warm-up load
*Lat pulldown		×	0.6	=	

Back Drill 4.   Practice Proper Technique

In this procedure, you are to perform 15 repetitions with the warm-up load determined in drill 2 (bent-over row, machine row, or seated row) or drill 3 (*lat pulldown). If you are an experienced lifter who decided to add the *lat pulldown, practice it last.

Review the photos and instructions for the exercise, focusing on proper grip and body positioning. Visualize the movement pattern through the full range of motion. Perform the movement with a slow, controlled velocity, remembering to exhale through the sticking point. Ask a qualified professional to observe and assess your technique.

Success Check

- Check movement pattern.
- Check velocity.
- Check breathing.

Back Drill 5. Determine Training Load

This practice procedure will help you determine an appropriate training load designed to produce 12 to 15 repetitions. For basic exercises, perform as many repetitions as possible with the calculated trial load from drill 2. Make sure that you perform the repetitions correctly. If you are doing the free-weight bent-over row, also check that your hips are lower than your back and that the bar touches at or near the nipples.

If you performed 12 to 15 repetitions with the trial load, then your trial load is your training load. Record this weight as your training load for this exercise in the workout chart (see page 146). If you did not perform 12 to 15 repetitions, go to drill 6 to make adjustments to the load.

Success Check

- Check that you are using the correct load.

- Maintain proper and safe technique during each repetition.

Back Drill 6. Make Needed Load Adjustments

If you performed fewer than 12 repetitions with your trial load, the load is too heavy, and you need to lighten it. On the other hand, if you performed more than 15 repetitions, the trial load is too light, and you need to increase it. Use figure 5.7 to determine the adjustment you need to make and the formula for making load adjustments.

Success Check

- Check correct use of load adjustment chart (figure 5.7).

- Write in your training load on the workout chart (see page 146).

Figure 5.7 Making adjustments to the training load for the back exercises.

Repetitions completed	Adjustment (pounds)
≤ 7	-15
8-9	-10
10-11	-5
16-17	+5
18-19	+10
≥ 20	+15

Trial load		Adjustment		Training load
	+		=	

SUCCESS SUMMARY FOR BACK EXERCISES

This step involved selecting one back exercise for which you have the needed equipment and perhaps one more if you have already been training. Using a proper grip, the correct body position, movement, and breathing patterns, and accurate warm-up and training loads will maximize your success.

After you have determined your training load and recorded it on your workout chart, you are ready to move on to step 6. In this step you will select exercises that develop the shoulder muscles. It includes three exercises and one *additional exercise, each with specific instructions on how they should be performed.

Before Taking the Next Step

Honestly answer each of the following questions. If you answer yes to all of the questions relevant to your level and exercise selection, you are ready to move on to step 6.

1. Have you selected a basic back exercise? If you are an experienced lifter, do you want to add the *lat pulldown?

2. Have you recorded your exercise selection (or selections) on the workout chart?

3. Have you determined a warm-up and training load for the exercise(s) you selected?

4. Have you recorded the training load(s) on the workout chart?

5. Have you learned the proper technique for performing the exercise(s) you selected?

Selecting Shoulder Exercises and Training Loads

Overhead pressing exercises using free weights, a pulley or pivot machine, or a cam machine are excellent for developing the front, middle, and posterior sections of the shoulder (anterior, middle, and posterior heads of the deltoid). They also develop the back of the upper arm (triceps). These exercises contribute to a stable shoulder joint and help balance the strength of the chest, neck, and upper back muscles.

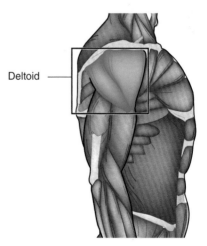

Deltoid

The free-weight standing press, sometimes called the military press, is generally considered to be the best shoulder exercise, although the free-weight *upright row is a good alternative because it does not involve (and therefore fatigue) the triceps.

If you have access to free weights, you are encouraged to select the standing press or the *upright row to develop your shoulders. If you have access to either a cam or a multi- or single-unit machine, choose either the shoulder press exercise or seated press exercise to develop your shoulders. These two exercises involve nearly the same movements but are performed with different types of machines.

STANDING PRESS

To prepare for this exercise, place the bar on a squat rack or set of supports at shoulder height. If racks or supports are not available, you must lift the bar from the floor using the techniques presented in step 2.

Grasp the bar in an overhand grip, with your hands equidistant from the center of the bar and slightly more than shoulder-width apart. With your elbows under the bar, your wrists should be in a slightly extended position. The bar should be resting on your shoulders, clavicles (collarbones), and hands (figure 6.1a).

MISSTEP

Your grip is too wide or uneven.

CORRECTION

Evenly space your hands shoulder-width apart, using the markings on the bar for reference.

Push the bar upward in a straight line above your shoulders at a slow to moderate speed until your elbows are fully extended (figure 6.1b). You will need to move your head slightly backward as the bar reaches chin level during the upward and downward movements. Otherwise, keep your head in a neutral position throughout this exercise. Avoid leaning back or hyperextending the spine, especially during the upward movement phase.

MISSTEP

You start the bar upward with a knee kick (flexion, then a quick extension).

CORRECTION

Start with your knees in a fully extended position and keep them that way throughout the upward and downward movements of the bar.

Pause momentarily at the top; then lower the bar slowly to the starting position (figure 6.1a). Do not bounce the bar on your upper chest or front shoulders. Inhale as you lower the bar and exhale as it passes through the sticking point during ascent. After the last repetition, rack the bar (not shown in figure 6.1). If you must lower the bar to the floor after completing the exercise, use the shoulder-to-floor lowering techniques presented in step 2.

CAUTION: Be careful not to hold your breath through the sticking point; doing so could cause you to pass out. Exhale as the bar moves through the sticking point.

As the spotter, stand directly behind your partner as close as you can without causing contact (figure 6.1a). With outstretched arms and your open hands under (but not touching) the bar, follow it as it moves up and down (figure 6.1b). Once your partner has given the "OK" signal after the last repetition, grasp the bar and help return it to the rack supports before releasing it (if a rack is available).

Figure 6.1   **FREE-WEIGHT STANDING PRESS**

Preparation

Spotter

1. Stand directly behind partner as close as possible without touching
2. Watch the bar
3. Keep feet shoulder-width apart

Lifter

1. Use an overhand grip, hands evenly spaced, shoulder width or slightly wider
2. Hold head upright, facing forward
3. Position elbows under bar, wrists extended
4. Hold bar in hands, resting it on shoulders and clavicles

Movement

Spotter

1. Keep hands close to bar, tracking movement
2. Assist only when necessary
3. Caution partner not to lean back or hold breath

Lifter

1. Push bar straight up
2. Keep torso erect
3. Exhale through sticking point
4. Pause at top of movement
5. Return to starting position while inhaling
6. Continue upward and downward movements until set is complete
7. Signal "OK" on last repetition

MISSTEP

Your eyes are closed during the exercise.

CORRECTION

Focus on an object straight ahead, especially when you reach the sticking point.

MISSTEP

Your arms extend unevenly.

CORRECTION

Keep both arms moving upward in unison by visually focusing and concentrating on the arm that lags behind.

Of the errors commonly seen in the standing press, leaning back too far is the most common. This typically occurs at the bar's sticking point. It should be avoided because it places extra stress on the low back. Think: *Torso, head, and bar form a straight line.*

SHOULDER PRESS

Position yourself on the seat of the cam machine with your back against the pad, your shoulders aligned under the handles, and your feet flat on the floor. Grasp the handles with a closed grip (figure 6.2a).

From this position, push the handles up to full elbow extension in a slow, controlled manner (figure 6.2b). Exhale when passing through the sticking point. Pause at full extension; then return to the starting position while inhaling (figure 6.2a).

MISSTEP

Your low back is not against the back pad.

CORRECTION

Slide back on the seat until your low back is pressed against the back pad.

MISSTEP

You hold your breath during the sticking point.

CORRECTION

Begin to exhale as soon as the bar nears the extended-elbow position.

The most common error made during the shoulder press is arching the low back when the sticking point is reached. The back should be kept flat against the pad because the arched position places too much stress on the low back. Concentrate on keeping your buttocks stationary and your low back pressed against the back pad.

Figure 6.2 **SHOULDER PRESS (CAM MACHINE)**

Preparation

1. Get into a seated position against back pad
2. Grasp the handles with a closed grip
3. Place feet flat on floor

Movement

1. Push up to full elbow extension
2. Keep elbows directly under wrists and torso erect
3. Exhale through sticking point of upward movement
4. Pause
5. Return to starting position while inhaling
6. Continue upward and downward movements until set is complete

SEATED PRESS

Sit erect on the stool of the multi- or single-unit weight machine so that the front of your shoulders is directly below the handles (figure 6.3a) with your feet flat on the floor. Grasp the handles with a closed grip slightly wider than shoulder-width apart.

Push the handles up until your elbows are fully extended (figure 6.3b). Keep your shoulders directly under the handles throughout the exercise. Keep your low back flat by pressing it into the back pad. Exhale as your elbows near the fully extended (sticking point) position. Pause when your elbows are fully extended; then slowly return to the starting position (figure 6.3a).

Figure 6.3 SEATED PRESS (MULTI- OR SINGLE-UNIT MACHINE)

Preparation
1. Sit erect on stool or seat so that front of shoulders is directly below handles
2. Grip handles with closed grip at approximately shoulder width
3. Place feet flat on floor

Movement
1. Push up to full elbow extension
2. Keep torso erect
3. Exhale during upward movement
4. Pause
5. Return to starting position while inhaling
6. Continue upward and downward movements until set is complete

MISSTEP

You hold your breath.

CORRECTION

Begin to exhale when the handles reach the sticking point.

The most common errors made during the seated press are hyperextending (excessively arching) the low back and failing to lower the handles to shoulder level. Keep the back flat by sitting erect on the seat by contracting your abdominal and low back muscles. Think: *Head, torso, and buttocks form a straight line.*

Failing to lower the handles to the starting position reduces the range through which the shoulder muscles are exercised, thus minimizing their development. Try to lower the handles so the weight plates lightly touch the rest of the weight stack. To keep the weight plates from banging against each other, control the handles' downward momentum and pause at shoulder level before pushing upward for the next repetition.

✳ UPRIGHT ROW

If you are an experienced lifter who wants to add a second shoulder exercise to your program, consider adding the *upright row. In addition, if you find that the first plate on the machine for the seated or shoulder press is too heavy, you can substitute the *upright row using an empty bar.

The *upright row also develops the deltoids, but it differs from other shoulder exercises because it uses a pulling motion and does not involve the triceps muscle. This exercise can be performed using a barbell, dumbbells, or the low-pulley station on a machine. Figure 6.4 shows a lifter using a barbell.

Grasp the barbell in an overhand grip, 6 to 8 inches (15-20 cm) apart (figure 6.4*a*). Stand with your torso erect, arms straight, and feet shoulder-width apart. Rest the bar on your thighs. (See step 2, page 18, for more information on lifting the bar from the floor to the thighs.)

Pull the bar up along your abdomen and chest (figure 6.4*b*). Keep your elbows higher than your wrists and point them out to the sides. Pull the bar up until your elbows are at shoulder height and exhale as the bar nears your shoulders. Pause briefly at the top of the movement.

Inhale as you lower the bar to the starting position (figure 6.4*a*) in a smooth motion. Pause at the bottom of the movement before beginning the next repetition.

MISSTEP
You allow your elbows to drop below your wrists.

CORRECTION
Keep your elbows high and pointed up as you raise the bar.

MISSTEP
You allow the bar to drop too quickly back to the starting position.

CORRECTION
Pause at the top position; then slowly return the bar to the starting position.

Figure 6.4   ✳ **UPRIGHT ROW**

Preparation

1. Use an overhand grip
2. Place hands 6 to 8 inches (15-20 cm) apart
3. Hold torso erect
4. Place feet shoulder-width apart
5. Fully extend elbows
6. Rest bar on thighs

Movement

1. Pull bar upward along abdomen and chest
2. Point elbows out and higher than wrists
3. Pull until elbows reach shoulder height
4. Exhale as bar nears shoulders
5. Pause briefly at top position
6. Return to starting position while inhaling
7. Continue upward and downward movements until set is complete

Shoulder Drill 1.   Choose One Exercise

After reading about the characteristics and techniques of the exercises and the type of equipment required for each, you are ready to put this information to use. Consider the availability of equipment and access to spotters in your situation; then select one of the following exercises to use in your program:

- Standing press (free weight)
- Shoulder press (cam machine)
- Seated press (multi- or single-unit machine)

Write in "Shoulders" in the "Muscle group" column on the workout chart and fill in the name of the exercise you selected in the "Exercise" column (see figure 11.1 on page 146). If you intend to include the free-weight *upright row, record it on the workout chart immediately after the previously selected shoulder exercise.

Success Check

- Consider availability of equipment.
- Consider need for a spotter and the availability of a qualified professional.
- Consider time available.
- Choose a shoulder exercise and write it on the workout chart.

Shoulder Drill 2.
Warm-Up and Trial Loads for Basic Exercises

The next practice procedure answers the question "How much weight or load should I use?" Using the coefficient associated with the shoulder exercise you selected and the formula shown in figure 6.5, determine the trial load. (See step 3, pages 33-34, for more information on using this formula.) Round your results down to the nearest 5-pound (2.3 kg) increment or to the closest weight-stack plate. Be sure to use the coefficient assigned to the exercise you selected. Use half of the amount determined for the trial load for your warm-up load in the exercise. These loads will be used in drills 4 and 5.

Success Check

- Determine your trial load by multiplying your body weight by the correct coefficient.

- Determine your warm-up load by dividing the trial load by two.

- Round down your trial and warm-up loads to the nearest 5-pound (2.3 kg) increment or to the closest weight-stack plate.

Figure 6.5   Calculations of the warm-up and trial loads for the shoulder exercises.

Female

Exercise	Body weight		Coefficient		Trial load	Warm-up load (Trial load ÷ 2)
FW–standing press		×	0.22	=		
C–shoulder press		×	0.25	=		
M–seated press		×	0.15	=		

Male

Exercise	Body weight		Coefficient		Trial load	Warm-up load (Trial load ÷ 2)
FW–standing press		×	0.38	=		
C–shoulder press		×	0.40	=		
M–seated press		×	0.35	=		

FW = free weight, C = cam, M = multi- or single-unit machine exercise.

Note: If you are a male who weighs more than 175 pounds (79.5 kg), record your body weight as 175 (79.5). If you are a female who weighs more than 140 pounds (63.6 kg), record your body weight as 140 (63.6).

Shoulder Drill 3.
Determine Trial Load for *Upright Row

If you are an experienced lifter who decided to add the *upright row, follow the directions to determine your trial load. (See step 3, pages 34-35 for more information.)

Based on your previous experience and knowledge of the weight that you can lift, select a weight that will allow you to perform 12 to 15 repetitions. Calculate the warm-up load by multiplying the trial load by 0.6 and round down to the nearest 5-pound (2.3 kg) increment or to the closest weight-stack plate (figure 6.6). These loads will be used in drill 4.

Success Check

- Select a weight that will allow 12 to 15 repetitions.

- Determine the warm-up load by multiplying the trial load by 0.6.

- Round down the warm-up load to the nearest 5-pound (2.3 kg) increment or to the closest weight-stack plate.

Figure 6.6   Calculation of the warm-up load for the *upright row.

Exercise	Estimated trial load for 12-15 repetitions				Warm-up load
*Upright row		×	0.6	=	

Shoulder Drill 4.   Practice Proper Technique

In this procedure, you are to perform 15 repetitions with the warm-up load determined in drill 2 (standing press, shoulder press, or seated press) or drill 3 (*upright row). If you are an experienced lifter who decided to add the *upright row, practice it last.

Review the photos and instructions for the exercise, focusing on proper grip and body positioning. Visualize the movement pattern through the full range of motion. Perform the movement with a slow, controlled velocity, remembering to exhale through the sticking point. Ask a qualified professional to observe and assess your technique.

If you selected the free-weight standing press, you need a spotter. You also need to practice the skills of spotting this exercise. Identify a spotter with whom you will take turns completing the drill.

Instead of performing 15 repetitions in a continuous manner, rack the bar after each repetition for practice. Alternate responsibilities so that you and your partner both have a chance to develop the proper techniques for performing and spotting this exercise. Ask a qualified professional to observe and assess your performance in the basic techniques.

Success Check

- For the standing press, all rackings are performed correctly.

- For all exercises, movement pattern, velocity, and breathing are correct.

Shoulder Drill 5.   **Determine Training Load**

This practice procedure will help you determine an appropriate training load designed to produce 12 to 15 repetitions. For basic exercises, perform as many repetitions as possible with the calculated trial load from drill 2. Make sure that you perform the repetitions correctly.

If you performed 12 to 15 repetitions with the trial load, then your trial load is your training load. Record this number

as your training load for this exercise on the workout chart (see page 146). If you did not perform 12 to 15 repetitions, go to drill 6 to make adjustments to the load.

Success Check

- Check that you are using the correct load.

- Maintain proper and safe technique during each repetition.

Shoulder Drill 6.
Make Needed Load Adjustments

If you performed fewer than 12 repetitions with your trial load, it is too heavy, and you need to lighten it. On the other hand, if you performed more than 15 repetitions, the trial load is too light, and you need to increase it. Use figure 6.7 to determine the adjustment you need to make and the formula for making load adjustments.

Success Check

- Check correct use of load adjustment chart (figure 6.7).

- Record your training load on the workout chart (see page 146).

Figure 6.7   Making adjustments to the training load for the shoulder exercises.

Repetitions completed	Adjustment (pounds)
≤ 7	-15
8-9	-10
10-11	-5
16-17	+5
18-19	+10
≥ 20	+15

Trial load		Adjustment		Training load
	+		=	

SUCCESS SUMMARY FOR SHOULDER EXERCISES

This step involved selecting one shoulder exercise for which you have the needed equipment and perhaps one more if you have already been training. Using a proper grip, the correct body position, movement, and breathing patterns, and accurate warm-up and training loads will maximize your success.

After you have determined your training load and recorded it on your workout chart, you are ready to move on to step 7. In this step you will select exercises that are designed for developing the arms, including four for the front of the arm and four for the back of the arm.

Before Taking the Next Step

Honestly answer each of the following questions. If you answer yes to all of the questions relevant to your level and exercise selection, you are ready to move on to step 7.

1. Have you selected a basic shoulder exercise? If you are an experienced lifter, do you want to add the *upright row?

2. Have you recorded your exercise selection (or selections) on the workout chart?

3. Have you determined a warm-up and training load for the exercise(s) you selected?

4. Have you recorded the training load(s) on the workout chart?

5. Have you learned the proper technique for performing the exercise(s) you selected?

6. If the exercise(s) you selected require a spotter, have you identified a qualified professional? Have you learned the proper spotting techniques?

Selecting Upper Arm Exercises and Training Loads

Exercises that develop the two muscle groups of the upper arm are very popular, especially with people who are just beginning a weight training program. These muscles respond quickly when properly trained, and changes in this muscle area are noticed sooner and more often than changes in other body parts. The anterior (front) and posterior (back) portions of the upper arm are known as the biceps (the traditional "show me your muscle" muscle) and the triceps, respectively.

The free-weight biceps curl or *alternating dumbbell biceps curl, the preacher curl using the cam-type machine, and the low-pulley biceps curl using a single- or

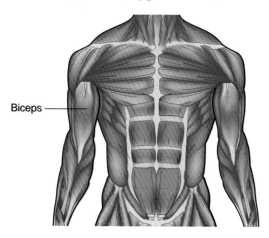

Biceps

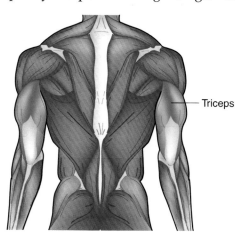

Triceps

multi-unit weight machine are ideal exercises to develop the front of the upper arm. They also develop the muscles in the front of the forearm.

The free-weight seated triceps extension or *supine triceps extension, the triceps extension using the cam machine, and the triceps pushdown on a multi- or single-unit weight machine are excellent exercises for developing the back of the upper arms.

When properly developed, the biceps and triceps muscles contribute to elbow-joint stabilization. Development of these muscles contributes to activities that require pulling (biceps) or pushing and throwing motions (triceps).

BICEPS EXERCISES

If you have access to free weights, you are encouraged to select the biceps curl or the *alternating dumbbell biceps curl to develop the front of your upper arms. If you have access to either a cam or multi- or single-unit machine, choose either the preacher curl or the low-pulley biceps curl exercise.

Biceps Curl

To get in the preparatory position, grasp the bar in an underhand grip with your hands about shoulder-width apart and evenly spaced (figure 7.1a). Press your upper arms against the sides of your torso, upper arms perpendicular to the floor with elbows fully extended. The bar should touch the front of your thighs in this position. Your back should be straight, your eyes should be looking straight ahead, and your knees should be slightly flexed to reduce stress on the low back.

MISSTEP

Your elbows are slightly flexed in the preparatory position.

CORRECTION

Stand erect with your shoulders back and your elbows fully extended.

Begin the upward movement phase by curling the bar upward toward your shoulders, keeping your elbows and upper arms perpendicular to the floor and close to the sides of your torso (figure 7.1b). Avoid allowing your elbows and upper arms to move back or out to the sides. Your body must remain straight and erect throughout the exercise—no rocking, swinging, or jerking should occur. Begin to exhale as the bar nears the sticking point and continue curling until the elbows are flexed, and the bar is near the front of the shoulders.

MISSTEP

Your upper arms move back as you lift the bar.

CORRECTION

Squeeze the insides of your upper arms against the sides of your torso.

MISSTEP

You use momentum to complete the repetition.

CORRECTION

Keep your upper body erect. If this problem continues, stand with your back against the wall.

MISSTEP

Your wrists hyperextend (roll back) as you complete the upward movement phase.

CORRECTION

Concentrate on keeping your wrists straight and rigid.

After reaching the top position, inhale as you slowly lower the bar back down to the starting position (figure 7.1a). Your elbows should be fully extended, and you should pause momentarily before curling the bar upward for the next repetition.

Figure 7.1 **BICEPS CURL (FREE WEIGHT)**

Preparation
1. Use an underhand grip, hands shoulder-width apart
2. Hold torso erect
3. Hold head up, facing forward
4. Keep upper arms against sides of torso, elbows extended
5. Allow bar to rest on front of thighs

Movement
1. Keep upper arms stationary
2. Keep elbows close to body
3. Do not rock, jerk, or swing body
4. Begin to exhale as bar nears shoulders
5. Curl bar to shoulders
6. Return to starting position while inhaling
7. Continue upward and downward movements until set is complete

Preacher Curl

Sit on the seat of the cam machine with your chest against the pad (figure 7.2a). Place your elbows on the pad in line with the axis of the cam, repositioning your arms if necessary. Adjust the seat so that your elbows are slightly lower than your shoulders with your feet flat on the floor.

MISSTEP

Your elbows are flexed at the start of the exercise.

CORRECTION

Start the exercise with your elbows fully extended; lower the seat if needed.

Grasp the handles in an underhand grip and begin the exercise at full elbow extension. Perform the exercise by curling the handles upward as far as possible, pausing briefly at the top position (figure 7.2b). Exhale as the handles pass through the sticking point.

MISSTEP

You use upper-torso movement to complete the curl.

CORRECTION

Keep the chest against the pad and the body stationary.

MISSTEP

You do not go through the full range of motion.

CORRECTION

Curl upward until your hands almost touch your shoulders.

Inhale as you slowly lower the handles to the starting position, being careful not to allow the elbows to hyperextend (figure 7.2a).

MISSTEP

The weight drops too quickly.

CORRECTION

Slowly lower the weight, being careful not to hyperextend your elbows.

Figure 7.2 **PREACHER CURL (CAM MACHINE)**

Preparation
1. Sit with chest against pad
2. Place elbows on pad in line with axis of cam
3. Adjust seat so that elbows are slightly lower than shoulders
4. Grasp handles with underhand grip

Movement
1. Curl upward as far as possible
2. Exhale through sticking point
3. Pause
4. Return to starting position while inhaling
5. Continue upward and downward movements until set is complete

Low-Pulley Biceps Curl

Stand and face the weight machine with your feet approximately 18 inches (46 cm) from the lowest pulley. Keep your torso erect with your shoulders pulled back and your chest out with your knees slightly flexed. If you begin with your knees locked, you will pull yourself forward as you pull the bar upward. Grasp the bar in an underhand grip and begin the exercise with your elbows fully extended (figure 7.3a).

MISSTEP
Your elbows are flexed at the start.

CORRECTION
Fully extend your elbows before starting and between each repetition.

Curl the bar until it almost touches your shoulders (figure 7.3b). Avoid allowing your upper arms to move backward or out to the sides. Exhale as you pass through the sticking point and inhale while lowering the bar (figure 7.3a).

MISSTEP

You allow the weight plates to drop quickly to the weight stack.

CORRECTION

Slowly lower the weight and allow the plates to lightly touch, not bang against, the rest of the weight stack.

MISSTEP

You do not go through the full range of motion.

CORRECTION

Raise the bar until it almost touches your shoulders and lower it to a fully extended elbow position.

Figure 7.3   LOW-PULLEY BICEPS CURL (MULTI- OR SINGLE-UNIT MACHINE)

Preparation

1. Hold torso erect, shoulders back, chest out
2. Slightly flex knees
3. Use underhand grip
4. Extend elbows fully

Movement

1. Curl bar to shoulder level
2. Keep upper arms stationary
3. Exhale as bar nears shoulders
4. Pause
5. Return to starting position while inhaling
6. Continue upward and downward movements until set is complete

*Alternating Dumbbell Biceps Curl

A common additional exercise for the biceps is the *alternating dumbbell biceps curl. This exercise is similar to the free-weight biceps curl except that it is performed with one arm at a time, using a dumbbell instead of a long bar. The major muscle area involved is the same (biceps brachii).

Grasp one dumbbell in each hand and stand with your feet shoulder-width part and your knees slightly flexed. Allow the dumbbells to hang at the sides of your body with your palms facing your legs (this places the dumbbell handles parallel to each other). Your elbows should be fully extended (figure 7.4a).

Beginning with your right arm, slowly curl the dumbbell up toward your right shoulder (figure 7.4b). As the dumbbell moves forward from the side of your right leg, rotate the handle so your palm faces up while keeping your elbow and upper arm perpendicular to the floor and close to the side of your torso. Do not lean back as you curl the dumbbell and exhale as the dumbbell nears your right shoulder. Pause at the top of the curl.

MISSTEP

Your elbow moves away from the side of your body as you curl the dumbbell upward.

CORRECTION

Press your upper arm and elbow against the side of your torso to keep it in position as the dumbbell is raised.

After reaching the top position, inhale as you slowly lower the dumbbell back down to the starting position, rotating it again as it passes by your thigh, until your elbow is fully extended (figure 7.4a). Repeat with the other arm.

MISSTEP

You allow the dumbbell to drop quickly back to the starting position.

CORRECTION

Slowly, with control, lower the dumbbell until the elbow is fully extended.

Figure 7.4 ✳ALTERNATING DUMBBELL BICEPS CURL (FREE WEIGHT)

Preparation

1. Stand erect with feet shoulder-width apart and flat on floor
2. Grasp dumbbells with arms next to sides of body
3. Elbows begin fully extended

Movement

1. Starting with right arm, slowly curl dumbbell toward right shoulder
2. Rotate handle as dumbbell moves in front of right leg
3. Continue curling dumbbell and rotating handle until palm faces up
4. Keep upper arms and body stationary
5. Exhale as dumbbell nears shoulder
6. Return to starting position while inhaling
7. Repeat with other arm
8. Continue upward and downward movements until set is complete

TRICEPS EXERCISES

If you have access to free weights, you may select the seated triceps extension or *supine triceps extension to develop the back of your upper arms. If you have access to either a cam or multi- or single-unit machine, select either the triceps extension or the triceps pushdown.

Seated Triceps Extension

Sit erect on the end of a bench with your buttocks in contact with the bench and both feet flat on the floor at or wider than shoulder-width apart. From this position, signal "OK" to the spotter to hand you the bar. Grasp the bar with a narrow overhand grip 6 to 8 inches (15-20 cm) apart. Move the bar to a position over your head and pause with the bar in a straight-elbow position with your wrists directly over your elbows (figure 7.5a).

CAUTION: Do not use a long barbell for the seated triceps extension exercise. A safer choice is a cambered bar because it is shorter and easier to keep balanced during the exercise.

With your upper arms stationary and perpendicular to the floor, flex your elbows to slowly lower the bar behind your head (figure 7.5b). Inhale as you lower the bar. Keep your upper arms parallel to each other; do not allow them to bow out.

Pause at the lowest bar position and then return to the starting position by extending your elbows to push the bar back up (figure 7.5a). Keep your upper arms stationary; do not let your elbows bow out. Exhale as the bar nears the top position. Signal the completion of the last repetition by saying "OK" to your spotter and smoothly hand off the bar.

MISSTEP

Your hands are too far apart.

CORRECTION

Space your hands no more than 8 inches (20 cm) apart on the bar.

MISSTEP

You lower the bar only to the top of your head.

CORRECTION

Perform the exercise in front of a mirror. Make sure you lower the bar to a position behind the head.

MISSTEP

Your elbows flare out as you push the bar overhead.

CORRECTION

Keep your upper arms next to your ears and point your elbows forward.

As the spotter, grasp the bar using a wide grip, lift the bar off the floor, straddle the bench to stand behind your partner, and allow your partner to grasp the bar between your hands. When you hear the "OK" command, guide the bar to a straight-elbow position over your partner's head. Before releasing the bar, be sure that your partner's elbows are completely straight. Practice to make the handoff as smooth as possible.

Follow the downward and upward motions (figure 7.5b) of the bar. As your partner's elbows straighten during the last repetition and after you hear the "OK" signal, assist by grasping the bar, using a wide grip, and return it to the floor.

Figure 7.5 SEATED TRICEPS EXTENSION (FREE WEIGHT)

Preparation

Spotter

1. Grasp bar using a wide grip
2. Stand directly behind partner, straddling bench
3. React to "OK" command from lifter
4. Hand bar to partner
5. Guide bar to straight-elbow position
6. Release bar smoothly

Lifter

1. Sit erect on bench with feet flat
2. Signal "OK" to spotter
3. Take bar from spotter
4. Grasp the bar with a narrow overhand grip, evenly spaced, 6 to 8 inches (15-20 cm) apart
5. Move to straight-elbow position over head

Movement

Spotter

1. Keep hands under bar to protect partner's head
2. Closely follow bar movement
3. Assist only when necessary
4. Grasp bar with wide grip after last repetition
5. Return bar to floor

Lifter

1. Lower bar to behind head
2. Keep elbows pointed forward
3. Inhale as bar is lowered
4. Pause in lowest position
5. Push bar to full extension
6. Keep elbows close to ears, pointing forward
7. Exhale as bar passes through sticking point
8. Continue downward and upward movements until set is complete
9. Signal "OK" on last repetition

Triceps Extension

Sit in the cam machine with your back firmly pressed against the low back pad and your chest against the chest pad. Adjust the seat so that your elbows are lower than your shoulders with your feet flat on the floor. Your elbows should be in line with the axis of the cam. Adjust the position of your upper arms so they are parallel to each other on the arm pad. Grasp the handles in a closed, neutral grip (figure 7.6a).

From this position, push with your hands until your elbows are extended (figure 7.6b). Do not allow your upper arms to lift off the pads. Pause in the extended position; then slowly return to the starting position (figure 7.6a). Exhale while pushing through the sticking point and inhale during the return.

MISSTEP
Your upper arms and elbows lift off the pads.

CORRECTION
Keep pressing your upper arms and elbows against the pads. Lighten the load, if necessary.

Figure 7.6   TRICEPS EXTENSION (CAM MACHINE)

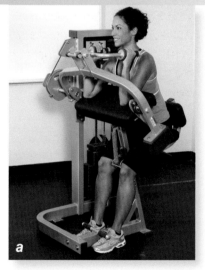 

Preparation
1. Place back firmly against low back pad and chest against chest pad
2. Adjust seat so that elbows are lower than shoulders
3. Place upper arms parallel to each other on arm pad
4. Grasp the handles in a closed, neutral grip

Movement
1. Extend elbows
2. Keep upper arms on arm pad, elbows pointing forward
3. Exhale through sticking point
4. Pause in extended elbow position
5. Return to starting position while inhaling
6. Continue forward and backward movements until set is complete

Triceps Pushdown

Stand erect with your feet approximately shoulder-width apart. Grasp the bar in an overhand grip with your hands 6 to 8 inches (15-20 cm) apart (figure 7.7a). Pull the bar down, flex your elbows, and press your upper arms firmly against the sides of your torso. Begin the exercise with the bar at chest height.

From this position, extend your elbows until they are straight, and the bar touches your body (figure 7.7b). Be sure to extend your elbows completely. Pause and then slowly return the bar to chest height without moving your upper arms and torso (figure 7.7a). Exhale as you press the bar down through the sticking point and inhale during the return.

MISSTEP

Your upper arms move away from your body.

CORRECTION

Squeeze your upper arms against the sides of your torso. Pause at both the fully extended and flexed elbow positions.

MISSTEP

You allow the bar to move above the shoulders.

CORRECTION

The bar should begin at chest height and be prevented from moving higher than shoulder level. Think: *Knuckles stay below the shoulders.*

MISSTEP

Your torso flexes forward as you push the bar down.

CORRECTION

Maintain a stable, upright position with your head, shoulders, hips, and feet in a straight vertical line. Lighten the load if necessary.

As you return the bar to chest height, take care not to allow it to move too quickly because this causes errors in technique and puts too much stress on the elbows. Slowly return the bar to the starting position in a controlled manner.

Figure 7.7 **TRICEPS PUSHDOWN (MULTI- OR SINGLE-UNIT MACHINE)**

Preparation
1. Stand erect
2. Place feet shoulder-width apart
3. Use overhand grip 6 to 8 inches (15 to 20 cm) apart
4. Squeeze upper arms against ribs
5. Begin with bar at chest height

Movement
1. Extend elbows until bar touches body
2. Do not move upper arms or torso
3. Exhale when passing through sticking point
4. Pause at fully-extended elbow position
5. Return to starting position while inhaling
6. Continue downward and upward movements until set is complete

*Supine Triceps Extension

If you are an experienced lifter who is ready for a second triceps exercise, consider adding the *supine triceps extension. Like the seated triceps extension, this exercise requires a spotter. It is a pushing exercise that is performed lying on your back, usually on a flat bench.

Lie on a bench and position your head, shoulders, and buttocks in contact with the bench and both feet flat on the floor about shoulder-width apart to complete the five points of contact. From this position, signal "OK" to the spotter to hand you the bar. Grasp the bar with an overhand grip evenly spaced about 8 inches (20 cm) apart. Move the bar to a position over your chest and pause with the bar in a straight-elbow position with your wrists directly over your elbows (figure 7.8a, page 95).

CAUTION: Do not use a long barbell for the *supine triceps extension exercise. A safer choice is a cambered bar because it is shorter and easier to keep balanced during the exercise.

Keeping your upper arms stationary and perpendicular to the floor, flex your elbows to slowly lower the bar toward your head (figure 7.8*b*). Inhale as you lower the bar. Keep your elbows pointing straight up; do not allow them to bow out. Continue lowering the bar until it approaches the top of your head (the actual location depends on the length of your forearms).

Pause at the lowest bar position and then reverse the motion by extending the elbows to push the bar back up to the starting position (figure 7.8*a*). Keep your upper arms stationary; do not let your elbows bow out. Exhale as the bar nears the top position. Signal the completion of the last repetition by saying "OK" to your spotter and smoothly hand off the bar.

MISSTEP

Your elbows move out and forward.

CORRECTION

Concentrate on keeping your upper arms stationary during the exercise.

MISSTEP

Your upper arms are not perpendicular to the floor during the exercise.

CORRECTION

Concentrate on keeping your elbows pointing up during the movement phases.

As the spotter, stand 2 to 6 inches (5-15 cm) from the head of the bench (figure 7.8*a*). Using the technique described in step 2 (see page 18), grasp the bar using a wide grip, lift the bar off the floor, stand at your partner's head, and allow your partner to grasp the bar between your hands. When you hear the "OK" command, guide the bar to a straight-elbow position over your partner's chest. Before releasing the bar, be sure that your partner's elbows are completely straight. Practice making the handoff as smooth as possible. If your handoff is too far forward or back, it will disturb your partner's stable position on the bench, which may contribute to a poor performance or injury.

Follow the downward motion of the bar with your open hands and eyes (figure 7.8*b*). Follow the bar back up to the starting position (figure 7.8*a*). As your partner's elbows straighten during the last repetition and after you hear the "OK" signal, assist by grasping the bar, using a wide grip, and then return it to the floor.

Figure 7.8 ✳**SUPINE TRICEPS EXTENSION (FREE WEIGHT)**

Preparation

Spotter
1. Grasp bar using a wide grip
2. Stand 2 to 6 inches (5-15 cm) from head of bench
3. React to "OK" command from lifter
4. Hand bar to partner
5. Guide bar to straight-elbow position
6. Release bar smoothly

Lifter
1. Create five points of contact: head, shoulders, buttocks on bench; both feet on floor
2. Signal "OK" to spotter
3. Take bar from spotter with an overhand grip, evenly spaced, 8 inches (20 cm) apart
4. Move to straight-elbow position over chest

Movement

Spotter
1. Keep hands under bar to protect partner's head
2. Closely follow bar movement
3. Assist only when necessary
4. Grasp bar with wide grip after last repetition
5. Return bar to floor

Lifter
1. Keep upper arms stationary
2. Keep elbows straight up, not flared out
3. Slowly lower bar while inhaling
4. Pause at lowest bar position
5. Push upward to extend elbows
6. Exhale during upward movement
7. Pause at straight-elbow position
8. Continue downward and upward movements until set is complete
9. Signal "OK" on last repetition

Arm Drill 1.   Choose Two Exercises

After reading about the characteristics and techniques involved in the exercises and the type of equipment required for each, you are ready to put to use what you have learned. Consider the availability of equipment and your situation; then select one biceps exercise and one triceps exercise to use in your program.

Biceps

- Biceps curl (free weight)
- Preacher curl (cam machine)
- Low-pulley biceps curl (multi- or single-unit machine)

Triceps

- Seated triceps extension (free weight)
- Triceps extension (cam machine)
- Triceps pushdown (multi- or single-unit machine)

Write in "Biceps" then "Triceps" in the "Muscle group" column on the workout chart and fill in the name of the exercises you selected in the "Exercise" column (see figure 11.1 on page 146). If you intend to include the free-weight *alternating dumbbell biceps curl (biceps) or free-weight *supine triceps extension (triceps), record it on the workout chart immediately after the arm exercises already selected.

Success Check

- Consider availability of equipment.
- Consider need for a spotter and the availability of a qualified professional.
- Consider time available.
- Choose two arm exercises and write them on the workout chart.

Arm Drill 2.
Warm-Up and Trial Loads for Basic Exercises

This practice procedure answers the question "How much weight or load should I use?" Using the coefficients associated with the arm exercises you selected and the formulas shown in figure 7.9, determine the trial load. (See step 3, pages 33-34), for more information on using this formula.) Round your results down to the nearest 5-pound (2.3 kg) increment or to the closest weight-stack plate. Be sure to use the coefficient assigned to the exercise you selected. Use one-half of the amount determined for the trial load for your warm-up load in the exercise. These loads will be used in drills 4 and 5.

Success Check

- Determine your trial load by multiplying your body weight by the correct coefficient.
- Determine your warm-up load by dividing the trial load by two.
- Round down your trial and warm-up loads to the nearest 5-pound (2.3 kg) increment or to the closest weight-stack plate.

Figure 7.9 Calculations of the warm-up and trial loads for the arm exercises.

Biceps

Female

Exercise	Body weight		Coefficient		Trial load	Warm-up load (Trial load ÷ 2)
FW–biceps curl		×	0.23	=		
C–preacher curl		×	0.12	=		
M–low-pulley biceps curl		×	0.15	=		

Male

Exercise	Body weight		Coefficient		Trial load	Warm-up load (Trial load ÷ 2)
FW–biceps curl		×	0.30	=		
C–preacher curl		×	0.20	=		
M–low-pulley biceps curl		×	0.25	=		

Triceps

Female

Exercise	Body weight		Coefficient		Trial load	Warm-up load (Trial load ÷ 2)
FW–seated triceps extension		×	0.12	=		
C–triceps extension		×	0.13	=		
M–triceps pushdown		×	0.19	=		

Male

Exercise	Body weight		Coefficient		Trial load	Warm-up load (Trial load ÷ 2)
FW–seated triceps extension		×	0.21	=		
C–triceps extension		×	0.35	=		
M–triceps pushdown		×	0.32	=		

FW = free weight, C = cam, M = multi- or single-unit machine exercise.

Note: If you are a male who weighs more than 175 pounds (79.5 kg), record your body weight as 175 (79.5). If you are a female who weighs more than 140 pounds (63.6 kg), record your body weight as 140 (63.6).

Arm Drill 3.
Determine Trial Loads for *Alternating Dumbbell Biceps Curl and *Supine Triceps Extension

If you are an experienced lifter who decides to add the *alternating dumbbell biceps curl or the *supine triceps extension, follow the directions to determine your trial load. (See step 3, pages 34-35, for more information.)

Based on your previous experience and knowledge of the weight that you can lift, select a weight that will allow you to perform 12 to 15 repetitions. Calculate the warm-up load by multiplying the trial load by 0.6 and round down to the nearest 5-pound (2.3 kg) increment

(figure 7.10). These loads will be used in drill 4.

Success Check

- Select a weight that will allow 12 to 15 repetitions.
- Determine the warm-up load by multiplying the trial load by 0.6.
- Round down the warm-up load to the nearest 5-pound (2.3 kg) increment.

Figure 7.10   Calculation of the warm-up load for the *alternating dumbbell biceps curl and the *supine triceps extension.

Exercise	Estimated trial load for 12-15 repetitions				Warm-up load
*Alternating dumbbell biceps curl		×	0.6	=	
*Supine triceps extension		×	0.6	=	

Arm Drill 4.   Practice Proper Technique

In this procedure you are to perform 15 repetitions with the warm-up load determined in drill 2 (biceps curl, preacher curl, or low-pulley biceps curl for the biceps; seated triceps extension, triceps extension, or triceps pushdown for the triceps) or drill 3 (*alternating dumbbell biceps curl for the biceps or *supine triceps extension for the triceps). If you are an experienced lifter who decided to add the *alternating dumbbell biceps curl or the *supine triceps extension, practice it last.

Review the photos and instructions for the exercise, focusing on proper grip and body positioning. Visualize the movement pattern through the full range of motion. Perform the movement with a slow, controlled velocity, remembering to exhale through the sticking point. Check your technique either by watching yourself in a

mirror or by asking a qualified professional to observe and assess your technique.

If you selected the free-weight seated triceps extension or the *supine triceps extension, you need a spotter. You also need to practice the skills of spotting these exercises. Identify a spotter with whom you will take turns completing the drill.

Instead of performing 15 repetitions in a continuous manner, return the bar to the floor after each repetition to practice getting in the right spotting position and properly handling the bar. Alternate responsibilities so that you and your partner both have a chance to develop the techniques that are required in performing and spotting these exercises. Ask a qualified professional to observe and assess your performance in the basic techniques.

Success Check

- For the free-weight seated triceps extension and the *supine triceps extension, all bar handoffs and bar returns are performed correctly.

- For all exercises, movement pattern, velocity, and breathing are correct.

Arm Drill 5. **Determine Training Load**

This practice procedure will help you determine an appropriate training load designed to produce 12 to 15 repetitions. For basic exercises, perform as many repetitions as possible with the calculated trial load from drill 2. Make sure that the repetitions are performed correctly.

If you performed 12 to 15 repetitions with your trial load, then your trial load is your training load. Record this number as your training load for this exercise in the workout chart (see page 146). If you did not perform 12 to 15 repetitions, go to drill 6 to make adjustments to the load.

Success Check

- Check that you are using the correct load.

- Maintain proper and safe technique during each repetition.

Arm Drill 6. **Make Needed Load Adjustments**

If you performed fewer than 12 repetitions with your trial load, the load is too heavy, and you need to lighten it. On the other hand, if you performed more than 15 repetitions, it is too light, and you need to increase it. Use figure 7.11 to determine the adjustment you need to make and the formula for making load adjustments.

Success Check

- Check correct use of load adjustment chart (figure 7.11).

- Write in your training load on the workout chart (see page 146).

Figure 7.11 Making adjustments to the training load for the arm exercises.

Repetitions completed	Adjustment (pounds)
≤ 7	-15
8-9	-10
10-11	-5
16-17	+5
18-19	+10
≥ 20	+15

Trial load		Adjustment		Training load
	+		=	

SUCCESS SUMMARY FOR ARM EXERCISES

This step involved selecting one arm exercise for the biceps and another for the triceps for which you have the needed equipment and perhaps one more for each if you have already been training. Using a proper grip, the correct body position, movement, and breathing patterns, and accurate warm-up and training loads, will maximize your success.

After you have determined your training load and recorded it on your workout chart, you are ready to move on to step 8. In this step, you will select exercises (classified as either multijoint or single-joint) that are designed for developing the legs.

Before Taking the Next Step

Honestly answer each of the following questions. If you answer yes to all of the questions relevant to your level and exercise selection, you are ready to move on to step 8.

1. Have you selected basic biceps and triceps exercises? If you are an advanced lifter, do you want to add the *alternating dumbbell biceps curl (biceps) or *supine triceps extension (triceps)?

2. Have you recorded your exercise selections on the workout chart?

3. Have you determined warm-up and training loads for the exercises you selected?

4. Have you recorded the training loads on the workout chart?

5. Have you learned the proper technique for performing the exercises you selected?

6. If an exercise you selected requires a spotter, have you identified a qualified professional? Have you learned the proper spotting techniques?

Selecting Leg Exercises and Training Loads

Exercises that develop the upper legs and hips are considered very physically demanding due to the large muscles involved. The area of the body trained by these exercises is sometimes referred to as the *power zone*. These muscles—the largest ones of the whole body—include the quadriceps (front of the thigh), hamstrings (back of the thigh), and gluteal muscles (the buttocks). They are responsible for our ability to run, jump, and make quick starts and fast stops, as well as lateral, backward, pushing, pulling, rotating, and kicking movements. They also stabilize the upper body during most of its movements. The importance of developing these muscles is obvious, and they should not be neglected in favor of the more visible muscles of the upper body.

The exercises in this step can be classified as either multijoint or single-joint. A *multijoint exercise* involves two or more joints of the body changing angles as the

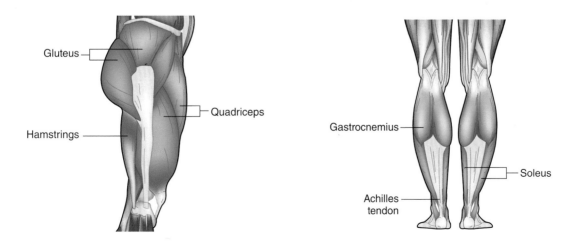

exercise is performed. This step includes the free-weight lunge, machine leg press, and *back squat (free weight) multijoint exercises. They are excellent for developing all of the large muscles of the upper legs and hips.

Some *additional exercises involve only one joint (a *single-joint exercise*); these focus on one muscle or body part area. The machine *knee extension trains the quadriceps, the machine *knee curl trains the hamstrings, and the free-weight *standing heel raise trains the back of the lower legs (the calves).

If you have access to free weights, you are encouraged to select the lunge or the *back squat to develop your legs. To isolate your calves, consider adding the *standing heel raise. If you have access to either a cam machine or a multi- or single-unit machine, choose the machine leg press exercise.

MULTIJOINT EXERCISES

Multijoint leg exercises require you to simultaneously extend the knee and hip joints. The quadriceps extend the knees, the hamstrings flex the knees and, with the help of the gluteal muscles, extend the hips.

The multijoint exercises featured in this step contribute to knee and hip-joint stabilization, muscular padding for protection of the hip, and lower-body sculpting. The leg and hip strength gained by training with these exercises is especially beneficial to those involved in athletic activities.

Lunge

Begin with your feet shoulder-width apart, eyes straight ahead, head up, shoulders back, chest out, and back straight (figure 8.1a). Do not lean your upper torso forward. This erect posture should be maintained throughout the exercise.

The forward movement phase begins with a controlled step forward with your preferred leg (figure 8.1b). Be careful not to under or overstride. Once in the stepped-out position, lower your hips (down, not forward) so the top of your forward thigh is parallel to the floor, and your forward knee is directly over your forward ankle (figure 8.1c). Your forward foot should be pointed straight ahead, with your back knee somewhat flexed and not quite touching the floor.

After pausing to gain balance, push off your forward foot and smoothly return to the starting position (figure 8.1a). Do not use the upper body to create momentum to move backward. Pause and then step forward with the other foot in the same manner. Continue alternating your legs until the set is completed. At first, you might have to slide or stutter step your forward foot to be able to return to the starting position. As you gain strength and develop better balance, this movement will not be necessary.

CAUTION: The lunge is a relatively difficult exercise to perform because of the balance required. First try lunges without weights to develop the needed balance. When you feel comfortable with the forward and backward movements and with your balance, begin using dumbbells (one in each hand) and eventually progress to using a barbell (as seen in figure 8.1).

MISSTEP

Your forward step is too short or too far out.

CORRECTION

Place your forward foot on the floor so that when you lower your hips, the forward knee is directly over your forward ankle. You may need to begin with small steps forward and gradually increase each stride until the thigh of the forward leg is parallel to the floor, and the lower leg is perpendicular to the floor.

MISSTEP

Your torso leans forward when you step forward, lower your hips, or both.

CORRECTION

Focus on keeping your torso erect and head facing forward. If your hips are not flexible enough to keep this erect position during the exercise, don't lower your hips as far down when you are in the stepped-out position. Also, be sure to perform the lower body stretching exercises described in step 2.

Figure 8.1   LUNGE (FREE WEIGHT)

Preparation
1. Stand erect with eyes straight ahead
2. Position head up, shoulders back, chest out, and back straight
3. Feet should be shoulder-width apart

Forward Movement
1. Inhale and take a controlled step straight ahead
2. Keep torso erect
3. Do not under or overstride
4. Pause in stepped-out position

(continued)

Figure 8.1 **LUNGE (FREE WEIGHT)** *(CONTINUED)*

Downward Movement and Return

1. Lower hips down until top of forward thigh is parallel to floor
2. Keep forward knee over forward ankle
3. Moderately flex back knee, but do not let it touch floor
4. Pause in lowest position
5. Push off with forward foot while exhaling to return to starting position
6. Maintain an erect torso
7. Pause before stepping forward with other leg
8. Continue alternating legs until set is complete

Leg Press

This exercise typically involves the use of a multi- or single-unit machine, although some equipment companies make a cam-type leg press machine. Begin by sitting in the machine and adjusting the seat so that your knees are flexed to 90 degrees. If you have trouble, use a mirror or ask someone to help you create a 90-degree angle. Sit erect with your low back pressed against the back of the seat, toes pointed slightly outward, and feet flat against the pedal surface slightly wider than shoulder-width apart (figure 8.2*a*). Grasp the handrails to stabilize your body.

Begin the forward movement phase by pushing your legs to an extended-knee position while maintaining an upright torso position (figure 8.2*b*). Do not let your knees move in toward each other as they are extended; keep a consistent space between them throughout the movement. Avoid twisting your body as you extend your legs and do not forcefully lock out your knees at the end of the movement. Exhale while pressing forward.

For the backward movement phase, allow your legs to move back toward your body without lifting your buttocks off the seat or allowing the plates to bang against the rest of the weight stack (figure 8.2*a*). Inhale as you return to the starting position. This movement should be performed in a slow, controlled manner.

MISSTEP

Your feet are not flat on the pedal surface.

CORRECTION

Think about pushing with the middle or back half of your foot.

MISSTEP
Your torso leans forward.

CORRECTION
Sit with your back and hips pushed against the seat.

MISSTEP
Your knees move in toward each other as you press the weight forward.

CORRECTION
Keep your knees over your feet during the movement; the distance between your knees should remain the same as you press the weight forward.

Most leg press errors involve the speed of movement. Many lifters have a tendency to press out too quickly, causing the knees to lock out. The danger is that you might hyperextend your knees and cause injury. Control your forward speed and concentrate on stopping your forward movement at a point just before your knees lock out. Another common error is letting the foot pedals free-fall back to the starting position. Just as you controlled your forward movement speed, also use a slow, controlled movement to return to the starting position.

Figure 8.2   LEG PRESS (MULTI- OR SINGLE-UNIT MACHINE)

Preparation
1. Sit erect with back pressed against back of seat
2. Adjust seat or chair to flex legs to 90 degrees
3. Place feet flat on pedal surface with toes pointed slightly outward
4. Feet should be slightly wider than shoulder-width apart
5. Grasp handrails

Movement
1. Push the pedals away by extending hips and knees
2. Maintain body position
3. Do not let knees move in toward each other
4. Avoid twisting body
5. Exhale during push
6. Pause at full extension without locking out knees
7. Return to starting position while inhaling
8. Continue forward and backward movements until set is complete

*Back Squat

The final multijoint exercise is the *back squat. This exercise targets all the major muscles of the lower body—quadriceps, hamstrings, and gluteals. In addition, many upper-body muscles are recruited to achieve an upright, *flat-back* (not rounded or hunched over) position, to keep the bar in place on the shoulder, and to provide protective support for the low back.

The *back squat is a more advanced exercise because of the upright, flat-back position (required to minimize stress on the low back), the placement of the barbell across the shoulders and upper back, and the balance needed throughout the whole exercise. A spotter is required. A common strategy when learning how to perform this exercise is to first try it with a long broomstick to develop the needed body position, bar placement, and overall balance. After you master the correct technique, progress to an empty bar, then to a bar with weight plates. Be sure to use locks.

Stand in the rack with feet flat on the floor, slightly wider than shoulder width (figure 8.3*a*, page 108). Grasp the bar in an overhand grip with your hands slightly more than shoulder-width apart. Duck under the bar and, with the help of the spotter, position the bar across your shoulders at the base of your neck. Keep your hips directly under the bar with your chest out, shoulders back, and head up.

From this position, signal "OK" to the spotter and slowly stand up, pause, and then take one or two steps backward to clear the supports. Reposition your feel to be slightly wider than shoulder-width apart with your toes pointed slightly outward. Again, position your hips directly under the bar with your chest out, shoulders back, and head up. Pause before beginning the downward movement phase.

For the downward movement phase, slowly squat (figure 8.3*b*, page 109). Do not lean forward; maintain an upright, flat-back position. Keep your feet flat on the floor and your knees aligned over your feet. Inhale as you descend and continue until your thighs are parallel to the floor.

MISSTEP
The bar is positioned too high on your neck.

CORRECTION
Place the bar on your shoulders at the base of your neck. You should be able to keep your head up even with the bar across your shoulders.

MISSTEP
You tip your head forward to look at the floor.

CORRECTION
Slightly tilt your head backward and focus your eyes slightly up with your chest out and shoulders back. However, do not look up at the ceiling.

MISSTEP

You allow your knees to move in front of your feet or toward each other.

CORRECTION

Keep your heels in full contact with the floor. Use a shallower squatting depth if needed.

Begin the upward movement by pushing with your legs. Keep your head up and chest out. Exhale through the sticking point as you extend your hips and knees and return to the starting position. Signal the completion of the last repetition by saying "OK" to your spotter. Pause and then walk forward until the bar comes into contact with the rack (figure 8.3c, page 109). Pause and then slowly squat down to place the bar on the supports. Be sure your hips remain directly under the bar with your chest out, shoulders back, and head up. Do not let the bar go until it is fully resting on the supports.

As the spotter, you should stand as close as you can to your partner without making contact. Alternatively, you can use two spotters; one at each end of the bar (as seen in figure 8.3). To assist your partner in removing the bar from the rack, grasp it with a closed grip. At your partner's "OK" command, carefully help lift the bar off the supports and take one or two steps backward as your partner also takes one or two steps backward to clear the supports (figure 8.3a, page 108). Before releasing the bar, be sure that your partner has the bar under control. Practice this procedure so that you can provide assistance without bumping your partner or the bar—either error could cause a loss of balance or a dropped bar.

Once the downward phase begins, squat with your partner and follow the bar's path with your open hands (figure 8.3b, page 109). Be sure to maintain the flat-back body position. During the upward phase, ascend with your open hands still under the bar.

As you ascend with your partner for the last repetition, prepare to help rack the bar. After your partner gives the "OK" signal, assist by grasping the bar with a closed grip and walking forward to help rack it (figure 8.3c, page 109). Be sure that the bar is fully resting on the supports before releasing it.

Figure 8.3 **BACK SQUAT (FREE WEIGHT)**

Preparation

Spotter

1. Stand close to partner (or ends of bar)
2. Use closed grip
3. React to "OK" command from partner
4. Assist in lifting bar off supports
5. Release bar smoothly
6. Take 1 or 2 steps backward with partner
7. Once partner is stationary, stand directly behind and close to partner (or ends of bar)

Lifter

1. Use an overhand grip, hands slightly wider than shoulder width
2. Position bar on shoulders at base of neck
3. Align hips directly under bar, with chest out, shoulders back, head up
4. Position feet flat on floor slightly wider than shoulder width
5. Signal "OK" to spotter
6. Slowly stand to move bar off supports
7. Take 1 or 2 steps backward
8. Reposition hips directly under bar, with chest out, shoulders back, head up
9. Reposition feet flat on floor slightly wider than shoulder width

Figure 8.3 **BACK SQUAT (FREE WEIGHT)** *(CONTINUED)*

Movement

Spotter
1. Squat with partner
2. Follow bar with open hands
3. Assist only when necessary

Lifter
1. Squat slowly
2. Maintain an upright, flat-back position
3. Keep feet flat on floor, knees in line with feet
4. Continue squatting until thighs are parallel to floor
5. Inhale during downward movement
6. Pause in lowest body position
7. Push up with legs to return to starting position
8. Keep head up and chest out
9. Exhale through sticking point
10. Continue downward and upward movements until set is complete
11. Signal "OK" on last repetition

Racking the Bar

Spotter
1. Grasp bar with closed grip
2. Walk 1 or 2 steps forward with partner
3. Guide bar to supports
4. Say "OK" when bar is racked

Lifter
1. Walk 1 or 2 steps forward until bar contacts rack
2. Align hips directly under bar, with chest out, shoulders back, head up
3. Squat down until bar is on supports

SINGLE-JOINT EXERCISES

If you are an experienced lifter who is ready for a more challenging leg program, consider one or more *additional leg exercises. At first, choose one of the single-joint exercises to complement the multijoint exercise you are already performing. A common approach is to add the machine *knee extension exercise (for the quadriceps muscle) and the machine *knee curl exercise (for the hamstring muscle) to a program that already includes either the free-weight lunge or the machine leg press. Later, as you become even more trained, consider replacing the lunge or leg press with the free-weight *back squat exercise. The *standing heel raise exercise can be added at any time.

*Knee Extension

Sit erect on the seat of the cam machine (figure 8.4*a*) with your back pressed against the back pad. Look straight ahead and keep your head up. Tuck your ankles behind the foot pads and position the instep of both feet against the pads. Grasp the edge of the seat or the handles of the machine.

Slowly extend your knees (figure 8.4*b*). Be sure to go through the complete range of motion. Exhale as you extend your knees and pause briefly at the top position.

Slowly lower the weight and return to the starting position (figure 8.4*a*). Keep a firm grip on the seat or handles to keep the buttocks in contact with the seat. Inhale as you lower the weight. Do not allow the weights to bang together at the bottom of the movement. Pause before beginning the next repetition.

MISSTEP

The backs of your knees hang off the front edge of the seat.

CORRECTION

Check that your knees are aligned with the axis of the machine and adjust the position of the back pad, if possible, so the backs of your knees are in contact with the front edge of the seat.

Figure 8.4 ✳**KNEE EXTENSION (CAM MACHINE)**

Preparation

1. Sit on seat
2. Place ankles behind pads
3. Position instep of feet against ankle pads
4. Sit erect with back against back pad
5. Hold head up, facing forward
6. Grip edge of seat or machine handles

Movement

1. Slowly extend knees through complete range of motion
2. Exhale while extending
3. Pause briefly in extended position
4. Return to starting position while inhaling
5. Keep buttocks in contact with seat
6. Continue upward and downward movements until set is complete

*Knee Curl

Lie face-down on the cam machine (figure 8.5a, page 112) with your thighs, hips, stomach, and chest in full contact with the bench. Your knees should hang off the edge of the thigh pad or bench. Tuck your ankles under the foot pads and position your Achilles tendons in contact with pads. Grasp the edge of the bench or the handles of the machine.

Slowly flex your knees to bring your heels as close to your buttocks as you can (figure 8.5b, page 112). Exhale as you flex your knees and pause briefly at the top position.

Slowly lower the weight and return to the starting position (figure 8.5a, page 112). Keep your hips and chest in contact with the bench by firmly gripping the handles or sides of the bench. Inhale as you lower the weight. Do not allow the weights to bang together at the bottom of the movement. Pause before beginning the next repetition.

MISSTEP

Your hips lift off the bench as you flex your knees.

CORRECTION

Check that your knees are aligned with the axis of the machine and keep your hips and chest in contact with the bench.

Figure 8.5 ✳KNEE CURL (CAM MACHINE)

Preparation
1. Lie face-down on bench
2. Position thighs, hips, stomach, and chest flat on bench
3. Hang knees off edge of bench
4. Place ankles under pads
5. Position Achilles tendons in contact with pads
6. Grip edge of seat or machine handles

Movement
1. Slowly flex knees through complete range of motion
2. Keep hips on bench
3. Exhale while flexing
4. Pause briefly in flexed position
5. Return to starting position while inhaling
6. Keep chest on bench
7. Continue upward and downward movements until set is complete

*Standing Heel Raise

This pushing exercise uses plantar flexion at the ankle joint to train the calf muscles, the soleus and gastrocnemius. The *standing heel raise can be performed with a barbell across the shoulders, with one or two dumbbells, with your body weight only, or in a standing machine (as shown in figure 8.6).

Dip your shoulders under the shoulder pads and place your feet hip-width apart with the balls of both feet near the front edge of the step (figure 8.6a). Keep your torso erect with your knees straight, but not forcefully locked out. Your eyes should focus straight ahead to help you maintain balance. Allow your heels to lower below the level of the step; you should feel no pain in your calves, only a stretch. This is the starting position.

Slowly point your toes to lift your heels as high as you can (figure 8.6b). Exhale as you ascend and pause briefly at the top of the movement.

Slowly allow your heels to lower back to the starting position (figure 8.6a). Again, allow your heels to lower below the level of the step in a gentle, stretched position. Maintain an upright position with your knees straight. Inhale as you lower your heels.

MISSTEP

Your knees flex and extend during the movement.

CORRECTION

Keep your knees straight—but not locked—throughout the exercise.

MISSTEP

Your ankles turn to the outside or your knees bow outward during the upward movement phase.

CORRECTION

Push up from the balls of the feet with attention focused on pushing up from the ball of the big toe of both feet.

Figure 8.6   ☀STANDING HEEL RAISE

Preparation

1. Dip shoulders under shoulder pads
2. Place balls of both feet hip-width apart near front edge of step
3. Stand erect with knees straight
4. Allow heels to lower below level of step in a gentle stretch

Movement

1. Push up from the balls of the feet to raise heels as high as possible
2. Exhale during upward movement
3. Keep knees straight
4. Pause at top of movement
5. Return to starting position while inhaling
6. Do not move torso or flex knees
7. Continue upward and downward movements until set is complete

Leg Drill 1.   Choose One Exercise

After reading about the characteristics and techniques of the exercises and the type of equipment required for each, you are ready to put to use what you have learned. Consider the availability of equipment and access to spotters in your situation; then select one of the following exercises to use in your program:

- Lunge (free weight)
- Leg press (multi- or single-unit weight machine)

Write in "Legs" in the "Muscle group" column on the workout chart and fill in the name of the exercise you selected in the "Exercise" column (see figure 11.1 on page 146). If you intend to include the machine *knee extension or *knee curl or the free-weight *back squat or *standing heel raise, record it on the workout chart immediately after the selected leg exercise.

Success Check

- Consider availability of equipment.
- Consider need for a spotter and the availability of a qualified professional.
- Consider time available.
- Choose a leg exercise and write it on the workout chart.

Leg Drill 2.
Warm-Up and Trial Loads for Basic Exercises

This practice procedure answers the question "How much weight or load should I use?" Using the coefficient associated with the leg exercise you selected and the formula shown in figure 8.7, determine the trial load. (See step 3, pages 33-34), for more information on using this formula.) Round off your results down to the closest 5-pound (2.3 kg) increment or to the closest weight-stack plate. For the lunge exercise (and the *standing heel raise if you choose to use two dumbbells), divide the loads you calculated by two to equal the weight of each individual dumbbell. Use half of the amount determined for the trial load for your warm-up load in the exercise. These loads will be used in drills 4 and 5.

Success Check

- Determine your trial load by multiplying your body weight by the correct coefficient.
- Determine your warm-up load by dividing your trial load by two.
- Round down your trial and warm-up loads to the nearest 5-pound (2.3 kg) increment or to the closest weight-stack plate.

Figure 8.7 Calculations of the warm-up and trial loads for the leg exercises.

Female

Exercise	Body weight		Coefficient		Trial load	Warm-up load (Trial load ÷ 2)
FW–lunge		×	0.10	=		
C–leg press		×	1.00	=		

Male

Exercise	Body weight		Coefficient		Trial load	Warm-up load (Trial load ÷ 2)
FW–lunge		×	0.10	=		
C–leg press		×	1.30	=		

FW = free weight, C = cam.

Note: If you are a male who weighs more than 175 pounds (79.5 kg), record your body weight as 175 (79.5). If you are a female who weighs more than 140 pounds (63.6 kg), record your body weight as 140 (63.6).

Leg Drill 3.
Determine Trial Loads for *Back Squat, *Knee Extension, *Knee Curl, and *Standing Heel Raise

If you are an experienced lifter who decided to add the *back squat, *knee extension, *knee curl, or *standing heel raise, follow the directions to determine your trial load. (See step 3, pages 34-35), for more information.)

Based on your previous experience and knowledge of the weight that you can lift, select a weight that will allow you to perform 12 to 15 repetitions. Calculate the warm-up load by multiplying the trial load by 0.6, and round down to the nearest 5-pound (2.3 kg) increment (figure 8.8). For the *standing heel raise, divide the loads you calculated by two to determine the weight of each dumbbell. These loads will be used in drill 4.

Success Check

- Select a weight that will allow 12 to 15 repetitions.

- Determine the warm-up load by multiplying the trial load by 0.6.

- Round down the warm-up load to the nearest 5-pound (2.3 kg) increment or to the closest weight-stack plate.

(continued)

Leg Drill 3. *(continued)*

Figure 8.8   Calculation of the warm-up load for the *back squat, *knee extension, *knee curl, or *standing heel raise.

Exercise	Estimated trial load for 12-15 repetitions				Warm-up load
*Back squat		×	0.6	=	
*Knee extension		×	0.6	=	
*Knee Curl		×	0.6	=	
*Standing Heel Raise		×	0.6	=	

Leg Drill 4.   Practice Proper Technique

In this procedure, you are to perform 15 repetitions with the warm-up load determined in drill 2 (lunge or leg press) or drill 3 (*back squat, *knee extension, *knee curl, or *standing heel raise). If you are an experienced lifter who decided to add the *back squat, practice it first. If you decided to add the *knee extension, *knee curl, or *standing heel raise exercise, practice it last.

Review the photos and instructions for the exercise, focusing on proper grip and body positioning. Visualize the movement pattern through the full range of motion. Perform the movement with a slow, controlled velocity, remembering to exhale through the sticking point. Ask a qualified professional to observe and assess your technique.

If you selected the free-weight *back squat, you need a spotter. You also need to practice the skills of spotting this exercise. Identify a spotter with whom you will take turns completing the drill. Instead of performing 15 repetitions in a continuous manner, practice racking the bar after each repetition. Alternate responsibilities so that you and your partner both have a chance to develop the techniques that are required in performing and spotting this exercise. Ask a qualified professional to observe and assess your performance in the basic techniques.

Success Check

- For the *back squat, all rackings are performed correctly.

- For all exercises, movement pattern, velocity, and breathing are correct.

Leg Drill 5. Determine Training Load

This practice procedure will help you determine an appropriate training load designed to produce 12 to 15 repetitions. If you selected the leg press, perform as many repetitions as possible with the calculated trial load from drill 2. Make sure that you perform the repetitions correctly.

If you performed 12 to 15 repetitions with the trial load, then your trial load is your training load. Record this number as your training load for this exercise on the workout chart (see page 146). If you did not perform 12 to 15 repetitions, go to drill 6 to make adjustments to the load.

CAUTION: If you selected the lunge or the *standing heel raise exercise, do not use the calculated load to perform a maximal number of repetitions because you will have extraordinarily sore muscles for the next several days. Instead, over the course of multiple weeks of consistent training, gradually increase the weight until the calculated training load is reached.

Success Check

- Check that you are using the correct load.
- Maintain proper and safe technique during each repetition.

Leg Drill 6. Make Needed Load Adjustments

If you performed fewer than 12 repetitions with your trial load, the load is too heavy, and you need to lighten it. On the other hand, if you performed more than 15 repetitions, the load is too light, and you need to increase it. Use figure 8.9 for the formula for making load adjustments to determine the adjustment you need to make.

Success Check

- Check correct use of load adjustment chart (figure 8.9).
- Write in your training load on the workout chart (see page 146).

Figure 8.9 Making adjustments to the training load for the leg exercises.

Repetitions completed	Adjustment (pounds)
≤ 7	-15
8-9	-10
10-11	-5
16-17	+5
18-19	+10
≥ 20	+15

Trial load		Adjustment		Training load
	+		=	

SUCCESS SUMMARY FOR LEG EXERCISES

This step involved selecting one leg exercise for which you have the needed equipment and perhaps one or two more if you have already been training. Using a proper grip, the correct body position, movement, and breathing patterns, and accurate warm-up and training loads will maximize your success.

After you have determined your training load and recorded it in your workout chart, you are ready to move on to step 9. In this step, you will select body weight or machine exercises that will develop the lower back, torso, and abdominal muscles (often called the *core* of the body).

Before Taking the Next Step

Honestly answer each of the following questions. If you answer yes to all of the questions relevant to your level and exercise selection, you are ready to move on to step 9.

1. Have you selected a basic leg exercise? If you are an advanced lifter, do you want to add the *back squat, *knee extension, *knee curl, or *standing heel raise?

2. Have you recorded your exercise selection(s) on the workout chart?

3. Have you determined warm-up and training loads for the exercise(s) you selected?

4. Have you recorded the training load(s) on the workout chart?

5. Have you learned the proper technique for performing the exercise(s) you selected?

6. If an exercise you selected requires a spotter, have you identified a qualified professional? Have you learned the proper spotting techniques?

Selecting Core Exercises and Training Loads

Previous editions of this text used the term "core exercises" to identify multijoint, large muscle exercises such as the bench press, shoulder press, and back squat. To reflect the recent attention given to improving the strength, endurance, and flexibility of the low back, torso, and abdominal muscles—the central section or *core* of the body—this edition now labels exercises that train those muscles as *core exercises*.

The core muscles are divided into three general areas—the front of the torso, the sides of the torso, and the low back—and include the rectus abdominis, transverse abdominis, external and internal obliques, and the erector spinae. The rectus abdominis and the transverse abdominis are the major supporting muscles of the front of the torso. They support and protect the internal abdominal organs and work with the low back muscles to align and support the spine. The external and internal obliques are on the sides of your torso side and wrap toward your waist. The internal obliques

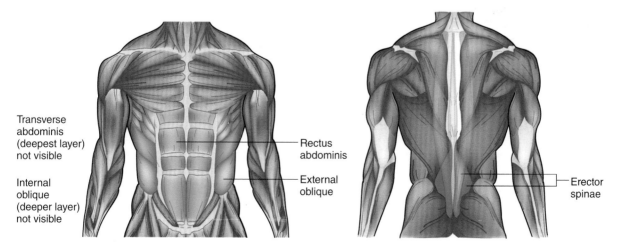

Transverse abdominis (deepest layer) not visible

Internal oblique (deeper layer) not visible

Rectus abdominis

External oblique

Erector spinae

are under the external obliques, and their fibers run in the opposite direction. The erector spinae muscles are actually a collection of muscles of varying length and thickness that run along your spine from right below the base of your neck to the base of your low back. Some sources also include in the core muscles of the upper torso, such as the latissimus dorsi and trapezius, and muscles that surround the hips, including the buttocks (gluteals) and hip flexors. Because these muscles are trained in other steps, exercises for them are not included in this step.

The core muscles are responsible for causing movement in three different general directions. If you are standing or sitting, your rectus abdominis and transverse abdominis flex your torso forward (such as when you bow to someone); your external and internal obliques rotate your torso from side-to-side, help you reach across your body toward the other side, and allow you to bend to the side; and your erector spinae arches your torso backward.

If you are lying down, your rectus abdominis and transverse abdominis lift your upper or lower body off the floor when you are lying face-up, your external and internal obliques twist your upper or lower body from side-to-side and lift your hips up when you are lying on your side, and your erector spinae lift your upper or lower body off the floor when you are lying face-down.

As mentioned in step 1, there is a variety of equipment that may be used when performing core exercises. Arguably the most common is the stability ball; an air-filled ball made of elastic soft vinyl and nylon with a diameter of about 55 to 75 centimeters (21.5-29.5 in.). It is called by many different names including balance ball, body ball, fitness ball, physioball, or Swiss ball. Several exercises in this step use a stability ball. If you choose one of those exercises, be sure that the ball is fully inflated (it should feel very firm when you push down on it). To choose the right ball size, sit on it (after it is fully inflated) with your feet flat on the floor. In this position, your thighs should be parallel to the ground.

The exercises in this step are the extended abdominal crunch, side plank, twisting trunk curl, back extension, and the *abdominal crunch. The extended abdominal crunch and the back extension involve a stability ball; be sure to choose one that is the proper size for you. The side plank and twisting trunk curl are no-weight exercises. All you need for these exercises is your own body. If you have access to a cam machine, you may select the *abdominal crunch to develop your rectus abdominis and transverse abdominis muscles. These machines come in various designs, so be sure to follow the signs or ask for assistance if the directions in this step do not match the machine in your facility.

CAUTION: A higher number of repetitions (up to 25-30) is encouraged to promote tone and muscular endurance. However, you should not sacrifice quality for quantity.

EXTENDED ABDOMINAL CRUNCH

Prepare for this exercise by lying face-up on a stability ball with the low-to-middle part of your back on the very top of the stability ball (figure 9.1a). In this position, your feet should be flat on the floor about hip-width apart with your thighs, hips, and lower abdomen approximately parallel to the floor. Fold your arms across your chest or place your hands behind your head (but don't pull on your neck).

Begin the upward movement phase by curling your torso to lift your shoulder blades off the ball (figure 9.1b). Be sure to exhale. This movement should be slow and controlled; do not use momentum created by lurching forward with the head, arms, or shoulders. Pause briefly at the most crunched position. Keep your feet on the floor and your thighs and hips motionless.

The downward movement phase follows the pause at the top. Inhale as you lower yourself back to the starting position (figure 9.1a). Your low back should remain in contact with the ball throughout the exercise with your feet flat on the floor.

Figure 9.1   EXTENDED ABDOMINAL CRUNCH

Preparation

1. Lie face-up on ball with low-to-middle back on very top of ball
2. Place feet flat on floor
3. Position thighs, hips, and lower abdomen approximately parallel to floor
4. Fold arms across chest or place hands behind head, but don't pull on neck

Movement

1. Curl chin to chest first
2. Continue curling torso to lift shoulder blades off ball
3. Do not jerk head, arms, or shoulders to help curl torso
4. Exhale during upward phase
5. Pause at highest position
6. Slowly return to starting position while inhaling
7. Pause at lowest position
8. Continue upward and downward movements until set is complete

MISSTEP

The stability ball rolls side-to-side or you slide off the side of the ball as you perform the exercise.

CORRECTION

Move your feet farther apart to create a wider base of support.

Most errors associated with the extended abdominal crunch exercise involve maintaining a stable body position on the ball. If you are not able to perform the exercise safely and correctly, your core muscles may not be strong enough. If so, then perform the exercise lying on a floor mat instead. This modified exercise is called the *bent-knee sit-up*; your feet should be flat on the floor with your knees flexed at 90 to 110 degrees. The rest of the exercise technique is the same as the extended abdominal crunch.

SIDE PLANK

There is a variety of plank exercises but to give specific attention to the external and internal obliques, perform the side plank exercise.

Prepare for this exercise by lying on your right side with only your right forearm and the right side of your hips and legs in contact with the floor. Place your left hand on your left hip or behind your head. Position your left leg across the top of your right leg so the inside edge of your left shoe contacts the floor ahead of your right foot (figure 9.2*a*).

Using the outside edge of your right shoe and the inside edge of your left shoe as fixed pivot points, perform the upward movement phase by contracting your core muscles to lift your hips straight up until your whole body is in an angled straight line (figure 9.2*b*). Exhale as you lift upwards with your body weight supported over your right forearm. Do not allow your head, shoulders, hips, or knees to tip forward or backward. If you want to increase the difficulty of the exercise, place your left leg and foot on top of your right leg and foot to create only one fixed pivot point (the outside edge of your right shoe).

The downward movement phase follows a pause at the top. Allow your core muscles to relax to lower the hips and torso back down to the starting position (figure 9.2*a*). Inhale before beginning the next repetition. For the next set, lie on your left side with only your left forearm and the left side of your hips and legs in contact with the floor. Continue to alternate sides with each set.

Figure 9.2 SIDE PLANK

Preparation
1. Lie on right side with right forearm and right side of hips and legs in contact with floor
2. Position left leg across the top of right leg with inside edge of left shoe in contact with the floor ahead of right foot
3. Place left hand on left hip or behind head

Figure 9.2 **SIDE PLANK** *(CONTINUED)*

Movement

1. Contract core muscles to lift hips straight up
2. Keep outside edge of right shoe and inside edge of left shoe in fixed position on floor
3. Continue until whole body is in an angled straight line
4. Exhale during upward phase
5. Pause at highest position
6. Relax core muscles to lower hips and torso back to starting position
7. Inhale during downward phase
8. Pause at lowest position
9. Continue upward and downward movements until set is complete
10. Switch to the left side for the next set

MISSTEP

Your hips sag toward the floor when you are in the highest body position.

CORRECTION

Contract your core muscles to keep your body stiff and straight from your head down to your feet.

If you find that this exercise is too easy over time, increase the difficulty by staying in the highest body position for 10 seconds or more.

TWISTING TRUNK CURL

This exercise has a similar movement pattern to the traditional sit-up exercise except you alternately curl your shoulders toward the *opposite* leg (the twisting motion) during the upward phase.

Prepare for this exercise by lying on your back with your feet flat on the floor (figure 9.3*a*). Your knees should be flexed at 90 to 110 degrees with your arms folded across your chest or behind your head (but don't pull on your neck).

Begin the upward movement phase by curling your chin to your chest and then contracting your abdominal muscles to lift your shoulders off the floor. While exhaling, immediately twist your torso so that your right shoulder (or elbow) goes toward your left knee (figure 9.3*b*). Pause at the top of the movement. Keep your low back on the floor and your legs and feet motionless.

Slowly untwist and uncurl your torso back down to the starting position (figure 9.3*a*). Keep your chin to your chest until your shoulders touch the floor. Inhale as you lower to the floor. On the next repetition, twist your torso so that your left shoulder (or elbow) goes toward your right knee. Continue alternating the direction that you twist with each repetition.

Figure 9.3   **TWISTING TRUNK CURL**

Preparation

1. Lie face-up on floor
2. Place feet flat on floor
3. Place knees at 90 to 110 degrees
4. Fold arms across chest or behind the head but not pulling on the neck

Movement

1. Curl chin to chest first
2. Immediately twist torso to move right shoulder or elbow toward left knee
3. Continue twist while curling torso to lift shoulder blades off floor
4. Exhale during upward phase
5. Pause at highest position
6. Slowly untwist and uncurl torso back down to starting position
7. Inhale during downward phase
8. Pause at lowest position
9. Continue alternating the twist direction with each repetition until set is complete

MISSTEP

Your buttocks lift off the floor just prior to the upward movement.

CORRECTION

Start each repetition with your head, shoulders, upper back, and low back in contact with the floor. As you twist and curl your torso, keep the rest of your body stationary.

Most errors associated with the twisting trunk curl involve speed. You will have a tendency to lurch forward and then quickly fall back to the starting position. Instead, keep the movements slow and controlled in both the upward and downward phases.

BACK EXTENSION

Prepare for this exercise by lying face-down on a stability ball with your navel on the very top of the stability ball (figure 9.4a). In this position, your feet should be at least 18 inches (46 cm) apart with your knees straight and balls of your feet flat on the floor. Clasp your hands behind your head.

Before you begin the upward movement phase, be sure the balls of your feet are firmly planted on the floor; that is a position that you need to maintain throughout the exercise. While exhaling, slowly lift your torso off the stability ball until your back is fully extended, and your chest is off the ball (figure 9.4b). At the highest body position, your head, shoulders, hips, knees, and feet should at least form a straight line. Better yet, you should lift your torso until your back is arched.

The downward movement phase follows a pause at the top. Inhale as you lower back to the starting position (figure 9.4a). Your lower stomach should remain in contact with the ball throughout the exercise with the balls of your feet in solid contact with the floor.

Figure 9.4 BACK EXTENSION

Preparation

1. Lie face-down on ball with navel on very top of ball
2. Place feet 18 inches (46 cm) apart
3. Position knees straight with balls of feet on floor
4. Clasp hands behind head

Movement

1. Lift torso off ball
2. Continue lifting torso until back is extended with chest off ball
3. Do not lift feet off floor
4. Exhale during upward phase
5. Pause at highest position
6. Return to starting position while inhaling
7. Pause at lowest position
8. Continue upward and downward movements until set is complete

MISSTEP

As you raise your torso, your knees bend or one or both of your feet lift up off the floor.

CORRECTION

Move your feet farther apart, slightly roll down off the top of the ball, or do a combination of both.

The primary challenge of the back extension exercise is the same as the one for the extended abdominal crunch exercise (as well as any exercise performed on a stability ball): keeping a stable body position. As explained for the extended abdominal crunch, if you are not able to keep your body in the right place on the ball, then you are at risk of falling off the ball and getting hurt. An alternative exercise is to perform the back extension while lying face-down on a floor mat and arching your back to lift up your head, torso, arms, legs, or any combination of these to train the erector spinae muscles.

✳ABDOMINAL CRUNCH

If you are an experienced lifter who is ready for a second core exercise, consider adding the *abdominal crunch. This is a core exercise for your abdominal muscles that is performed in a cam machine. Most fitness facilities have an abdominal crunch station, but the machine may not look or function like figure 9.5. Be sure to follow the signs or ask for assistance if the directions in this step do not match the machine in your facility.

Prepare for this exercise by sitting erect on the seat of the cam machine with your shoulders and upper arms firmly against the chest or shoulder pads. Adjust the height of the seat so that the machine's axis of rotation is level with the middle of your torso. Place your ankles behind the roller pad and your hands crossed in front of you or holding on the handles (figure 9.5a).

While exhaling, lean forward and then down solely by contracting your abdominal muscles (figure 9.5b). Be sure you do not use your legs or arms to pull on the chest or shoulder pads. Pause in the fully contracted position and then inhale while you slowly return to the starting position (figure 9.5a).

Figure 9.5 ✳**ABDOMINAL CRUNCH (CAM MACHINE)**

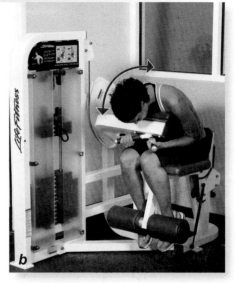

Preparation

1. Sit erect with shoulders and upper arms firmly against pads
2. Adjust seat so axis of rotation is mid-torso level
3. Place ankles behind roller pads
4. Cross arms or hold handles

Movement

1. Lean forward and down by contracting abdominal muscles
2. Keep legs and arms relaxed
3. Exhale during downward movement
4. Pause in fully crunched position
5. Return to starting position while inhaling
6. Continue downward and upward movements until set is complete

MISSTEP

You pull on the chest or shoulder pads with your hands.

CORRECTION

Concentrate on contracting only your abdominal muscles without using any other muscles to help you flex your torso forward and down.

CAUTION: Be sure to not use so much weight that you involve muscles other than your abdominals to perform the exercise. The heavier load may place a higher stress on your low back.

Core Drill 1. **Choose Two Exercises**

After reading about the characteristics and techniques of the exercises and the type of equipment required for each, you are ready to put to use what you have learned. Consider what equipment is available to you and then select two of the following exercises to use in your program:

- Extended abdominal crunch
- Side plank
- Twisting trunk curl
- Back extension

Write in "Core" in the "Muscle group" column on the workout chart and fill in the name of the exercises you selected in the "Exercise" column (see figure 11.1 on page 146). If you intend to include the *abdominal crunch, record it on the workout chart immediately after the core exercises previously selected.

Success Check

- Consider availability of equipment.
- Consider time available.
- Choose two core exercises and record them on the workout chart.

Core Drill 2. **Warm-Up and Trial Loads for the *Abdominal Crunch**

This practice procedure will answer the question "How much weight or load should I use?" If you chose the extended abdominal crunch, side plank, twisting trunk curl, or back extension, you will not need to determine the warm-up, trial, and training loads. Continue to drill 3 and ignore comments concerning warm-up and training loads. If you chose the *abdominal crunch, continue with the following procedures.

For the *abdominal crunch exercise, use the formula shown in figure 9.6 to determine the trial load. (See step 3, pages 34-35, for more information on using this formula.) Round off your results down to the closest 5-pound (2.3 kg) increment or to the closest weight-stack plate. Use half of the amount determined for the trial load for your warm-up load in the exercise. These loads will be used in drills 3 and 4.

Success Check

- Determine your trial load for the *abdominal crunch by multiplying your body weight by the coefficient.
- Determine your warm-up load by dividing your trial load by two.
- Round down your trial and warm-up loads to the nearest 5-pound (2.3 kg) increment or to the closest weight-stack plate.

Figure 9.6   Calculations of the warm-up and trial load for the *abdominal crunch.

Female

Exercise	Body weight		Coefficient		Trial load	Warm-up load (Trial load ÷ 2)
C–*abdominal crunch		×	0.20	=		

Male

Exercise	Body weight		Coefficient		Trial load	Warm-up load (Trial load ÷ 2)
C–*abdominal crunch		×	0.20	=		

C = cam.

Note: If you are a male who weighs more than 175 pounds (79.5 kg), record your body weight as 175 (79.5). If you are a female who weighs more than 140 pounds (63.6 kg), record your body weight as 140 (63.6).

Core Drill 3.   **Practice Proper Technique**

In this procedure, you are to perform 12 to 15 repetitions of the exercises you have chosen. If you chose the *abdominal crunch, use the warm-up load determined in drill 2.

Review the photos and instructions for proper body positioning. Visualize the movement pattern through the full range of motion. Perform the movement with a slow, controlled velocity, remembering to exhale through the sticking point. Ask a qualified professional to observe and assess your technique.

Success Check

- Check movement pattern.
- Check velocity of movements.
- Check breathing.

Core Drill 4.
Determine Training Load for the *Abdominal Crunch

If you chose the extended abdominal crunch, side plank, twisting trunk curl, or back extension, you do not need to determine warm-up, trial, or training loads. Skip drills 4 and 5 and proceed to the success summary.

This practice procedure will help you determine an appropriate training load designed to produce 12 to 15 repetitions for the *abdominal crunch. Use the calculated trial load from drill 2 and perform as many repetitions as possible with this load, **up to a maximum of 25.** Make sure that you perform the repetitions correctly.

If you performed 12 to 15 repetitions with the trial load, then your trial load is your training load. Record this number as your training load for this exercise on the workout chart (see page 146). If you did not perform 12 to 15 repetitions, go to drill 5 to make adjustments to the load.

Success Check

- Check for correct load.
- Maintain proper and safe technique during each repetition.

129

Core Drill 5.
Make Needed Load Adjustments for the *Abdominal Crunch

If you performed fewer than 12 repetitions with your trial load, the load is too heavy, and you need to lighten it. On the other hand, if you performed more than 15 repetitions, the load is too light, and you need to increase it. Use figure 9.7 to determine the adjustment you need to make and the formula for making load adjustments.

Success Check

- Check correct use of load-adjustment chart (figure 9.7).
- Observe the "CAUTION" on page 127.
- Record your training load on the workout chart (see page 146).

Figure 9.7 Making adjustments to the training load for the *abdominal crunch.

Repetitions completed	Adjustment (pounds)
≤ 7	-15
8-9	-10
10-11	-5
16-17	+5
18-19	+10
≥ 20	+15

Trial load		Adjustment		Training load
	+		=	

SUCCESS SUMMARY FOR CORE EXERCISES

In this step, you learned how to perform five exercises that can be used to strengthen the core muscles. Regardless of which exercises you selected, be sure to perform them in a slow, controlled manner and complete 12 to 25 repetitions of each during a workout, depending on the core exercise selected.

After you have determined your exercises and training loads (if applicable) and recorded that information in your workout chart, you are ready to move on to step 10. In this step, you will select total-body exercises for your program. You may select from two exercises: the hang clean and the push press. Both of these involve the use of a barbell, and each requires a higher level of muscular coordination than any of the exercises included in steps 4 through 9. If you are new to weight training, you will want to wait a couple of months before adding these exercises to your workouts. If you are experienced, adding one or both of them to your workout will provide you with a more well-rounded and challenging program.

Before Taking the Next Step

Honestly answer each of the following questions. If you answer yes to all of the questions relevant to your level and exercise selection, you are ready to move on to step 10.

1. Have you selected two core exercises?

2. Have you recorded your exercise selections on the workout chart?

3. If you chose the *abdominal crunch, have you determined warm-up and training loads?

4. Did you record your training load on the workout chart?

5. Have you learned the proper technique for performing the exercises you selected?

Selecting Total-Body Exercises and Training Loads

In this step, you have an opportunity to add one or two total-body barbell exercises—the hang clean and the push press—to your basic program. Total-body exercises train major muscles of the upper and lower body simultaneously. These exercises involve quick, powerful movement, which is especially important for athletes involved in sports that have an explosive or speed–strength component such as sprinting, jumping, throwing, kicking, or punching.

Total-body exercises involve many muscle groups, and so a high level of muscular coordination is required to perform them correctly. Thus, if you are just beginning a weight training program, total-body exercises included in this step are not appropriate for you. To give you time to get stronger and learn general weight-training techniques, it is best to wait at least six weeks before adding one of these exercises.

If you choose to include a total-body exercise, perform it *first* during your workout. Because these exercises involve many muscle groups and require a high level of muscular coordination for correct technique, you need your muscles to be as fresh as possible. By performing a total-body exercise first, you can give attention to proper technique when you are least fatigued.

Unlike other steps, total-body exercises use free weights only, so you will need a barbell, weight plates, and two locks. Also, because the exercises are performed quickly and require extra attention to proper technique, they must be performed in an area away from others who are training. The area should have some floor protection in case you drop the bar quickly.

CAUTION: A spotter should *not* be used in these exercises because if something goes wrong, a spotter attempting to help or catch the bar could easily be injured or could cause injury to you. Do not ask someone to spot you in these exercises. If you experience balance or technique problems while performing them, simply allow the bar to drop while you back away from its downward path.

HANG CLEAN

In the hang clean exercise, the bar moves from the thighs to the shoulders in one quick, powerful jumping movement. Initially, the bar is on the thighs, just above the knees, not on the floor. The upward phase requires a forceful, rapid extension of the hips, knees, and ankles followed by shrugging the shoulders and pulling with the arms to lift the bar to the front of the shoulders.

Begin this exercise with the bar at a midthigh position (called the *hang* position) (figure 10.1*a*, page 136). The techniques used to reach the midthigh position are the same as the preparation and upward movement (floor-to-thigh) phases described in step 2.

From this starting position, rapidly jump straight up (figure 10.1*b*, page 136). Completely extend the knees and hips. Think about jumping up, pushing through the floor, and fully lengthening your lower body. Immediately follow the jump with a strong shoulder-shrugging motion. Up to this point your arms should be like ropes that attach the bar to your shoulders. In other words, don't bend your elbows yet to pull the bar up. However, at the *end* of the shrugging motion, your elbows flex, moving up and out to the side, to continue pulling the bar up as high as possible.

MISSTEP
The bar swings away from your thighs and hips.

CORRECTION
Concentrate on pulling the bar straight up and keeping it close to your thighs and hips.

MISSTEP
You rely on your arms to lift the bar off your thighs.

CORRECTION
Do not think about your arms doing any active work until after you have jumped up.

After the bar reaches its highest point (figure 10.1*c*, page 136), quickly shift your body under it to catch the weight while rapidly rotating your elbows down, then under, and then up in front of the bar as it touches your shoulders and clavicles (collarbones) (figure 10.1*d*, page 137). Do not let your elbows flex too soon; be sure to wait to do that until the shrug is at its highest point. As your elbows rotate around the bar, flex your knees and catch the barbell on the front of your shoulders. At the same time, your knees should act like shock absorbers to smoothly cushion the downward momentum. Never catch the weight with your knees fully extended because doing so could injure your back. Move your upper arms parallel to the floor, and after gaining a balanced position, finish the exercise by standing erect. Exhale as the bar lands on your shoulders.

MISSTEP

Your knees are straight when you catch the bar.

CORRECTION

Concentrate on flexing your knees, which provides "give" to your shoulders as you rack the bar on them to lessen much of the impact.

To return the bar to the midthigh (hang) position, slowly and with control "unrack" the bar and allow it to descend until it reaches your thighs (figure 10.1*e*, page 137). Simultaneously, flex your hips and knees to reduce the impact on your thighs. Your back should remain straight with your shoulders pulled back, and the bar close to your chest and abdominal area. After the last repetition of the set, squat down to lower the bar past your knees and back onto the floor.

Figure 10.1 **HANG CLEAN**

Preparation
1. Properly lift bar from floor to thighs
2. Start exercise from midthigh position
3. Inhale

Jump and Shrug
1. Jump up explosively
2. Keep bar close to body as hips drive forward
3. Keep elbows straight
4. Fully extend knees and hips
5. Rapidly shrug the shoulders
6. Shrug as high as possible
7. Keep elbows straight

Highest Bar Height
1. Flex elbows and move them up and to side
2. Keep elbows above wrists
3. Continue pulling bar as high as possible

Figure 10.1   **HANG CLEAN** *(CONTINUED)*

Catch

1. Rotate elbows down, under, then up in front of bar
2. Catch (rack) bar on front of shoulders
3. Flex knees and hips to absorb bar's impact
4. Exhale
5. Move upper arms to be parallel to floor
6. Gain balance and stand up straight

Unrack

1. Unrack bar from shoulders
2. Flex knees and hips
3. Allow bar to lower to thighs
4. Keep shoulders back and back flat
5. Keep bar close to chest and abdomen
6. Pause at hang position
7. Continue upward and downward movements until set is complete
8. After final repetition, allow bar to lower past knees
9. Squat to set bar on floor
10. Keep bar close to thighs, knees, and shins

Because of the complexity of this exercise, you may perform multiple errors in one repetition or develop technique flaws. Be diligent about perfecting your technique with this or any total-body exercise. Many of the common errors and corrections seen with this exercise are similar to those described in the "Lifting the Bar Off the Floor" section of step 2 (see page 18).

PUSH PRESS

In the push press exercise, the bar moves from the shoulders to overhead in one quick and powerful jumping movement, similar to the hang clean. For this exercise, begin with the bar where it ends during the hang clean—at the front of the shoulders. The upward phase resembles the standing press (see figure 6.1), but the push press requires a forceful, rapid extension of the hips, knees, and ankles, followed by a pushing motion of the arms to lift the bar to a stable position over the head with the elbows fully extended. Inhalation occurs as the bar is returned to the shoulders between each repetition.

You will need to use the techniques you learned in step 2 and in the hang clean exercise (figure 10.1) to properly lift the bar off the floor up to the shoulders before you can actually begin the push press exercise. Alternatively, you can lift the bar out of a squat rack with supports already positioned at shoulder level.

The bar should be resting on your shoulders, clavicles, and hands (figure 10.2a). From this starting position, flex the hips and knees at a slow to moderate speed to move the bar in a straight path downward (figure 10.2b). This downward movement is *not* a full squat but rather a "dip" to a depth not to exceed the catch position of the hang clean. Do not lean forward or backward as you dip. Keep your torso erect and your head in a neutral position and do not change the position of your arms.

Immediately after reaching the lowest position of the dip, immediately reverse the movement by rapidly jumping up with your hips, knees, and ankles (figure 10.2c). Be sure to fully extend your knees and hips by the end of the upward drive. As your lower body joints reach full extension, slightly tip your head backward to allow the bar to pass by your chin (or else it will hit you). At this point (and not earlier) you begin pushing upward with your arms. To be sure that the bar travels straight up, be sure to jump straight up with your torso erect.

Catch the bar directly overhead with fully extended elbows and your hips and knees flexed to absorb the weight (figure 10.2d, page 140). Having your knees flexed provides give as you rack the bar on your shoulders, dissipating much of the impact. Your torso should be erect with your head in a neutral position directly under the bar, with your eyes focused forward. To keep your torso from leaning back when you catch the bar, think: *Torso, head, and bar form a straight line.* Once the bar is balanced overhead, stand up to a fully erect position by extending your hips and knees.

MISSTEP

Your arms extend unevenly.

CORRECTION

Keep both of your arms extending in unison by concentrating on the arm that lags behind.

MISSTEP

The bar is behind or slightly ahead of your head in the catch position.

CORRECTION

Catch the bar directly over the head with fully extended elbows, an erect torso, and the head in a neutral position.

To return the bar to the beginning position, slowly and with control allow it to descend until it reaches your shoulders and then stand up straight (figure 10.2*e*). Exhale as the bar reaches your shoulders and simultaneously flex your hips and knees to reduce the impact. Your back should remain straight with your shoulders pulled back and your chest held up and out. After the last repetition of the set, lower the bar to your thighs and then squat down to set it on the floor.

Figure 10.2   PUSH PRESS

Preparation
1. Properly lift bar from floor to thighs
2. Properly lift bar from thighs to shoulders
3. Start exercise with bar at front of shoulders
4. Inhale

Dip
1. Flex hips and knees at a slow to moderate speed
2. Move bar downward in straight path
3. Keep torso erect and head in neutral position
4. Do not change position of arms
5. Do not dip too low

Drive
1. Jump up explosively
2. Tip head back slightly
3. Fully extend knees and hips
4. Push up with arms
5. Keep eyes focused forward

(continued)

Figure 10.2 **PUSH PRESS** *(CONTINUED)*

Catch

1. Catch bar directly overhead with fully extended elbows
2. Flex knees and hips to absorb bar's impact
3. Keep torso erect and eyes focused forward
4. Gain balance and stand up straight
5. Exhale

Lower

1. Allow bar to lower to shoulders
2. Inhale as bar reaches shoulders
3. Flex knees and hips
4. Keep shoulders back and back flat
5. Pause
6. Continue upward and downward movements until set is complete
7. After final repetition, unrack bar from shoulders
8. Allow bar to lower to thighs
9. Keep bar close to chest and abdomen
10. Allow bar to lower past knees
11. Squat to set bar on floor
12. Keep bar close to thighs, knees, and shins

Like the hang clean, this exercise can be a challenge to learn and master. You may perform several technique mistakes at one time. Common errors and corrections are similar to those described for the hang clean and the standing press.

Total-Body Drill 1. Choose One Exercise

After reading about the characteristics and techniques of these two total-body exercises and the type of equipment they require, you are ready to put to use what you have learned. Consider the availability of equipment and then select one of the following exercises to use in your program:

- Hang clean
- Push press

Write in "Total-body" in the "Muscle group" column on the workout chart and fill in the name of the exercise you selected in the "Exercise" column (see figure 11.1 on page 146).

CAUTION: Performing any total-body exercise first in your workout is extremely important (regardless of where you wrote in the exercise on your workout chart).

Success Check

- Consider availability of equipment.
- Consider availability of a designated area away from other lifters.
- Consider time available.
- Choose a total-body exercise and record it on the workout chart.

Total-Body Drill 2.
Warm-Up and Trial Loads for Total-Body Exercises

This practice procedure answers the question "How much weight or load should I use?" If you are an experienced lifter who is ready to add a total-body exercise, follow the directions to determine the trial load.

In steps 4 through 9, you determined trial and warm-up loads that would allow you to perform 12 to 15 repetitions. Because total-body exercises involve multiple large and small muscle groups of the upper and lower body and require a high level of skill to perform correctly, they can cause fatigue very quickly. In that tired state, even a well-trained lifter will not be able to repeatedly perform explosive, quick movements; as a result, the quality of the exercise can severely decrease. Total-body exercises that are performed too slowly, with too much weight, or for too many repetitions lose much of their effectiveness. Therefore, for your warm-up, trial, and even your workout sets, limit the number of repetitions to 6 to 8 for the hang clean and the push press.

The most accurate way to determine warm-up and trial loads for total-body exercises requires you to have previously performed the hang clean or the push press to give you an idea of how much load you can handle and still produce explosive, quick repetitions.

If a total-body exercise is new to you, go back to step 6 and determine warm-up and trial loads for the standing press (see page 77). If you did not select the standing press as your shoulder exercise from step 6, go back and read the technique points that accompany figure 6.1.

Complete the shoulder drill 2 for the standing press and write down the trial load. When doing the hang clean or the push press, **perform only 6 to 8 repetitions with the warm-up load**—not 12 to 15 repetitions. That way you can be sure that you will be able to perform the exercises powerfully and with good technique without excessive fatigue. Use the formula shown in figure 10.3 to determine the warm-up load.

(continued)

141

Total-Body Drill 2. *(continued)*

Success Check

- Determine a trial load based on shoulder drill 2 for the standing press (see step 6).

- Determine the warm-up load by multiplying the trial load by 0.6.

- Round off the warm-up load to the nearest 5-pound (2.3 kg) increment.

Figure 10.3   Calculations of the warm-up and trial loads for the total-body exercises.

Exercise	Estimated trial load (from the standing press)				Warm-up load (for 6-8 repetitions)
Hang clean		×	0.6	=	
Push press		×	0.6	=	

Total-Body Drill 3.   **Practice Proper Technique**

In this procedure, you are to perform 6 to 8 repetitions with the warm-up load determined in drill 2. Be sure you practice the total-body exercise *before* any other exercise.

Review the photos and instructions for the exercise. Visualize the movement pattern through the full range of motion. Asking a qualified professional to observe and assess your technique is especially important for a total-body exercise.

Success Check

- Check movement pattern.
- Check velocity.
- Check breathing.

Total-Body Drill 4.   **Determine Training Load**

Now go back to shoulder drill 5 of step 6 and use the trial load of the standing press to determine the training load for that exercise.

Next, add 10 pounds (4.5 kg) to the standing press training load. This load now becomes the training load you should use for the hang clean or the push press. In previous steps, this practice procedure helped you determine an appropriate training load designed to produce 12 to 15 repetitions. Remember, though, that the highest repetition range for a total-body exercise is 6 to 8 per set. Therefore, use the hang clean or the push press training load you just determined and try to perform 6 to 8 repetitions with correct exercise technique.

If you performed 6 to 8 repetitions with the training load, then record this number as your training load for your selected total-body exercise on the workout chart (see figure 11.1 on page 146), and skip total-body drill 5.

If you did not perform 6 to 8 repetitions, go to drill 5 to make adjustments to the load.

Success Check

- Check that you are using the correct load.

- Maintain proper and safe technique during each repetition.

Total-Body Drill 5.
Make Needed Load Adjustments

If you performed fewer than 6 repetitions, the load is too heavy, and you need to lighten it. On the other hand, if you performed more than 8 repetitions, the load is too light, and you need to increase it. Figure 10.4 has been modified for the total-body exercises. Use it to determine the adjustment you need to make. Again, keep in mind that the highest repetition range for a total-body exercise is 6 to 8 per set.

Success Check

- Check correct use of load adjustment chart.
- Record your training load on the workout chart.

Figure 10.4   Making adjustments to the training load for the total-body exercises.

Repetitions completed	Adjustment (pounds)
1	-15
2-3	-10
4-5	-5
9-10	+5
11-12	+10
≥ 13	+15

Trial load		Adjustment		Training load
	+		=	

SUCCESS SUMMARY FOR TOTAL-BODY EXERCISES

If you are new to weight training, you may have decided to wait until you are more experienced before adding the hang clean or push press to your workout. If you are more experienced and have added one or both of these exercises, you have taken your program to the next level. Using a proper grip, the correct body position, movement, and breathing patterns, and accurate warm-up and training loads will maximize your success.

After you have determined your training load for one or both total-body exercises and recorded it on your workout chart, you are ready to move on to step 11. This step provides instruction on how to approach your first workout now that you have selected all of the exercises for your program.

Before Taking the Next Step

Honestly answer each of the following questions. If you answer yes to all of the questions relevant to your level and exercise selection, you are ready to move on to step 11.

1. Have you selected a total-body exercise?

2. Have you recorded your exercise selection(s) on the workout chart?

3. Have you determined a warm-up and training load for the exercise(s) you selected?

4. Have you recorded the training load(s) on the workout chart?

5. Have you learned the proper technique for performing the exercise(s) you selected?

Completing Your First Workout

Now the fun really begins because this is when you start training! This step takes you through a series of tasks that are necessary to complete your first workout and to make appropriate changes in the ones that follow. Each workout should contain three parts: a proper warm-up, at least one exercise for each of the seven muscle groups addressed in steps 4 through 9, and a proper cool-down. (It is assumed that you are just starting a weight training program and are not yet trained enough to perform one of the total-body exercises from step 10.)

Completing this step results in a well-balanced basic program that gets you started on a training schedule. You don't have to worry about other exercises to include, in which order to do them, how many repetitions to perform or sets to complete, or when to make load changes—these decisions have already been made for you. You should follow this basic program for at least six weeks before changing or customizing it in any way. It is designed to slowly improve your muscular fitness and give your body time to adapt to the new demands being placed on it.

BASIC PROGRAM

By this point, you should have filled out much of the information needed for the workout chart (see figure 11.1). You should have selected an exercise for each of the seven muscle groups and determined a training load for each exercise. This is your basic program; in this step, you will use it to begin your journey to muscular fitness.

Weight training workout chart (three days a week)

Muscle group	Exercise	Training load	Set	Week Day 1		Day 2		Day 3	
1			Wt.						
			Reps						
2			Wt.						
			Reps						
3			Wt.						
			Reps						
4			Wt.						
			Reps						
5			Wt.						
			Reps						
6			Wt.						
			Reps						
7			Wt.						
			Reps						
8			Wt.						
			Reps						
9			Wt.						
			Reps						
10			Wt.						
			Reps						
11			Wt.						
			Reps						
12			Wt.						
			Reps						
Body weight									
Date									
Comments									

From T.R. Baechle and R.W. Earle, 2012, *Weight training: steps to success*, 4th ed. (Champaign, IL.: Human Kinetics).

Figure 11.1 Weight training workout chart for a three-days-a-week program.

Make six copies of the workout chart to record your basic program results for six weeks. The drills at the end of this step will help you determine when and how to make needed changes to your workouts. Remember to properly warm up before each workout and cool down afterward.

For maximum benefits, make a commitment to train three times a week and allow yourself one day of rest between workouts. For example, try a Monday/Wednesday/Friday or a Tuesday/Thursday/Saturday schedule. If you can train only twice a week, allow no more than three days between sessions—a Monday/Thursday, Tuesday/Saturday, or Wednesday/Sunday regime. With consistent training, you will notice that as your muscular fitness improves, so will your ability to recover from the fatigue of each set and each workout.

The basic program begins with one set of 12 to 15 repetitions for the first workout, two sets of 12 to 15 repetitions for workouts 2 through 4, and three sets of 12 to 15 repetitions for workouts 5 through 18. The strategy is that the first four workouts will provide an appropriate level of initial stress to prepare your body for the more strenuous workouts to follow.

Pay attention to the length of the rest periods between sets and exercises; try to be consistent. The recovery time between each set and exercise should be 1 minute until workout 5, when you can consider shortening it to 45 or 30 seconds. Shortening the rest period will not only improve your level of muscular endurance, it also reduces the amount of time needed to complete a workout. The concern, however, is that if you do not rest long enough, you will not be able to complete the targeted number of repetitions. The result would be that you do not accomplish what you set out to do—which is to perform more repetitions of each exercise.

When you are able to perform two or more repetitions above the intended number (17 or more) in the last set on two consecutive training days (the *two-for-two rule*), it is time to increase the load. If you are unable to perform 12 repetitions in two consecutive training sessions, you need to decrease the load. Refer to the load adjustment chart shown in table 11.1 and make appropriate changes to the load.

Table 11.1   Load Adjustments

Repetitions completed	Adjustment (pounds)
≤ 7	-15
8-9	-10
10-11	-5
16-17	+5
18-19	+10
≥ 20	+15

Keep in mind two very important points while training. First, all repetitions should be performed with excellent technique—do not sacrifice technique for additional repetitions. The quality of the technique used to perform each repetition is more important than the number of repetitions performed. Give each repetition in each set your best effort and apply the two-for-two rule to keep the number of repetitions in each set between 12 and 15.

Charting Your Program Drill 1. Workout 1

For your first workout, perform one set of each exercise in the order listed on your workout chart. If the training loads are correct, you should be able to perform 12 to 15 repetitions in each set; if not, make adjustments as described in practice procedure 5 in step 3 (see pages 37-38). On your workout chart, record the completed number of repetitions in each set under the heading "Day 1." Figure 11.2 illustrates where to write in loads and repetitions performed. After completing an exercise set, rest approximately 1 minute before starting the next exercise.

If you select any of the *additional exercises included in steps 4 through 9, remember to write them on the workout chart immediately after the basic exercise selected for that step.

Success Check

- Check that you are using the correct loads.
- Be sure that all of the bars are loaded evenly.
- Secure the weight plates on the bars and selection keys in the weight stacks.
- Use proper exercise and, if necessary, spotting techniques.
- Make appropriate load adjustments, if necessary.

Weight training workout chart (three days a week)

Load goes here

Set 1

Number of reps goes here

Workout day

	Muscle group	Exercise	Training Load	Set	Week			Day 2	
					Day 1				
					1	2	3	1	2
1	Chest	Bench press	90	Wt.	90				
				Reps	13				
2	Back	Bent-over row	80	Wt.	80				
				Reps	12				
3	Shoulders	Standing press	60	Wt.	60				
				Reps	15				
4	Biceps	Biceps curl	55	Wt.	55				
				Reps	15				
5	Triceps	Triceps pushdown	30	Wt.	30				
				Reps	12				
6	Legs	Leg press	165	Wt.	165				
				Reps	15				
7	Core	Twisting trunk curl	—	Wt.	—				
				Reps	20				
8	Core	Back extension	—	Wt.	—				
				Reps	20				

Figure 11.2 Recording loads and repetitions.

Charting Your Program Drill 2.
Workouts 2 Through 4

If you are training with a partner, arrange your workouts so that you take turns performing an exercise until both of you have completed the desired number of sets. For workouts 2 through 4, perform two sets of each of the exercises in the order listed on your workout chart. Again, if the training loads are correct, you should be able to perform 12 to 15 repetitions in a set. If not, you will need to make adjustments as described in practice procedure 5 in step 3 (see pages 37-38).

After completing an exercise set, rest 1 minute before starting the next set. On your workout chart, record the repetitions and sets you completed in the proper boxes. See figure 11.3 for an example of how to record your repetitions and sets for workouts 2 through 4. Complete drill 3 for workouts 5 through 18.

Success Check

- Monitor your rest periods between sets and exercises.
- Use proper exercise and spotting techniques.

Weight Training Workout Chart (three days a week)

	Muscle group	Exercise	Training load	Set	Week — Day 1 (1)	(2)	(3)	Week — Day 2 (1)	(2)	(3)	Week — Day 3 (1)	(2)	(3)	Week — Day 1 (1)	(2)	(3)	Week — Day 2 (1)	(2)	(3)
1	Chest	Bench press	90	Wt.	90			90	90		90	90		90	90		90	90	90
				Reps	13			12	12		14	12		15	14		16	15	12
2	Back	Bent-over row	80	Wt.	80			80	80		80	80		80	80		80	80	80
				Reps	12			13	12		14	13		14	14		15	14	12
3	Shoulders	Standing press	60	Wt.	60			60	60		60	60		60	60		65	65	65
				Reps	15			15	13		16	15		17	17		15	12	12
4	Biceps	Biceps curl	55	Wt.	55			55	55		55	55		55	55		55	55	55
				Reps	15			14	14		15	14		16	15		17	16	15
5	Triceps	Triceps pushdown	30	Wt.	30			30	30		30	30		30	30		30	30	30
				Reps	12			12	11		14	12		15	15		17	15	13
6	Legs	Leg press	165	Wt.	165			165	165		170	170		170	170		170	170	170
				Reps	15			17	17		14	13		16	15		18	16	15
7	Core	Twisting trunk curl	—	Wt.	—														
				Reps	20			25	20		25	23		30	25		30	30	25
8	Core	Back extension	—	Wt.	—														
				Reps	20			25	20		25	23		30	25		30	30	25

2 sets in workouts 2, 3, 4

Start 3 sets in workout 5 and continue through workout 18

(continued)

Weight Training Workout Chart *(continued)*

9				Wt.																			
				Reps																			
10				Wt.																			
				Reps																			
11				Wt.																			
				Reps																			
12				Wt.																			
				Reps																			
Body weight					140		141		140		142		141										
Date					9/23		9/25		9/27		9/30		10/2										
Comments				1 set first workout, 2 sets in workouts 2, 3, 4 3 sets starting in workout 5																			

Figure 11.3 Sample record of workouts 2 through 4 followed by workouts 5 through 18.

Charting Your Program Drill 3.
Workouts 5 Through 18

Starting at workout 5, perform three sets of each exercise. The challenge is to keep the loads heavy or light enough so that you can perform 12 to 15 repetitions with excellent technique. Ask your training partner to use the numbered technique points in steps 4 through 9 to evaluate your technique and provide feedback. Be especially concerned with breathing and controlling the speed of movement throughout the range of each exercise. Consider shortening the rest periods between sets and exercises to 45 or possibly even 30 seconds.

Record all three sets on your workout chart. Use table 11.2 to determine when and how to make changes to your program.

Success Check

- Focus on the quality of exercise technique rather than the number of repetitions you perform.

- Apply the two-for-two rule to keep repetitions between 12 and 15 in each set.

Table 11.2 Making Workout Changes

Variable	Workouts 2-4	Workouts 5-18
Repetitions	12-15	12-15
Sets	2 sets	3 sets
Rest period length	60 seconds	30-45 seconds
Load	Continue to make changes in the loads so that they are heavy or light enough to produce 12-15 repetitions.	

SUCCESS SUMMARY FOR THE BASIC PROGRAM

In this step you learned how to transfer the exercises you selected for your program to the workout sheet to begin training. You also learned how to record training information on your workout sheet. Keep recording this information in the weeks ahead—you will be impressed when you see your progress!

When you complete workout 18, which will be in six weeks if you are working out three days a week, you should modify your program. To learn how, read and complete the tasks described in steps 12, 13, and 14. These steps describe how you can change your program so that it continues to meet your needs and stimulate ongoing improvement.

Before Taking the Next Step

Honestly answer each of the following questions. If you answer yes to all of them, you are ready to move on to step 12.

1. Have you completed 18 workouts using your basic program?

2. Have you recorded your workouts on your workout chart?

3. Do you know how to modify loads so that you can complete 12 to 15 repetitions for each exercise?

Applying Program Design Principles

This step will help you understand the logic of designing a well-conceived weight training program. If you have trained before, the information provided here will give you a chance to determine how well your previous program followed recommended training principles. The elements of exercise selection, exercise arrangement, loads, repetitions, sets, length of rest period, and training frequency—collectively referred to as *program design variables*—are the foundation on which effective weight training programs are built. These seven variables are grouped into the following three sections of this step:

1. Select and arrange exercises

2. Manipulate training loads, number of repetitions, number of sets, and the length of rest periods

3. Decide training frequency

Just as certain ingredients in your favorite meals must be included in proper amounts and at the correct time, so too must the sets, repetitions, and loads in your workouts. The workout recipe, referred to as the *program design,* is what ultimately determines the success of your weight training program (along with your commitment to training). The exciting thing about learning about program design variables is that, once learned, you can then design your own program.

SELECT AND ARRANGE EXERCISES

The exercises you select will determine which muscles become stronger, more enduring, and thicker. In addition, how you arrange, or *order*, the exercises in your program will affect the intensity of your workouts.

Selecting Exercises

An advanced program may include as many as 15 to 20 exercises. However, a beginning or basic program (which is what you are following) need only include one exercise for each muscle group:

- chest (pectoralis major)

- shoulders (deltoids)

- back (latissimus dorsi, trapezius, rhomboids)

- biceps (biceps brachii)

- triceps (triceps brachii)

- legs (quadriceps, hamstrings, gluteals)

- core (rectus abdominis, transverse abdominis, external and internal obliques, erector spinae)

In steps 4 through 9, you selected one exercise for each muscle group if you were new to weight training and one more *additional exercise if you were trained. You can now consider adding a second exercise for each muscle group or an exercise for a muscle not specifically worked in the basic program, such as the forearm. The result is an even more rounded program.

Also, if you are training to improve your athletic performance, consider adding one or both of the total-body exercises described in step 10. They train upper and lower body muscles simultaneously and involve quick, powerful movements that are important for athletes involved in sports such as sprinting, jumping, throwing, kicking, or punching.

Finally, you may also want to consider exchanging one of the basic exercises for one of the others described in each step, especially if the change means you will now perform a free-weight version of a machine-based exercise. Before making a final decision about which exercises to select, be sure you understand the exercise techniques involved and the following concepts and principles.

- **Apply the specificity concept.** Your task is to identify the muscle groups you want to develop and then determine which exercises will recruit or use those muscles. This involves applying the *specificity concept*. This important concept refers to training in a manner that will produce outcomes specific to that method. For example, developing the chest muscles requires an exercise that recruits the pectoralis major muscle; choosing a leg exercise to train the chest muscles, for example, does not follow the specificity concept because muscles other than the pectoralis major are trained.

Figure 12.1 Effect of changing body position to alter muscle involvement. *(a)* When a flat bench is used for the bench press exercise, the midchest is more involved. *(b)* When a decline bench is used instead, the lower section of the chest is more involved. *(c)* Applying the specificity concept, these changes in body position influence muscle involvement.

Even the specific angle at which muscles are called into action determines if, and to what extent, they will be stimulated during an exercise. For example, figure 12.1 illustrates how a change in body position changes the angle at which the barbell is lowered and pushed upward from the chest. The angle of the bar's path dictates whether the middle or lower portion of the chest muscles becomes more or less involved in the exercise.

The type and width of the grip are as important as body position because they, too, change the angle at which muscles become involved and thus affect the training results. For example, using a wide grip for the bench press exercise places a greater stress on the chest muscles than using a narrow grip. That is why performing exercises exactly as they are described is so important.

- **Create muscle balance.** It is important to select exercises that create strong joints, a proportional physique, and good posture. A common method is to choose exercises that train opposing muscle groups or body-part areas such as:

  - Chest and upper back
  - Front of the upper arm (biceps) and back of the upper arm (triceps)
  - Front (palm side) of the forearm and back (knuckle side) of the forearm
  - Abdomen and low back
  - Quadriceps and hamstrings
  - Front of the lower leg (shin) and back of the lower leg (calf)

- **Know what equipment is available.** Determine the equipment needs for each exercise before making a final decision. You may not have the needed equipment to perform an exercise.

- **Determine if you need a spotter.** Is a spotter needed for an exercise you are considering adding to your program? If one is needed but is not available, choose a different exercise that trains the same muscle group.

- **Know how much time you have to train.** The more exercises you decide to include in your program, the longer your workouts will take. It is a common mistake to choose too many exercises! Plan for approximately two minutes per set unless you want a program that is designed to develop strength. If strength is your goal, you'll need to plan on about four minutes per set because the rest period is longer between sets and exercises. Also, the more sets you want to do, the longer the workout will last. This is discussed in greater detail later in this step.

Arranging Exercises

There are many ways to arrange exercises in a workout. Their order affects the intensity of training and is therefore an important consideration. For instance, alternating upper- and lower-body exercises produces a lower intensity level on the upper body or the lower body muscles than performing all of the upper-body exercises or all of the lower-body exercises one after the other.

Exercises that train larger muscles and involve two or more joints changing angles as the exercises are performed are called *multijoint exercises* (abbreviated as "MJEs" throughout this book). This type of exercise is more intense than those that isolate one muscle and involve movement at only one joint (called *single-joint exercises* and abbreviated as "SJEs"). The two most common ways to arrange these exercises are to either perform MJEs before SJEs or alternate exercises that involve a pushing (PS) movement with exercises that involve a pulling (PL) movement.

- **Perform MJEs before SJEs.** Performing all of the MJEs before the SJEs is a well-accepted approach. For example, rather than training the triceps with the triceps extension (a SJE) and then the chest with the bench press (a MJE), it is recommended that you perform the bench press exercise first. Note that although the overall size of the upper arm can appear to be large, the front and back of the arm are considered separate, smaller muscle groups. An example of the sequence for performing MJEs before SJEs is shown in table 12.1.

Table 12.1 Exercise Arrangement: MJEs First

Exercise	Type	Muscle group
Lunge	MJE	Legs (thigh and hip)
Bench press	MJE	Chest
Lat pulldown	MJE	Back
Triceps extension	SJE	Back of the upper arm
Biceps curl	SJE	Front of the upper arm
Standing heel raise	SJE	Calf

- **Alternate PS exercises with PL exercises.** You may also arrange exercises so that those that extend (straighten) joints alternate with those that flex (bend) joints. Extension exercises require you to push, whereas flexion exercises require you to pull—thus the name of this arrangement is to alternate PS with PL. An example is to perform the triceps extension (a PS exercise) followed by the biceps curl (a PL exercise). This is a good arrangement because the same muscle or body area is not trained back-to-back; that is, the same muscle group is not worked two or more times in succession. This arrangement should give your muscles sufficient time to recover. An example of this method of arranging exercises is shown in table 12.2.

Table 12.2   Exercise Arrangement: Alternate Push (PS) With Pull (PL)

Exercise	Type	Muscle group
Bench press	PS	Chest
Lat pulldown	PL	Back
Seated press	PS	Shoulder
Biceps curl	PL	Front of the upper arm
Triceps extension	PS	Back of the upper arm
Knee curl	PL	Legs (back of the thigh)
Knee extension	PS	Legs (front of the thigh)

There are two more exercise arrangement options that need to be considered because they affect the intensity of your workout.

- **Sets performed in succession versus alternating sets.** When you are going to perform more than one set of an exercise, you will need to decide if you will perform them one after another (in succession) or alternate them with other exercises. The following shows an example of two exercises performed for three sets in succession and alternated:

    - In succession: Shoulder press (set 1), shoulder press (set 2), shoulder press (set 3); biceps curl (set 1), biceps curl (set 2), biceps curl (set 3)
    - Alternated: Shoulder press (set 1), biceps curl (set 1), repeated until three sets of each exercise are performed

In each of these arrangements, three sets of the shoulder press and the biceps curl exercises are performed, each with a different intervening rest period and activity. Most people prefer the in-succession arrangement because it provides a greater (and more challenging) training effect.

- **Triceps and biceps exercises after other upper-body exercises.** When arranging exercises in your program, be sure that a triceps exercise is not performed before other pushing exercises such as the bench press or the shoulder press. These two MJEs rely on assistance from elbow-extension strength from the triceps muscles. When triceps exercises precede pushing chest or shoulder exercises, they fatigue the triceps and reduce the number of repetitions that can be performed and the desired effect on the chest or shoulder muscles. The same logic applies to biceps exercises. Pulling exercises that involve flexion of the elbow, such as the lat pulldown, depend on strength from the biceps muscles. Performing the biceps curl before the lat pulldown will fatigue the biceps and reduce the number of lat pulldown repetitions that can be performed.

Selecting and Arranging Exercises Drill 1.
Specificity Concept Quiz

Review the exercises in steps 4 through 10. In figure 12.2, demonstrate your understanding of the specificity concept by marking in the left-hand column a "C" (to mean "correct") where an exercise and the primary muscle group it trains are correctly matched and an "I" (for "incorrect") where they are not. Can you find the five that are incorrect? The answers are on page 201.

Success Check

- Apply knowledge of the muscle group locations.
- Apply knowledge of exercises in steps 4 through 10.

Figure 12.2   Which five pairs are incorrectly matched?

C / I?		Exercise	Primary muscle group trained
	1.	Back squat	Legs (thigh and hip)
	2.	Supine triceps extension	Back of the upper arm
	3.	Standing press	Back
	4.	Standing heel raise	Calf
	5.	Lunge	Legs (thigh and hip)
	6.	Side plank	Shoulders
	7.	Bent-over row	Upper back
	8.	Trunk curl	Core
	9.	Shoulder shrug	Shoulders
	10.	Upright row	Back
	11.	Preacher curl	Front of the upper arm
	12.	Knee curl	Legs (back of the thigh)
	13.	Lat pulldown	Chest
	14.	Knee extension	Legs (front of the thigh)
	15.	Hang clean	Shoulders

Selecting and Arranging Exercises Drill 2.
Balanced (Paired) Exercises Quiz

Identify the one correct and two incorrectly paired exercises. Use the letter "C" to identify the correctly paired exercises. Use an "I" to identify the two pairs that are incorrect and then correct them. Answers are on page 202.

__ 1. Knee extension—back squat

__ 2. Extended abdominal crunch—back extension

__ 3. Dumbbell chest fly—upright row

Success Check

- Apply knowledge of muscle balance.
- Apply knowledge of exercises in steps 4 through 10.

Selecting and Arranging Exercises Drill 3.
Arranging Exercises Quiz

Before you are able to fully understand how to arrange exercises in a workout, you need to be able to classify exercises by type. Consider the muscle groups involved, how many joints change angles as the exercise is performed, and the push-pull movement patterns of each exercises listed in figure 12.3. Then identify the type of exercise by correctly placing an "X" in the MJE or the SLE column and an "X" in the PS or the PL column (each exercise will have two "X's"). Answers are on page 202.

Success Check

- Apply knowledge of multiple and single-joint exercises.
- Apply knowledge of push-pull movement patterns.
- Apply knowledge of exercises in steps 4 through 10.

Figure 12.3   Identify the MJEs and SJEs and the PS and PL exercises.

	Exercise	MJE	SJE	PS	PL
1.	Back squat				
2.	Supine triceps extension				
3.	Standing press				
4.	Standing heel raise				
5.	Lunge				
6.	Side plank				
7.	Bent-over row				
8.	Trunk curl				
9.	Shoulder shrug				
10.	Upright row				
11.	Preacher curl				
12.	Knee curl				
13.	Lat pulldown				
14.	Knee extension				
15.	Hang clean				

MANIPULATE PROGRAM VARIABLES

Now that you have a better understanding of exercise selection and arrangement, you need to decide on training load, repetitions, sets, and rest period length. Of these, determining training loads is the most challenging.

Training Loads

Opinions differ concerning how to handle this program design variable; however, the general consensus is that decisions should be based on the specificity concept and the *overload principle.* The overload principle asserts that each workout should place a demand on the muscles that is greater than what they are used to. Training that incorporates this principle challenges the body to meet and adapt to greater-than-normal physiological stress. As it does, it creates a new threshold that requires even greater stress to overload the involved muscles. Introducing overload in a systematic manner is sometimes referred to as *progressive overload.*

Methods for Determining Training Loads

Determining how much load to use is one of the most confusing aspects of a weight training program—and it's probably the most important one because the load determines the number of repetitions you will be able to perform and the amount of rest you need between sets and exercises. It also influences decisions concerning the number of sets and the frequency of workouts. Two approaches can be taken to determine the amount of load to use in training.

In steps 4 through 9, you used your body weight to determine initial training loads for the basic exercises. The calculations were designed to produce light loads so that you could concentrate on developing correct technique and avoid undue stress on bones and joint structures. Your goal was to calculate a load that resulted in 12 to 15 repetitions. This method of determining a load is referred to as a *12- to 15RM method* for assigning loads. The letter *R* is an abbreviation for "repetition" and the *M* stands for "maximum," meaning the maximum amount of weight that you can lift with proper technique for 12 to 15 repetitions.

Another method is the *1RM method*—a single (1) repetition (R) maximum (M) effort. Said another way, it is the maximum amount of weight that you can lift for one repetition in an exercise. Although not a perfect method (you are estimating or predicting that maximum load), it is more accurate than using body weight to determine initial training loads, especially if you have good exercise technique and are conditioned to safely handle heavier loads. It is not appropriate for a beginner, however, because it requires greater skill and a level of conditioning developed only after consistently following a weight training program for six weeks or more, depending on what shape you were in when you started.

CAUTION: The 1RM method of determining training loads should be used only with a certain advanced group of MJEs that train the largest muscle groups because they can withstand the heavy loads. In other words, determining a 1RM is *not* recommended for *all* MJEs; only the advanced group of MJEs that train the chest, shoulders, and legs as well as the total body qualify for this method.

The MJEs included in steps 4 through 10 are:

- Bench press (free weight) and chest press (multi- or single-unit machine) from step 4

- Standing press (free weight), shoulder press (cam machine), and seated press (multi- or single-unit machine) from step 6

- Lunge (free weight), leg press (multi- or single-unit machine), and *back squat (free weight) from step 8

- Hang clean and push press from step 10

CAUTION: Before attempting the 1RM method, be sure you have perfected your exercise technique and have weight trained for at least six weeks.

Regardless of the load and repetitions assigned for MJEs, remember to keep the number of repetitions at 12 to 15 for all SJEs. A possible exception is to gradually increase the number of repetitions to 15 to 30 per set in the core exercises performed without weights; the rationale is that since you are using a light load (your upper-body weight), it should be easier to perform a greater number of repetitions.

There are 10 procedures involved in estimating or predicting the 1RM.

1. The MJE you have selected is _____.

2. Warm up by performing 1 set of 10 repetitions with your current 12 to 15RM load. Your current 12 to 15RM load is ____ pounds (____ kg).

3. Add 10 pounds (4.5 kg) or a weight-stack plate that is closest to that weight. Your current 12 to 15RM load plus 10 pounds (4.5 kg) = _____ pounds (_____ kg).

4. Perform 3 repetitions with this load.

5. Add 10 more pounds (4.5 kg) or the next heaviest weight-stack plate = _____ pounds (_____ kg).

6. Rest for 2 to 5 minutes and perform as many repetitions as possible with this load. Give it your best effort!

7. Using table 12.3, fill in the name of the exercise, the repetitions completed, and the load lifted.

8. Refer to table 12.4, "Prediction of 1RM." Based on the number of repetitions you completed, circle the repetition factor number in the right-hand column of that table.

9. Record the circled repetition factor in table 12.3.

10. Multiply the repetition factor by the load used to obtain the predicted 1RM. Be sure to round the load to the nearest 5 pounds (2.3 kg) or weight-stack plate.

Table 12.3 Predicting the 1RM for MJEs

MJE:	
Repetitions completed:	

Load used:		Repetition factor from table 12.4:		Predicted 1RM:
	×		=	
Predicted 1RM (rounded to the nearest 5 pounds [2.3 kg]/weight-stack plate) = _____				

Table 12.4 Prediction of 1RM

Repetitions completed	Repetition factor
1	1.00
2	1.07
3	1.10
4	1.13
5	1.16
6	1.20
7	1.23
8	1.27
9	1.32
10	1.36

Adapted, by permission, from V.P. Lombardi, 1989, *Beginning weight training: The safe and effective way* (Dubuque, IA: William C. Brown), 201. © The McGraw-Hill Companies, Inc.

Figure 12.4 provides an example of applying the 10 procedures for predicting the 1RM for the free-weight bench press. In this example, six repetitions are performed with 120 pounds (54.4 kg). The repetition factor for six repetitions is 1.20, which when multiplied by 120 equals 144 pounds (65.3 kg). Rounding 144 off to the nearest 5-pound (2.3 kg) increment results in a predicted 1RM of 145 pounds (65.8 kg).

MJE:	Free-weight bench press
Repetitions completed:	6

Load used:		Repetition factor from table 12.4:		Predicted 1RM:
120	×	1.20	=	144

Predicted 1RM (rounded to the nearest 5 pounds [2.3 kg]/weight-stack plate) = 145

Repetitions completed	Repetition factor
1	1.00
2	1.07
3	1.10
4	1.13
5	1.16
6	1.20
7	1.23
8	1.27
9	1.32
10	1.36

Adapted, by permission, from V.P. Lombardi, 1989, *Beginning weight training: The safe and effective way* (Dubuque, IA: William C. Brown), 201. © The McGraw-Hill Companies, Inc.

Figure 12.4   Predicting a 1RM for a chest MJE.

To use the 1RM to determine a training load, multiply the 1RM by a percentage. To continue the example from figure 12.4 (a predicted 1RM in the bench press of 145 pounds [65.8 kg]), if you decide to use a 75 percent training load, the formula for calculating the training load is $1RM \times 0.75$ or $145 \times 0.75 = 108.75$ pounds (rounded down to 105 pounds [47.7 kg]. See CAUTION on page 169). This process will be discussed in detail in the "Application of the Specificity Concept" section of this step.

1RM Load *Self-Assessment Quiz*

Mark the correct choice in each of the following statements. Answers are on page 202.

1. 1RM refers to the [___ 1-repetition maximum ___ 1-minute rest minimum].

2. The [___ lunge ___ knee extension] is an example of a MJE.

3. The procedure for predicting the 1RM includes a total of [___ 10 ___ 20] pounds that are added to your 12- to 15RM load when performing as many repetitions as possible.

Increasing Loads

Lifting heavier loads as soon as you are able to complete the required number of repetitions is important. However, changes should not be made too soon. Wait until you can complete two or more repetitions more than the intended number in the last set of two consecutive workouts (the *two-for-two rule*; see step 11). When you have met the two-for-two rule, instead of referring to the load adjustment table (found at the end of steps 4 to 9), simply increase loads by 2.5 or 5 pounds (1.1 or 2.2 kg). The load adjustment chart was used initially to assist with large fluctuations in the number of repetitions performed. You will now find that fluctuations are much smaller and that using the two-for-two rule with a 2.5- or 5-pound increase works well, with two exceptions:

- You may need to make heavier increases for MJEs. Be aware, though, that underestimating the increase needed is better than overestimating it.

- Smaller load increments are appropriate for SJEs. Use 1.25- to 2.5-pound (0.6 to 1.1 kg) plates to increase loads in arm (biceps, triceps), forearm, calf, and neck exercises.

Increasing Loads *Self-Assessment Quiz*

Mark the correct choice in each of the following statements. Answers are on page 203.

1. The two-for-two rule concerns [___ resting 2 minutes after the second set of every exercise ___ completing 2 or more repetitions above the goal in the last set in two consecutive workouts].

2. Load increases for the bench press and squat exercises are likely to be [___ heavier ___ lighter] than those for the biceps and triceps exercises.

Number of Repetitions

The number of repetitions you will be able to perform is directly related to the load you select. As the loads become heavier, the number of repetitions possible becomes fewer; as the loads become lighter, the number of repetitions possible becomes greater. Assuming that a good effort is given in each set of exercises, the primary factor that dictates the number of repetitions is the load selected.

Number of Repetitions *Self-Assessment Quiz*

Mark the correct choice in each of the following statements. Answers are on page 203.

1. Heavier loads are associated with a [___ greater ___ fewer] number of repetitions.

2. The number of repetitions that can be completed is primarily based on the [___ load ___ exercise].

Number of Sets

Some controversy exists as to whether multiple (two or more) sets are better than single sets for developing strength, muscular size, or muscular endurance. While one-set training works exceptionally well during the early stages (10 weeks or fewer) of training, growing research supports adding more sets to the programs of well-trained individuals.

It seems reasonable to expect that the multiple-set approach to training provides a better stimulus for continued development. The rationale is that a single set of an exercise will not recruit all the fibers in a muscle and that performing additional sets will recruit more fibers. This is because muscle fibers that were involved in the first set will not be sufficiently recovered and therefore will rely on fresh fibers (not previously stimulated) for assistance, especially if succeeding sets use an increased load.

When three or more sets are performed, the likelihood of recruiting additional fibers becomes even greater. Further support for multiple sets comes from observations of the programs followed by successful competitive weightlifters, powerlifters, and bodybuilders. These competitors rely on multiple sets to achieve a high degree of development. As you will see later, your goals for training should influence the number of sets you perform.

Another consideration in determining the number of sets is the amount of time you have for training. For instance, if you choose to rest for one minute between exercises in your program (for a goal of muscular size), you should plan on a minimum of two minutes per exercise (a minimum of 60 seconds to complete the exercise, plus 60 seconds of rest). Thus your program of seven exercises, in which you perform one set of each, should take 14 minutes. If you increase the number of sets to two, and then to three, your workout time will increase to 28 and 42 minutes, respectively (assuming a 60-second rest period after each set). The actual time for rest between sets, as you will read soon, may vary from 30 seconds to 5 minutes.

Number of Sets *Self-Assessment Quiz*

Mark the correct choice in each of the following statements. Answers are on page 203.

1. The fewest number of sets recommended for continued development is [___ 1 ___ 2].

2. The basis for multiple-set training is that the additional sets are thought to [___ recruit ___ relax] a greater number of muscle fibers.

Length of the Rest Period

The impact of the rest period between sets and exercises on the intensity of training is not usually recognized, but it should be. Longer rest periods provide time for the energizers of muscle contraction to rebuild, enabling muscles to exert greater force. If the amount of work is the same, and the rest periods are shortened, the intensity of training increases. The length of time between sets and exercises has a direct impact on the outcomes of training.

CAUTION: Moving too rapidly from one exercise or set to another often reduces the number of repetitions you are able to perform because of inadequate recovery time, and you may become dizzy and nauseated.

Length of the Rest Period
Self-Assessment Quiz

Mark the correct choice in each of the following statements. Answers are on page 203.

1. Longer rest periods enable you to exert [___ more ___ less] force.

2. The length of the rest period has [___ an effect ___ no effect] on the outcome of training.

Application of the Specificity Concept

The earlier discussion of the specificity concept addressed only the issue of exercise selection, but this concept is broader in scope as it relates to program design. Table 12.5 shows a continuum or range from 100 to 65 percent of the 1RM and the number of repetitions associated with each percentage presented. For instance, selecting a load that represents 85 percent of the 1RM should yield 6 repetitions, whereas 67 percent of 1RM should yield about 12 repetitions. Knowledge of this inverse relationship is helpful when selecting loads if a specific number of repetitions is desired.

Loads, repetitions, sets, and rest periods are manipulated using the specificity concept in designing three different programs: muscular endurance, hypertrophy, and strength. Table 12.6 also illustrates a continuum on which the variables for the percentage of 1RM, number of repetitions and sets, and length of the rest period are presented. It reveals that muscular endurance programs (as compared to other programs) should include lighter loads (67 percent of 1RM or less), permit 12 to 20 repetitions, involve fewer sets (2 or 3), and have shorter rest periods (20 to 30 seconds). In contrast, programs designed to develop strength should include heavier loads (85 to 100 percent of 1RM) with fewer repetitions (1 to 6), more sets (3 to 5, possibly more), and longer rest periods between sets (2 to 5 minutes). Programs designed to develop hypertrophy (muscular size increases) have repetitions, sets, and rest periods assignments that fall between the guidelines for developing muscle endurance and strength.

Table 12.5   Percent of 1RM–Repetition Relationship

% of 1RM	Estimated number of repetitions that can be performed
100	1
95	2
93	3
90	4
87	5
85	6
83	7
80	8
77	9
75	10
70	11
67	12
65	15

Reprinted, by permission, from R.W. Earle and T.R. Baechle, 2004, Resistance training program design. In *NSCA's essentials of personal training*, edited by R.W. Earle and T.R. Baechle (Champaign, IL: Human Kinetics), 371.

Table 12.6   Specificity Concept Applied to Program Design Variables

Relative loading	Outcome of training	% of 1RM	Repetitions	Sets	Rest period length
Light	Muscular endurance	60-67	12-20	2-3	20-30 seconds
Moderate	Hypertrophy	67-85	6-12	3-6	30-90 seconds
Heavy	Muscular strength	85-100	1-6	3-5	2-5 minutes

Muscular Endurance Program

The program you have been following in this book so far is designed to develop muscular endurance. You will notice some similarities between it and the program for muscular endurance in table 12.6. The loads you are using now may permit you to perform 15, but not quite 20, repetitions. Also, your rest periods should be close to the suggested 30 seconds if you have made an effort to shorten them. If you choose in step 14 to continue with your muscular endurance program, do not increase the load until you are able to perform 20 repetitions in the last set in two consecutive workouts and keep the rest periods at 20 to 30 seconds. Except for specific situations, such as training for competitive aerobic endurance events, rest periods of less than 20 seconds are not recommended or needed.

Muscular Endurance Program
Self-Assessment Quiz

Write or mark the correct choices in each of the following statements. Answers are on page 203.

1. The guidelines to use when designing a program for muscular endurance are:

   a. Relative loading _____

   b. Percentage of 1RM load _____

   c. Repetitions _____

   d. Sets _____

2. Unless there is a specific reason to do otherwise, the appropriate amount of rest between sets and exercises in a muscular endurance program is [___ 10 to 15 seconds ___ 20 to 30 seconds].

Hypertrophy Program

If you decide in step 14 to emphasize hypertrophy, refer to table 12.7 to see one method of implementing the guidelines in tables 12.5 and 12.6. The example uses a 1RM of 200 pounds (90.9 kg) in the leg press exercise. To allow 10 repetitions per set, use 75 percent of the 1RM. This calculation (200 × 0.75) equals 150 pounds (68.2 kg).

Table 12.7   Sample Hypertrophy Program: Multiple Set–Same Load Training

Set	Goal repetitions	1RM × %1RM = training × load
1	10	200 × 0.75 = 150 pounds (68.2 kg)
2	10	200 × 0.75 = 150 pounds (68.2 kg)
3	10	200 × 0.75 = 150 pounds (68.2 kg)

1RM in the leg press = 200 pounds (90.9 kg); length of rest between sets = 30-90 seconds

Success in a hypertrophy program is associated with the use of moderate loads (67 to 85 percent of 1RM), a medium number of repetitions (6 to 12) per set, 3 to 6 sets, and moderate rest periods (30 to 90 seconds between sets). A simple method for estimating 67 to 85 percent loads is to add 5 to 10 pounds (2.3 to 4.5 kg) to the loads you are currently using. Do this only with MJEs; keep the loads for the SJEs the same and apply the two-for-two rule when making load adjustments.

You may notice that successful bodybuilders usually perform many sets and do not rest very long between them. Thus they combine the multiple-set program described earlier in this step with the rest period and load guidelines presented in table 12.6 to promote hypertrophy.

Two unique methods implemented in many hypertrophy programs are the *superset* and the *compound set*. A superset consists of two exercises that train opposing muscle groups that are performed without rest between them; for example, one set of the biceps curl exercise followed immediately by one set of the triceps extension exercise. A compound set is two exercises that train the same muscle group performed consecutively without rest between them. An example is one set of the barbell biceps curl exercise followed immediately by one set of the dumbbell biceps curl exercise. The fact that these approaches deviate from the rest periods shown in table 12.6 does not mean that they are ineffective. The time frames indicated are only guidelines; program design variables can be manipulated in many ways to produce positive outcomes.

Hypertrophy Program *Self-Assessment Quiz*

Write or mark the correct answer in each of the following statements. Answers are on page 203.

1. The guidelines to use when designing a program for hypertrophy are:

    a. Relative loading _____

    b. Percentage of 1RM load _____

    c. Repetitions _____

    d. Sets _____

    e. Length of the rest period _____

2. When two exercises for opposing muscle groups are performed without rest, this arrangement is referred to as a [___ superset ___ compound set].

Muscular Strength Program

Programs can be designed in many ways to produce significant strength gains. The two presented here are commonly used by successful powerlifters and weightlifters and are most appropriately applied to MJEs.

The first method is *pyramid training*. If you decide in step 14 to change your program to develop muscular strength, refer to table 12.8 to see one method of applying the guidelines presented in tables 12.5 and 12.6. The example uses a 1RM of 225 pounds (102.3 kg) in the back squat exercise. To calculate a load that will produce the goal of 6 repetitions in the first set, use 85 percent of the 1RM. (The second and third sets will be discussed later.) This calculation (225 × 0.85) equals 191.25 pounds (86.9 kg) which is rounded down to 190 pounds (86.4 kg).

CAUTION: For all calculations, it is best to round down even if the next closest increment is reached by rounding up. The lower load will just result in meeting the two-for-two rule sooner than if the load was heavier.

Another method that may get you close to 85 percent of a 1RM load is to add 10 to 15 pounds (4.5 to 6.8 kg) to what you are using currently in your MJEs. Remember to keep the SJEs loads the same and apply the two-for-two rule when making load adjustments.

Now, to incorporate the concept of progressive overload, you can use what is referred to as *light to heavy pyramid training*, in which each succeeding set becomes heavier; see the second and third sets in table 12.8, for examples. Increase the 85 percent of the 1RM (190 pounds [86.4 kg]) load to 90 percent of the 1RM (200 pounds [90.9 kg]) in the second set, and to 95 percent of the 1RM (210 pounds [95.5 kg]) in the third set. Between each set, rest for 2 to 5 minutes. Use this approach with the MJEs and perform 3 sets of 8 to 12 repetitions in the SJEs. (Heavy loads place too much stress on the smaller muscles and joints.) Forcing yourself to lift progressively heavier loads from set to set provides the stimulus for dramatic strength gains. As training continues and the intensity of workouts increases, a time will come when training with very heavy loads is appropriate only on designated days. This will be discussed further in step 13.

Table 12.8   Sample Muscular Strength Program: Pyramid Training

Set	Goal repetitions	1RM × %1RM = training load
1	6	225 × 0.85 = 190 pounds (86.4 kg)*
2	4	225 × 0.90 = 200 pounds (90.9 kg)**
3	2	225 × 0.95 = 210 pounds (95.5 kg)***

1RM in the back squat = 225 pounds (102.3 kg); length of rest between sets = 2-5 minutes

* Rounded down from 191.25 pounds (86.9 kg)

** Rounded down from 202.5 pounds (92 kg)

*** Rounded down from 213.75 pounds (97.2 kg)

Multiple sets–same load training is another popular approach used to develop strength. With this method you perform 3 to 5 sets of 2 to 6 repetitions with the same load in the MJEs and 3 sets of 8 to 12 repetitions in the SJEs. The program can be made more aggressive by decreasing the goal repetitions, which means you must use heavier loads. To modify the pyramid training example from table 12.8 (a 1RM in the back squat of 225 pounds [102.3 kg]), see table 12.9. Notice how the percentages of the 1RM are associated with the goal repetitions of 4, 3, and 2 at the bottom of table 12.9. You will find that completing the specified number of repetitions in set 1 is usually easy, set 2 is more difficult, and set 3 is very difficult, if not impossible. With continued training, sets 2 and 3 will become easier, and eventually you will need to increase the loads.

Table 12.9   Muscular Strength Program: Multiple Sets–Same Load Training

Set	Goal repetitions	1RM × %1RM = training load
1	6	225 × 0.85 = 190 pounds (86.4 kg)*
2	6	225 × 0.85 = 190 pounds (86.4 kg)*
3	6	225 × 0.85 = 190 pounds (86.4 kg)*

1RM in the back squat = 225 pounds (102.3 kg); length of rest between sets = 2-5 minutes

* Rounded down from 191.25 pounds (86.9 kg)

Use 90% of 1RM for goal repetitions of 4.

Use 93% of 1RM for goal repetitions of 3.

Use 95% of 1RM for goal repetitions of 2.

Muscular Strength Program
Self-Assessment Quiz

Write or mark the correct answer in each of the following statements. Number 4 has two answers. Answers are on page 204.

1. The guidelines to use when designing a program for muscular strength are:

    a. Relative loading _____

    b. Percentage of 1RM load _____

    c. Repetitions _____

    d. Sets _____

    e. Length of the rest period _____

2. Given a 1RM of 200 pounds (90.9 kg) and a goal of muscular strength development, the lightest load for a first set should be [___ 170 pounds (77.3 kg) ___ 140 pounds (63.6 kg)].

3. The use of sequentially heavier loads in each set of the pyramid training approach demonstrates the use of the [___ two-for-two rule ___ progressive overload principle].

4. The two muscular strength development programs described here have been referred to as [___ 1RM ___ pyramid ___ multiple set–same load ___ overload].

5. The heavy loads of a muscular strength program are not used with [___ MJEs ___ SJEs] because they place too much stress on the involved muscle and joint structures.

Manipulating Program Variables Drill 1.
Loads, Repetitions, Sets, and Rest Periods

You have learned how the specificity concept and overload principle are used in determining loads, and what the implications of these loads are on the number of repetitions and sets and on the length of the rest periods between exercises and sets. As a review, fill in the missing information in figure 12.5. Answers can be found in table 12.6, page 167.

Success Check

- Apply the specificity concept to determine the relative loading, training outcome, percent of 1RM, repetitions, sets, and rest period length.

Figure 12.5 Practice with applying the specificity concept to the program design variables.

Relative loading	Outcome of training	% of 1RM	Repetitions	Sets	Rest period length
	Muscular endurance		12-20		20-30 seconds
Moderate		67-85		3-6	
	Muscular strength		1-6		2-5 minutes

Manipulating Program Variables Drill 2.
Determining Load Ranges

This drill will give you experience in determining training loads, using either a predicted or actual 1RM, and in applying what you've learned about training loads. Using 85 pounds (38.6 kg) as the 1RM and the example shown for a hypertrophy program, determine the training load ranges for a muscular strength and a muscular endurance program. Remember to round down to the nearest 5 pounds (2.3 kg) or closest weight-stack plate. Write your answers in the blanks in figure 12.6. Answers are on page 204.

Success Check

- Remember the percentage of the 1RM associated with specific training outcomes.
- Round down load to nearest 5 pounds (2.3 kg) or closest weight-stack plate.

Figure 12.6 Practice with determining training load ranges for muscular strength and muscular endurance programs.

Goal	1RM		Training load (%)		Training load range*
Hypertrophy	85 pounds (38.6 kg)	×	65 to 85 %	=	55 to 70
Muscular strength	85 pounds (38.6 kg)	×	%	=	to
Muscular endurance	85 pounds (38.6 kg)	×	%	=	to

*Round down load to nearest 5 pounds (2.3 kg) or closest weight-stack plate.

DECIDE TRAINING FREQUENCY

Training frequency is the last design variable to be covered before you will be challenged to design your own program. The question that needs to be answered is "How often should I train?" The frequency of your training, just like the application of the overload principle, is an essential element in determining the proper intensity for a successful training program.

To be effective, you must train on a regular, consistent basis. Sporadic training short-circuits your body's ability to adapt. Know, though, that rest days between training days are as important as the actual training. Your body needs time to recover, to move the waste products of exercise out of the muscles and nutrients in so that muscles that are torn down from training can rebuild and increase in endurance, size, or strength. Rest and nutritious foods are essential to ongoing success.

Often people who are new to weight training become so excited with the changes in their strength and appearance that they start training on scheduled rest days. More is not always better, especially during the beginning stages of your program! If you are relatively new to weight training, you will need to insert rest days between training days evenly throughout the week. The result is a schedule that permits two to three workouts of the same exercises per week. As you become more accustomed to training, you can include additional exercises. Eventually, your program will include too many exercises to perform all in one workout, so you may decide to add another training day each week and redistribute (split up) the exercises across more workouts. This will make the length of each workout more reasonable and provide variety to your program.

For beginners, allowing at least 48 hours between workouts that train the same muscles is important. The result is a *three-days-a-week program*. Typically, this means training on Monday, Wednesday, and Friday; Tuesday, Thursday, and Saturday; or Sunday, Tuesday, and Thursday. In a three-days-a-week program, all exercises are performed each training day.

A *split program* is a more advanced method of training that involves performing some of the exercises two days a week (for example, Monday and Thursday) and the others on two other days (for example, Tuesday and Friday). A split program typically involves more exercises and sets; it requires four training days as shown in table 12.10. On the left half of this table (Option A), exercises are split into upper body and lower body. Option B illustrates another common split-program option in which exercises for the chest, shoulders, and arms are performed on different days than leg and back exercises. Notice that in both options the exercises have been arranged so that PS and PL exercises are alternated, and triceps and biceps exercises follow the upper body PS and PL exercises, respectively. Also, MJEs are performed before SJEs within the upper body exercise list and within the lower body exercise list.

A split program offers several advantages. It spreads the exercises in your workout over four days instead of three, usually reducing the amount of time required to complete each workout. This allows you to add more exercises and sets while keeping workout time reasonable. Because you can add more exercises, you can emphasize development in specific muscle groups, should you decide to do so. The program's disadvantage is that you must train four days a week instead of three.

Frequency of Training *Self-Assessment Quiz*

Mark the correct choices in each of the following statements. Answers are on page 204.

1. Creating the proper stimulus for improvement depends on using the overload principle and training [___ on a regular basis ___ in a sporadic manner].

2. Compared to a split program, a three-days-a-week program typically includes a [___ greater ___ fewer] number of exercises.

3. Compared to a three-days-a-week program, the workouts in a split program usually take [___ less ___ more] time to complete.

4. A [___ split ___ three-days-a-week] program offers the best opportunity for emphasizing development in specific muscle groups.

Table 12.10   Four-Days-a-Week Split Training Program

OPTION A		OPTION B	
Monday and Thursday (upper body)		**Monday and Thursday (chest, shoulders, arms)**	
Exercise	**Type**	**Exercise**	**Type**
Bench press	MJ, PS	Chest press	MJ, PS
Lat pulldown	MJ, PL	Upright row	MJ, PL
Standing press	MJ, PS	Standing press	MJ, PS
Biceps curl	SJ, PL	Preacher curl	SJ, PL
Triceps extension	SJ, PS	Triceps pushdown	SJ, PS
Extended abdominal crunch	SJ*, PL	Twisting trunk curl	SJ*, PL
Tuesday and Friday (lower body)		**Tuesday and Friday (legs and back)**	
Exercise	**Type**	**Exercise**	**Type**
Lunge	MJ, PS	Leg press	MJ, PS
Knee curl	SJ, PL	Knee curl	SJ, PL
Knee extension	SJ, PS	Knee extension	SJ, PS
Standing heel raise	SJ, PS**	Standing heel raise	SJ, PS**
		Seated heel raise	SJ, PS**
		Bent-over row	MJ, PL
		Lat pulldown	MJ, PL***

*All core exercises are loosely classified as single-joint exercises.

**All calf exercises are PS exercises.

***All upper-back exercises are PL exercises so you cannot alternate with PS upper-back exercises (because there are none).

SUCCESS SUMMARY FOR PROGRAM DESIGN PRINCIPLES

A clear understanding of how to apply the specificity concept and the overload principle is the basis for well-conceived programs. Understanding and incorporating the guidelines for loads, repetitions, sets, and rest period length in designing muscular endurance, hypertrophy, and muscular strength programs are the keys to meeting your specific needs.

When selecting exercises, keep in mind the specificity concept, available equipment, and spotter requirements for each exercise. Also, include at least one exercise for each of the seven muscle groups and remember to select balanced pairs of exercises. Include additional exercises if you want to emphasize the development of certain muscle groups but not so many that workouts take too long. Lastly, remember that how you arrange exercises and the order in which you perform them also has an impact on the intensity of your overall program.

Training on a regular basis is essential to the success of your weight training program. Beginning programs typically begin with two or three workout days a week and may evolve into a four-days-a-week split program. The greater time commitment in split programs is offset by the advantages of being able to emphasize certain body parts because of the extra training time.

Your ability to recover from workout sessions is critical to your future training successes—more is not always better. Finally, muscles need to be nourished, especially after a challenging workout. Eating nutritious meals is essential for muscle repair and increases in size and strength.

Step 13 provides strategies on how to modify or vary the program you have been following to avoid a plateau in your progress and keep you moving toward your weight training goals. A common way to vary your program is to incorporate purposeful changes in training intensity.

Before Taking the Next Step

Honestly answer each of the following questions. If you answer yes to all of the questions, you are ready to move on to step 13.

1. Have you completed all of the self-assessment quizzes and checked your answers?

2. Do you understand how to manipulate training variables for different types of programs—muscular endurance, hypertrophy, and muscular strength?

3. Do you understand the specificity principle and how to apply it to create your program?

Learning How to Manipulate Training Variables to Maximize Results

This step builds on the discussion in step 12 of applying program design principles associated with exercise selection, arrangement, loads, repetitions, sets, rest periods, and training frequency by describing how these program design elements can be manipulated to maximize training outcomes.

If you perform the same number of sets and repetitions on the same days each week and with the same loads week after week, a plateau in strength will occur, and you will not meet your goals for training. The program design variables need to be systematically varied in order to promote continued improvements and avoid overtraining.

Although performing greater numbers of repetitions and sets and lifting heavier loads is necessary in order for improvement to continue, performing too many repetitions and sets with aggressive loads and without adequate rest periods can result in injury, extended muscle soreness, and aggravated joint problems. The goal, therefore, is to design programs that vary the overall intensity of training and provide the needed overload and rest to produce maximum improvements without injury.

Training variation involves efficiently manipulating the variables of

- training frequency,
- exercise selection,
- exercise arrangement,
- number of repetitions per set,
- number of sets, and
- length of the rest periods.

Programs that are designed to vary the intensity of training give special attention to the loads assigned or calculated for the large muscle multi-joint exercises (MJEs) discussed in step 12. Further, you may recall that a certain advanced group of MJEs—those that train the chest, shoulders, and legs as well as the total-body—qualify for the 1RM method of determining training loads because they train the largest muscle groups, which are better able to withstand the rigors of weight training than smaller muscle groups. Those MJEs were also identified as being appropriate for the heavier loads used in pyramid training as part of a muscular strength program. Be aware that the MJEs mentioned in the discussions and examples of this step refer to that advanced group of MJEs, not all MJEs (and definitely not the SJEs).

Some of the common strategies used to vary the intensity of workouts are to

- lift heavy, light, and medium loads on different days of the week;
- increase loads from week to week; or
- change loads in a cyclical or repeated manner every two to four weeks.

These strategies can be applied to MJEs and programs designed to increase muscular strength and hypertrophy because they typically involve performing three or more sets of the MJEs. (The loads used for SJEs should continue to allow 8 to 12 repetitions and follow the two-for-two rule to gradually increase the loads.) Although the discussion here focuses on the loads assigned for the various programs, you should realize that the number of repetitions and sets can also be manipulated to vary training intensities.

WITHIN-THE-WEEK VARIATIONS

There are three primary methods of designing a program that includes changes in the loads lifted during one training week. Again, remember that any numerical or relative loading guidelines refer to changes made to MJEs only.

Three Days a Week, Same Load in Each Set

Table 13.1 shows you an example of a three-days-a-week workout program in which heavy (H), light (L), and medium (M) loads are varied within the week. The loads used in a particular day's workout do not change (thus the "same load in each set" name). The table uses abbreviations: 3 × 6 means 3 sets of 6 repetitions and 2 × 8-12 indicates that you should perform 2 sets of 8 to 12 repetitions. If you completed 3 sets of 8 to 10 repetitions with 120 pounds (54.5 kg), you would write it like this: 120 × 3 × 8-10.

Notice that in table 13.1 only the MJEs are associated with the letters *H, L,* or *M* designating the use of heavy (85 percent of 1RM for 6 repetitions), light (75 percent of 1RM for 10 repetitions), and medium (80 percent of 1RM for 8 repetitions) loads, respectively. The SJEs use loads that permit 8 to 12 repetitions. Even though you may be able to, do *not* perform more than 10 repetitions on your light day or more than 8 repetitions on your medium day. Notice that Monday (in table 13.1's example), the most intense training day, is followed by the least intense training day, which is then followed by a medium-intensity day so that your body has a chance to recover. This pattern repeats itself in all the training-program examples provided in this step.

Table 13.1   Within-the-Week Training Load Variation—Three Days a Week, Same Load Each Set

Exercise	Monday	Wednesday	Friday
Chest press*	H: 3 × 6	L: 3 × 10	M: 3 × 8
Bent-over row	2 × 8-12	2 × 8-12	2 × 8-12
Standing press*	H: 3 × 6	L: 3 × 10	M: 3 × 8
Biceps curl	2 × 8-12	2 × 8-12	2 × 8-12
Triceps extension	2 × 8-12	2 × 8-12	2 × 8-12
Back squat*	H: 3 × 6	L: 3 × 10	M: 3 × 8
Twisting trunk curl	2 × 15-30	2 × 15-30	2 × 15-30

*Advanced MJEs (the number of sets does not include warm-up sets)
Heavy (H) = 85% 1RM; light (L) = 75% 1RM; medium (M) = 80% 1RM

Three-Days-a-Week Pyramid Approach

In step 12 you learned about the use of the pyramid approach in which progressive load increases occur from one set to another until all sets for a specific exercise are completed. In table 13.2 you will recognize these progressive increases, but you should note that the loads used vary from 80 to 95 percent of 1RM on Monday (H), from 67 to 80 percent on Wednesday (L), and from 75 to 85 percent on Friday (M). The example uses a 1RM of 150 pounds (68.2 kg) and the loads are rounded down to the nearest 5-pound (2.3 kg) increment.

Table 13.2   Within-the-Week Training Load Variation—Three Days a Week, Pyramid Approach

Monday—heavy (H)		Wednesday—light (L)		Friday—medium (M)	
% 1RM	Load* (pounds) × sets × repetitions	% 1RM	Load* (pounds) × sets × repetitions	% 1RM	Load* (pounds) × sets × repetitions
80	120 × 1 × 8	67	100 × 1 × 12	75	110 × 1 × 10
85	125 × 1 × 6	75	110 × 1 × 10	80	120 × 1 × 8
95	135 × 1 × 4	80	120 × 1 × 8	85	125 × 1 × 6

*Current 1RM = 150 pounds (68.2 kg)

Four-Days-a-Week Heavy-Light Split Approach

Tables 13.3 and 13.4 show how a four-days-a-week (split) program can be organized to vary heavy and light loads within the week. Table 13.3 shows the assignment of loads on Monday and Thursday for the chest, shoulders, and triceps. Table 13.4 shows load assignments on Tuesday and Friday for the legs, back, and biceps. Again, it is important not to perform more than 12 repetitions on your light day even if you are able to.

Table 13.3 Monday-Thursday Split Program—Chest, Shoulders, and Triceps

Exercise	Monday	Thursday
Bench press*	H: 4 × 6	L: 3 × 12
Dumbbell chest fly	4 × 8-12	3 × 8-12
Shoulder press*	H: 4 × 6	L: 3 × 12
Triceps pushdown	4 × 8-12	3 × 8-12
Extended abdominal crunch	2 × 15-30	2 × 15-30

*Advanced MJEs (the number of sets does not include warm-up sets)
Heavy (H) = 85% 1RM; light (L) = 67% 1RM

Table 13.4 Tuesday-Friday Split Program—Legs, Back, and Biceps

Exercise	Tuesday	Friday
Back squat*	H: 4 × 6	L: 3 × 12
Knee curl	4 × 8-12	3 × 8-12
Standing heel raise	4 × 8-12	3 × 8-12
Lat pulldown	4 × 8-12	3 × 8-12
Seated row	4 × 8-12	3 × 8-12
Low-pulley biceps curl	4 × 8-12	3 × 8-12

*Advanced MJE (the number of sets does not include warm-up sets)
Heavy (H) = 85% 1RM; light (L) = 67% 1RM

WEEK-TO-WEEK VARIATIONS

Table 13.5 shows two ways to increase loads on a weekly basis. Option A involves simply scheduling a small percent increase each week. Option B also shows a small percentage of increase (Monday) each week, followed by the use of light and medium loads on Wednesday and Friday, respectively. Remember that the percentages shown apply only to MJEs.

Table 13.5   Within- and Between-Weeks Training Load Variation

OPTION A: SAME LOAD EACH SET, INCREASES BETWEEN WEEKS			
Week	Monday	Wednesday	Friday
1	80% 1RM	80% 1RM	80% 1RM
2	83% 1RM	83% 1RM	83% 1RM
3	86% 1RM	86% 1RM	86% 1RM
OPTION B: WITHIN- AND BETWEEN-WEEK LOAD VARIATIONS			
Week	Monday	Wednesday	Friday
1	80% 1RM	70% 1RM	75% 1RM
2	83% 1RM	73% 1RM	78% 1RM
3	86% 1RM	76% 1RM	81% 1RM

CYCLICAL TRAINING VARIATIONS

The strategies previously explained in this step describe how to vary the intensity of your weight training program. If, however, you were to continue following one of those programs for an extended period of time, you would most likely experience a plateau or an overtraining injury. Remember the earlier emphasis on the need for proper rest? Programs that continue to increase loads, repetitions, or sets without scheduling rest time will not produce optimal gains. To counteract that risk, you should follow the concept of *periodization*, which refers to the purposeful scheduling or cycling of high-intensity training periods and low-intensity training periods.

A typical periodization strategy divides a program into time periods. The largest division is a *macrocycle,* which usually lasts an entire training year but may range from one month to four years (for Olympic athletes, for example). Within the macrocycle are two or more *mesocycles* that last several weeks to several months. Each mesocycle is divided into two or more *microcycles,* each of which is usually one week long. These cycles are incorporated into two general types of periodization models, *linear* and *undulating.* In the linear model, the intensity (load) is consistently increased over time while the volume (sets and repetitions) is reduced. The non-linear or undulating model is characterized by the intensity and volume being from varied day to day and from workout to workout.

The training program described in table 13.6 represents an eight-week cycle (for advanced MJEs only) that includes load variations within the week (undulating) and load increases after every three weeks (linear) until the eighth week.

Follow the guidelines for loading and sets for each heavy, light, and medium training day. On Friday of the third and sixth weeks, complete the following procedures as an abbreviated way to determine a new 1RM to use when calculating the new training loads:

1. Warm up as usual, then use Friday's loads in sets 1 and 2 (and 3 for week 6), but perform only 5 and 3 repetitions (6, 4, and 2 repetitions for week 6), respectively.

2. If you are using the pyramid method, perform as many repetitions as possible with the heaviest load used thus far in this cycle (specific to the exercise being tested). If you are using the same load in each set, increase the load lifted in the last set by 10 pounds (4.5 kg) and perform as many repetitions as possible.

3. Predict the 1RM using the procedures you learned in step 12 (see page 160). A shortcut method for identifying training loads is described in the next section.

In the fourth and seventh weeks, the loads lifted are based on new calculations using the newly tested 1RMs that were determined during the Friday workout of the third and sixth weeks. Notice that the eighth week involves lighter loads and fewer sets (resulting in less intensive workouts), providing an opportunity for the body to recover as well as to increase strength levels in succeeding weeks. The number of sets may also be increased after each three-week period. A four-days-a-week program could be cycled in a similar way.

Table 13.6 Eight-Week Training Cycle

Week	Sets	Monday	Wednesday	Friday
1	3	H	L	M
2	3	H	L	M
3	3	M	L	Testing
4*	4	H	L	M
5	4	H	L	M
6	4	M	L	Testing
7*	4	H	L	M
8	2	L	L	L
9	Retest 1RM in the advanced MJEs and repeat 8-week cycle with new training loads			

*Begin using loads based on new 1RM from previous Friday's testing.
Heavy (H) = 85% 1RM; light (L) = 67% 1RM; medium (M) = 75% 1RM

SHORTCUT FOR DETERMINING TRAINING LOADS

Instead of multiplying the 1RM by the desired training percentage to determine training loads as you did in step 12, refer to table 13.7 and follow these steps:

1. Locate and circle your 1RM value in the "1RM" column.

2. Identify the desired training percentage (65 to 95 percent).

3. Follow the percentage column down until it meets the row for your 1RM and circle that number—this is your training load.

Table 13.7 Training Load Determination

Line	1RM	Training load percentage*											
		65%	67%	70%	75%	77%	80%	83%	85%	87%	90%	93%	95%
1	20	13	13	14	15	15	16	17	17	17	18	19	19
2	25	16	17	18	19	19	20	21	21	22	23	23	24
3	30	20	20	21	23	23	24	25	26	26	27	28	29
4	35	23	23	25	26	27	28	29	30	30	32	33	33
5	40	26	27	28	30	31	32	33	34	35	36	37	38
6	45	29	30	32	34	35	36	37	38	39	41	42	43
7	50	33	34	35	38	39	40	42	43	44	45	47	48
8	55	36	37	39	41	42	44	46	47	48	50	51	52
9	60	39	40	42	45	46	48	50	51	52	54	56	57
10	65	42	44	46	49	50	52	54	55	57	59	60	62
11	70	46	47	49	53	54	56	58	60	61	63	65	67
12	75	49	50	53	56	58	60	62	64	65	68	70	71
13	80	52	54	56	60	62	64	66	68	70	72	74	76
14	85	55	57	60	64	65	68	71	72	74	77	79	81
15	90	59	60	63	68	69	72	75	77	78	81	84	86
16	95	62	64	67	71	73	76	79	81	83	86	88	90
17	100	65	67	70	75	77	80	83	85	87	90	93	95
18	105	68	70	74	79	81	84	87	89	91	95	98	100
19	110	72	74	77	83	85	88	91	94	96	99	102	105
20	115	75	77	81	86	89	92	95	98	100	104	107	109
21	120	78	80	84	90	92	96	100	102	104	108	112	114
22	125	81	84	88	94	96	100	104	106	109	113	116	119
23	130	85	87	91	98	100	104	108	111	113	117	121	124
24	135	88	90	95	101	104	108	112	115	117	122	126	128
25	140	91	94	98	105	108	112	116	119	122	126	130	133
26	145	94	97	102	109	112	116	120	123	126	131	135	138
27	150	98	101	105	113	116	120	125	128	131	135	140	143
28	155	101	104	109	116	119	124	129	132	135	140	144	147
29	160	104	107	112	120	123	128	133	136	139	144	149	152
30	165	107	111	116	124	127	132	137	140	144	149	153	157
31	170	111	114	119	128	131	136	141	145	148	153	158	162
32	175	114	117	123	131	135	140	145	149	152	158	163	166

(continued)

Table 13.7 (continued)

Line	1RM	Training load percentage*											
		65%	67%	70%	75%	77%	80%	83%	85%	87%	90%	93%	95%
33	180	117	121	126	135	139	144	149	153	157	162	167	171
34	185	120	124	130	139	142	148	154	157	161	167	172	176
35	190	124	127	133	143	146	152	158	162	165	171	177	181
36	195	127	131	137	146	150	156	162	166	170	176	181	185
37	200	130	134	140	150	154	160	166	170	174	180	186	190
38	210	137	141	147	158	162	168	174	179	183	189	195	200
39	220	143	147	154	165	169	176	183	187	191	198	205	209
40	230	150	154	161	173	177	184	191	196	200	207	214	219
41	240	156	161	168	180	185	192	199	204	209	216	223	228
42	250	163	168	175	188	193	200	208	213	218	225	233	238
43	260	169	174	182	195	200	208	216	221	226	234	242	247
44	270	176	181	189	203	208	216	224	230	235	243	251	257
45	280	182	188	196	210	216	224	232	238	244	252	260	266
46	290	189	194	203	218	223	232	241	247	252	261	270	276
47	300	195	201	210	225	231	240	249	255	261	270	279	285
48	310	202	208	217	233	239	248	257	264	270	279	288	295
49	320	208	214	224	240	246	256	266	272	278	288	298	304
50	330	215	221	231	248	254	264	274	281	287	297	307	314
51	340	221	228	238	255	262	272	282	289	296	306	316	323
52	350	228	235	245	263	270	280	291	298	305	315	326	333
53	360	234	241	252	270	277	288	299	306	313	324	335	342
54	370	241	248	259	278	285	296	307	315	322	333	344	352
55	380	247	255	266	285	293	304	315	323	331	342	353	361
56	390	254	261	273	293	300	312	324	332	339	351	363	371
57	400	260	268	280	300	308	320	332	340	348	360	372	380

*After locating the training load, round it down to the nearest 5-pound (2.3-kg) increment or weight-stack plate. To convert the training load into kilograms, use the conversion chart found on page 212.

Figure 13.1 shows an example of this shortcut. In the example, the lifter completed seven repetitions with 90 pounds (40.9 kg) and wants a training load that represents 80 percent of 1RM. Completing seven repetitions with 90 pounds (40.9 kg) equals a 1RM of 110 pounds (50 kg) using the procedures to predict the 1RM explained in step 12 (see page 160). In table 13.7, under the column heading "1RM," 110 pounds (50 kg) is found on line 19. The number at the intersection of line 19 and the 80 percent column is the calculated training load (88), which is rounded down to the nearest 5 pounds (2.3 kg) or weight-stack plate (85 pounds [38.6 kg]).

Repetitions completed	Repetition factor
1	1.00
2	1.07
3	1.10
4	1.13
5	1.16
6	1.20
(7) reps →	(1.23) → × 90 = 110 lbs (rounded)
8	1.27
9	1.32
10	1.36

Adapted, by permission, from V.P. Lombardi, 1989, *Beginning weight training: The safe and effective way* (Dubuque, IA: William C. Brown), 201. © The McGraw-Hill Companies, Inc.

Line	1RM	65%	67%	70%	75%	77%	80%	83%	85%	87%	90
1	20	13	13	14	15	15	16	17	17	17	
2	25	16	17	18	19	19	20	21	21	22	
3	30	20	20	21	23	23	24	25	26	26	
4	35	23	23	25	26	27	28	29	30	30	
5	40	26	27	28	30	31	32	33	34	?	
6	45	29	30	32	34	35	36	37	38		
7	50	33	34	35	38	39	40	42	43		
8	55	36	37	39	41	42	44	46	47		
9	60	39	40	42	45	46	48	50	51		
10	65	42	44	46	49	50	52	54	55		
11	70	46	47	49	53	54	56	58	60		
12	75	49	50	53	56	58	60	62	64		
13	80	52	54	56	60	62	64	66	68		
14	85	55	57	60	64	65	68	71	72		
15	90	59	60	63	68	69	72	75	77		
16	95	62	64	67	71	73	76	79	81		
17	100	65	67	70	75	77	80	83	85		
18	105	68	70	74	79	81	84	87	89		
19	110	72	74	77	83	85	(88)	91	94		
20	115	75	77	81	86	89	92	95	98	1	

Training load percentage*

88 rounded down to the nearest 5 lbs. = 85 lb. training load

Figure 13.1 A shortcut for determining training loads.

Regardless of the method you use to create variations in intensity, you should perform as many repetitions of the MJEs as possible on the heavy days of your workout schedule, but keep them within the designated ranges during the Wednesday (light) and Friday (medium) workouts. This means that even though you may be capable of performing more repetitions with the lighter Wednesday and Friday loads, don't do it! In the SJEs, use the two-for-two rule for increasing loads.

Program Variation *Self-Assessment Quiz*

Mark the correct choice in each of the following statements. Answers are on page 205.

1. The repetitions performed on light and medium training days allow you to [___ apply the overload principle ___ recover from the overloading].

2. You should perform [___ the designated number of repetitions ___ as many repetitions as possible] on heavy training days.

3. The two variables that have been manipulated in the eight-week training cycle in table 13.6 are [___ repetitions and sets ___ loads and sets].

Maximizing Training Drill 1. **Shortcut Method**

This drill is designed to give you experience in the shortcut method of determining training loads using table 13.7. Assume that you performed the "as many repetitions as possible test" with 150 pounds (68.2 kg) and were able to complete 8 repetitions. If you want to use 75 percent of 1RM, what is the correct training load? Remember to use the procedures for predicting the 1RM from step 12 first (refer to the example in figure 12.4, page 163), and then use this 1RM value and the 75 percent 1RM column of table 13.7 to locate the correct training load. Round this value down to the nearest 5-pound (2.3 kg) increment or weight-stack plate. The answer is on page 205.

Success Check

- Associate the number of repetitions completed with the repetition factor (see table 12.4).

- Multiply the repetition factor by the load lifted to determine the 1RM.

- Locate and circle where your 1RM value is located in the "1RM" column (see table 13.7).

- Identify the desired training percentage column.

- Identify the intersecting point.

- Round this value down to determine the training load.

Maximizing Training Drill 2.
Determining Training Loads in a Program

To give you another opportunity to determine training loads, fill in training loads for the program shown in figure 13.2. In this drill, assume that five repetitions were performed with 105 pounds (47.7 kg). Answers are on page 205.

Success Check

- Associate the number of repetitions completed with the repetition factor (see table 12.4, page 163).

- Multiply the repetition factor by the load lifted to determine the 1RM.

- Locate and circle the 1RM value on table 13.7.

- Multiply the desired training percentage by the 1RM.

- Round this value down to determine the training load.

Figure 13.2   Practice determining training loads.

	Monday (H)	Wednesday (L)	Friday (M)
Week 1	80% 1RM = _____	67% 1RM = _____	75% 1RM = _____

SUCCESS SUMMARY FOR PROGRAM VARIABLES

Training intensity can be varied in many ways, but the most common methods involve manipulating the amount of the load, the number of sets and repetitions, and the number of training days. The use of periodization programs that include aggressive training weeks followed by a week (or weeks) of less aggressive training provide an appropriate overload and an opportunity for the body to recover and make significant gains.

As you become more experienced, you may want to learn more about periodization. Detailed discussions can be found in the texts by Baechle and Earle (2008) and Earle and Baechle (2004).

Step 14, the last step, allows you to apply everything you have learned about developing your own weight training program. You will be prompted to use your knowledge about the program design variables described in the last two steps and apply the overload and specificity concepts to design a program that meets your needs. Enjoy the challenge!

Before Taking the Next Step

Honestly answer each of the following questions. If you answer yes to all of the questions, you are ready to move on to step 14.

1. Have you completed the self-assessment quiz and the drills and checked your answers?

2. Do you understand how to manipulate training variables to maximize training?

3. Can you calculate new training loads using table 12.4 and table 13.7?

Designing Your Own Program

This is your chance to apply all that you have learned to create your own weight training program. In this step, you will use your knowledge of program design variables and apply the specificity and overload concepts to design a program that meets your needs. If you follow the procedures in this step as they are presented, you will develop a well-conceived, individualized weight training program. You may also use these tasks to assess your level of comprehension about how to design a weight training program.

Follow this sequence when developing your program:

1. Determine the goal of your training program.

2. Select the exercises you will perform.

3. Decide the frequency of your training sessions.

4. Place your exercises in order.

5. Calculate your training loads.

6. Determine how many repetitions to perform.

7. Decide how many sets of each exercise to complete.

8. Determine how long to rest between sets and exercises.

9. Choose how you will add variety to the program.

DETERMINE YOUR TRAINING GOAL

Think about why you want to weight train and the outcomes that you most desire to experience from training. Below, place a check mark next to your most important training goal; then read the paragraphs that follow to understand which type of program is most aligned with that goal.

The most important goal that I have for training is to improve my (choose one)

- ☐ Muscular endurance
- ☐ Hypertrophy
- ☐ Muscular strength
- ☐ General muscular toning
- ☐ Body composition (reproportioning)
- ☐ Other (describe: _____)

Choosing a single training goal will help you focus your efforts and maximize your results, but it does not prevent you from selecting another training goal when you are ready to make a change later!

- **Goal: Muscular endurance.** As you have learned, your present program is designed to improve muscular endurance. If this is the outcome you want from training, you will not need to make many changes. Simply try to increase the number of repetitions from 15 to 20 and increase the numbers of sets for all exercises. If possible, also try to reduce the length of time you rest between sets and exercises; doing so will definitely contribute to higher level of muscular endurance.

- **Goal: Hypertrophy.** To gain muscle size, you need to use loads that will keep your repetitions between 8 and 12, and you probably will need to include more exercises and complete more sets. You may *want* to initially focus on developing the chest and arms but try to avoid the common tendency of spending too much time on these muscles and not spending enough time developing the legs. Also, be aware that as you increase the number of exercises, sets (to as many as six per exercise), and the number of training days, the amount of time you will need to commit to your program will increase substantially.

- **Goal: Muscular strength.** If muscular strength is your goal, you will need to handle loads that are quite a bit heavier than those you are currently using. An important thing to remember (from step 12) is that to safely and effectively handle the heavier loads associated with developing strength, you must have fairly long rest periods (2 to 5 minutes) between sets. A common mistake is to rush through sets. Doing so slows recovery and compromises your ability to exert a maximum effort in succeeding sets. Additionally, remember that only your MJEs should be assigned heavy loads (85 percent of 1RM or heavier), and lifting those loads will require several warm-up sets and a spotter.

- **Goal: General muscle toning.** Follow the guidelines presented for muscular endurance programs to meet this goal. If you do not experience satisfactory changes in muscle tone from that type of program, switch to a program designed to produce hypertrophy.

- **Goal: Body composition (reproportioning).** If reproportioning your body is your goal, it is likely that you believe you are carrying too much body fat, not enough muscle, or both. Consider doing three things: Follow a hypertrophy training program to increase muscle mass, select your foods more carefully, and begin an aerobic exercise program to increase the number of calories you expend. For the hypertrophy program, simply follow the guidelines presented in this text. When selecting foods, make sure that you eat a balanced diet, increase your intake of complex carbohydrates, and decrease your intake of fats. Most normal diets will supply the needed amount of protein. For more information on nutrition, refer to the book by Clark (2008). For directions on how to design an aerobic exercise program, use the text by Baechle and Earle (2005).

- **Goal: Other.** If you have special needs, such as improving athletic performance in weightlifting, powerlifting, or other sports activities, read the chapter by Baechle and Conroy (1996), and texts by Baechle and Earle (2008), Earle and Baechle (2004), and journals published by the National Strength and Conditioning Association. You will find helpful guidelines for designing and implementing programs for young athletes in the text by Faigenbaum and Westcott (2009). If your interest is bodybuilding, consult the text by Evans (2011). The texts by Westcott and Baechle (2007) and Baechle and Westcott (2010) will be helpful for those interested in programs designed specifically for older populations. The book by Baechle and Earle (2005) is helpful if you are looking for sample programs for body shaping, muscle toning, strength, or cross-training.

SELECT EXERCISES

The exercises included in your current program are few, but they work all seven of the muscle groups. It is a basic program that will benefit from the addition of exercises areas as you become better trained and more experienced.

If your goal is to increase muscular endurance, size, or strength in a particular body part, adding another exercise that is designed to train those muscles is a good idea. If you add exercises, do not select more than two per muscle group at this time, and do not include more than a total of 12 exercises if you are following a three-days-a-week program. As you will remember from step 12, the four-days-a-week split program allows you to add more exercises. Thus you may choose to include three exercises for a particular body part if you decide to follow a four-days-a-week program.

Using table 14.1, decide for which of the muscle groups listed you want to select exercises or to which you want to add emphasis (meaning you already have one

Table 14.1 Exercise Selection

Days	Muscle area	Exercises	
	Total body		
	Chest		
	Back		
	Shoulders		
	Biceps		
	Triceps		
	Legs (thigh and hip)		
	Calves		
	Core		

exercise for this muscle area, and you want to add one more). Before completing this task, you may want to refer to steps 3 through 10 to review the explanations and descriptions of the various free-weight and machine exercises. Remember to consider the equipment needed and the spotter requirements. After considering your goals, write the name of the exercise to the right of the appropriate muscle areas.

DECIDE ON TRAINING FREQUENCY

Decide whether you are going to use a three-days-a-week or four-days-a-week (split) program. If you decide on a split program, determine how you will divide the exercises among the four days. You may need to reconsider the number of exercises you have selected. Remember, you can include more exercises in a split program than in a three-days-a-week program.

Choose how often you plan to weight train:

- Three-days-a-week program (If you chose this option, skip to the next section on "Arranging Exercises.")

- Four-days-a-week split program (If you chose this option, go down to the next line.)

For a split program, choose which schedule you will follow:

- Chest, shoulders, and triceps on two days; legs, back, and biceps on two other days

- Upper body on two days; lower body on two other days

Once you make these decisions, go back to table 14.1 and, under the "Days" column, write down the days of the week that you will train each muscle area.

ARRANGE EXERCISES

Next decide how you will arrange these exercises within a workout. Step 12 pointed out several options. Choose which arrangement you plan to use:

- Perform MJEs before SJEs.

- Alternate PS exercises with PL exercises.

Now look again at the exercises that you want to include in your program and decide how you will determine the order in which you will perform them. Rewrite, in order, the exercises from table 14.1 in table 14.2, using the left-hand column if you plan to follow a three-days-a-week program and the right-hand column for a four-days-a-week split program.

Table 14.2 Exercise Arrangement

THREE-DAYS-A-WEEK PROGRAM		FOUR-DAYS-A-WEEK SPLIT PROGRAM	
Order	Exercise	Order	Exercise
1		Monday/Thursday* exercises	
2		1	
3		2	
4		3	
5		4	
6		5	
7		6	
8		7	
9		Tuesday/Friday* exercises	
10		8	
11		9	
12		10	
		11	
		12	
		13	
		14	

*Or whatever days you plan to train each group of muscle areas for your split program.

Now copy the exercises in the proper order from table 14.2 on the chart in figure 14.1 (for a three-days-a-week program) or figure 14.2 (for a four-days-a-week program). The four-days-a-week chart assumes that you are training on Mondays/Thursdays and Tuesdays/Fridays.

Weight training workout chart (three days a week)

Name _____

	Muscle group	Exercise	Load × sets × reps	Set	Day 1					Day 2					Day 3				
					1	2	3	4	5	1	2	3	4	5	1	2	3	4	5
1				Wt.															
				Reps															
2				Wt.															
				Reps															
3				Wt.															
				Reps															
4				Wt.															
				Reps															
5				Wt.															
				Reps															
6				Wt.															
				Reps															
7				Wt.															
				Reps															
8				Wt.															
				Reps															
9				Wt.															
				Reps															
10				Wt.															
				Reps															
11				Wt.															
				Reps															
12				Wt.															
				Reps															

(Column heading: Week)

Body weight _____

Date _____

Comments _____

From T.R. Baechle and R.W. Earle, 2012, *Weight training: steps to success*, 4th ed. (Champaign, IL: Human Kinetics).

Figure 14.1 Workout charts for a three-days-a-week program.

Weight training workout chart (four days a week)

Name _____

Week _____

Monday/Thursday exercises	Load × sets × reps	Set	Day 1—Monday					Day 3—Thursday				
			1	2	3	4	5	1	2	3	4	5
1		Wt.										
		Reps										
2		Wt.										
		Reps										
3		Wt.										
		Reps										
4		Wt.										
		Reps										
5		Wt.										
		Reps										
6		Wt.										
		Reps										
7		Wt.										
		Reps										

Tuesday/Friday exercises	Load × sets × reps	Set	Day 2—Tuesday					Day 4—Friday				
			1	2	3	4	5	1	2	3	4	5
8		Wt.										
		Reps										
9		Wt.										
		Reps										
10		Wt.										
		Reps										
11		Wt.										
		Reps										
12		Wt.										
		Reps										
13		Wt.										
		Reps										
14		Wt.										
		Reps										

Body weight

Date

Comments

From T.R. Baechle and R.W. Earle, 2012, *Weight training: steps to success*, 4th ed. (Champaign, IL: Human Kinetics).

Figure 14.2 Workout chart for a four-days-a-week program

CALCULATE YOUR TRAINING LOADS

Based on the specificity concept, the overload principle, your primary training goal, and the type of exercise (multijoint or single-joint), determine the warm-up and training load for each exercise.

First select your approach. Review the methods for determining training loads presented in step 12. Decide which approach you will take when deciding on the amount of load to use for each exercise:

- 12- to 15RM method

- 1RM method

You may want to use both methods, especially if you are well trained and want to begin a program that provides higher intensities in the advanced MJEs. If so, you should make a list of which exercises will be assigned loads from which method.

If you are following a muscular strength program, you need to identify the approach you will follow:

- Pyramid training

- Multiple sets, same load training

Now determine starting loads. Using the guidelines presented in step 12, calculate the loads for the exercises selected. To save time, you can use the shortcut method of determining training loads from step 13 on page 182. Record these loads on the chart in figure 14.1 (for a three-days-a-week program) or figure 14.2 (for a four-days-a-week split program) in the "Load × sets × reps" box. Leave room for the sets and repetitions numbers. Do this now, but take your time because this process is the most important of all the steps in creating your program.

DECIDE HOW MANY REPETITIONS TO PERFORM

Based on your training goal, the load calculations from the previous task, and table 12.6 (see page 167), determine the number of repetitions you intend to perform in each set for each exercise:

- 12 to 20 repetitions

- 6 to 12 repetitions

- 1 to 6 repetitions for MJEs and 8 to 12 repetitions for SJEs

- Other (describe: _____)

Fill in the number of repetitions for each exercise in the "Load × sets × reps" box next to the loads you just wrote in. Leave room for the number of sets.

DECIDE HOW MANY SETS OF EACH EXERCISE TO COMPLETE

Depending on your training status, training goal, available time to work out, and information in table 12.6 (see page 167), decide on the number of sets you plan to perform in each exercise listed on your workout chart in the "Load × sets × reps" box. You might want to assign more sets to the MJEs.

DECIDE ON THE LENGTH OF REST PERIODS

Based on your training goal and table 12.6 (see page 167), decide how much rest you will allow yourself between sets and exercises:

- 20 to 30 seconds (for muscular endurance)
- 30 to 90 seconds (for hypertrophy or with SJEs in the muscular strength program)
- 2 to 5 minutes (for muscular strength)

CAUTION: Allow yourself a little extra time between sets of a new exercise so that you do not become too fatigued and perform it incorrectly.

DECIDE HOW TO VARY THE PROGRAM

Consult step 13, if necessary, and then decide which method you will use to vary the load intensities:

- Within-the-week variation
- Between weeks or week-to-week variation
- Cyclical variation (periodization)

If you chose the within-the-week variation, decide which approach you will take to vary the loads lifted in the MJEs:

- Same load in each set (heavy, light, medium days)
- Pyramid approach
- Heavy-light split approach

If you chose the between-week variation, decide which method you will follow to vary the load intensities in the MJEs:

- Same load in each set with increases between weeks
- Within- and between-week load variations

197

If you chose the cyclical variation, decide when you will make load increases for the MJEs:

- Weekly

- Every two weeks

- Other (describe: _____)

Now decide how you plan to make load increases for the MJEs:

- Increase loads by a specified percentage. (How much? ___ percent)

- Increase loads based on retesting. (How often to retest? Every ___ weeks)

Finally, decide on the number of training weeks that you will complete before a week of low-intensity training is scheduled:

- 4 weeks

- 5 weeks

- 6 weeks

Program Design Drill.
Design an Eight-Week Program

Depending on which method of program variation you plan to follow, on a separate sheet of paper, fill in the loads, repetitions, and sets for all exercises for an eight-week period. Use the Success Check points below to make sure that you have considered all of the important program design variables.

Success Check

- Select one primary training goal.
- Select exercises.
- Decide training frequency.
- Arrange exercises.
- Calculate training loads.
- Determine number of repetitions to perform.
- Determine number of sets of each exercise to complete.
- Decide on the length of the rest periods.
- Decide how to vary the program.

SUCCESS SUMMARY FOR CREATING YOUR PROGRAM

The activities included in this step required you to apply everything you have learned about designing a weight training program. You are capable of designing a program that meets your current needs, but you may want to look ahead and consider how to modify or manipulate the program design variables during the next year.

In the process of learning about equipment, exercise techniques, and program design variables, you likely gained a better appreciation of the expertise required to devise weight training programs for athletes in various sports and individuals within special populations (prepubescents, seniors, pregnant women, and those with osteoporosis, hypertension, or injuries). If you fall into one of these categories or if you are training such individuals, you may want to refer to the texts by Baechle and Westcott (2010) or Earle and Baechle (2004).

Remember, no program will allow you to reach your training goal unless you approach it with a positive attitude. If you train hard, train smart, and eat sensibly, you are guaranteed success and the opportunity to enjoy wearing your workouts proudly.

Answer Key

STEP 3—ANSWERS

Practice Procedures Drill *Practice Procedure Quiz*

1. b
2. b
3. c
4. c
5. b
6. b
7. a

STEP 12—ANSWERS

Selecting and Arranging Exercises Drill 1
Specificity Concept Quiz

C / I?		Exercise	Primary muscle group trained
C	1.	Back squat	Legs (thigh and hip)
C	2.	Supine triceps extension	Back of the upper arm
I	3.	Standing press	Back
C	4.	Standing heel raise	Calf
C	5.	Lunge	Legs (thigh and hip)
I	6.	Side plank	Shoulders
C	7.	Bent-over row	Upper back
C	8.	Trunk curl	Core
C	9.	Shoulder shrug	Shoulders
I	10.	Upright row	Back
C	11.	Preacher curl	Front of the upper arm
C	12.	Knee curl	Legs (back of the thigh)
I	13.	Lat pulldown	Chest
C	14.	Knee extension	Legs (front of the thigh)
I	15.	Hang clean	Shoulders

STEP 12—ANSWERS *(CONTINUED)*

Selecting and Arranging Exercises Drill 2
Balanced (Paired) Exercises Quiz

1. I; Knee extension—Knee curl

2. C

3. I; Dumbbell chest fly—Bent-over row (or Machine row or Seated row)

Selecting and Arranging Exercises Drill 3
Arranging Exercises Quiz

	Exercise	MJE	SJE	PS	PL
1.	Back squat	X		X	
2.	Supine triceps extension		X	X	
3.	Standing press	X		X	
4.	Standing heel raise		X	X	
5.	Lunge	X		X	
6.	Side plank		X		X
7.	Bent-over row	X†			X
8.	Trunk curl		X		X
9.	Shoulder shrug		X		X
10.	Upright row	X†			X
11.	Preacher curl		X		X
12.	Knee curl		X		X
13.	Lat pulldown	X†			X
14.	Knee extension		X	X	
15.	Hang clean	X		Both; a total-body exercise	

NOTE: The quiz for drill 3 (Arranging Exercises) appears in step 12 before the "Manipulate Program Variables" section, which is where you learn that only a certain group of MJEs qualify for the 1RM method of determining training loads. All other MJEs, such as those marked with a "†", still involve two or more joints changing angles as the exercise is performed, but they are not recommended for 1RM testing.

1RM Load *Self-Assessment Quiz*

1. 1-repetition maximum

2. lunge

3. 20

Increasing Loads *Self-Assessment Quiz*

1. completing 2 or more repetitions above the goal in the last set in two consecutive workouts

2. heavier

Number of Repetitions *Self-Assessment Quiz*

1. fewer

2. load

Number of Sets *Self-Assessment Quiz*

1. 2

2. recruit

Length of the Rest Period *Self-Assessment Quiz*

1. more

2. an effect

Muscular Endurance Program *Self-Assessment Quiz*

1a. light

1b. 60-67%

1c. 12-20

1d. 2-3

2. 20 to 30 seconds

Hypertrophy Program *Self-Assessment Quiz*

1a. moderate

1b. 67-85%

1c. 6-12

1d. 3-6

1e. 30-90 seconds

2. superset

Muscular Strength Program *Self-Assessment Quiz*

1a. heavy

1b. 85-100%

1c. 1-6

1d. 3-5

1e. 2-5 minutes

2. 170 pounds (77.3 kg)

3. progressive overload principle

4. pyramid; multiple set–same load

5. SJEs

Manipulating Program Variables Drill 2
Determining Load Ranges

Goal	1RM		Training load (%)		Training load range*
Hypertrophy	85 pounds (38.6 kg)	×	67-85%	=	55 pounds (25 kg) to 70 pounds (31.8 kg)
Muscular strength	85 pounds (38.6 kg)	×	85-100%	=	70 pounds (31.8 kg) to 85 pounds (38.6 kg)
Muscular endurance	85 pounds (38.6 kg)	×	60-67%	=	50 pounds (22.7 kg) to 55 pounds (25 kg)

*Round down load to nearest 5 pounds (2.3 kg) or closest weight-stack plate.

Frequency of Training *Self-Assessment Quiz*

1. on a regular basis

2. fewer

3. less

4. split

STEP 13—ANSWERS

Program Variation *Self-Assessment Quiz*

1. recover from the overloading

2. as many repetitions as possible

3. loads and sets

Maximizing Training Drill 1 *Shortcut Method*

The load that should be lifted to perform as many repetitions as possible is 150 pounds (68.2 kg). Using table 12.4, we find that the repetition factor for 8 repetitions is 1.27. We multiply 150 pounds by 1.27 to get 190.5 pounds (86.6 kg). On table 13.7, 190 pounds is on line 35. Line 35 intersects with the 75 percent column at 143. Rounded down, this number equals a training load of 140 pounds (63.6 kg).

Maximizing Training Drill 2 *Determining Training Loads in a Program*

The load used is 105 pounds (47.7 kg), with gives us a repetition factor of 1.16 for 5 repetitions, according to table 12.4. If we multiply 105 pounds by 1.16, we get 121.8 pounds (55.4 kg), which rounds to 120 pounds (54.5 kg) as the predicted 1RM. We find 120 pounds on line 21 in table 13.7. For a training load of 80 percent, find the number at the junction of line 21 and 80 percent in table 13.7 (96, rounded down to 95 [43.2 kg]). For a training load of 67 percent, find the number at the junction of line 21 and 67 percent in table 13.7 (80 pounds [36.4 kg]). For a training load of 75 percent, find the number at the junction of line 21 and 75 percent in table 13.7 (90 pounds [40.9 kg]).

	Monday (H)	Wednesday (L)	Friday (M)
Week 1	80% 1RM = 95 pounds (43.2 kg)	67% 1RM = 80 pounds (36.4 kg)	75% 1RM = 90 pounds (40.9 kg)

Glossary

1RM method—The process of determining the maximum amount of weight that a lifter can lift for one repetition in an exercise.

absolute strength—A comparative expression of strength based on actual load lifted.

aerobic—In the presence of oxygen.

aerobic capacity—A measurement of physical fitness based on maximum oxygen uptake.

aerobic energy system—The metabolic pathway that requires oxygen for the production of adenosine triphosphate (ATP).

aerobic exercise—Exercise during which muscle cells receive enough oxygen to continue at a steady state. Some examples are walking, biking, running, swimming, and cross-country skiing.

all-or-none law—A muscle fiber that is stimulated by the brain will contract maximally or not at all; a stimulus of insufficient intensity will not elicit a contraction.

alternated grip—A grip in which one hand is supinated and the other hand is pronated so that both thumbs point in the same direction; also called a *mixed grip*.

amino acids—Nitrogen-containing compounds that form the building blocks of protein.

anabolic effects—Tissue building that is conducive to the constructive process of metabolism.

anabolic steroid—Testosterone, or a substance resembling it, which stimulates body growth anabolically.

anaerobic—In the absence of oxygen.

anaerobic exercise—Exercise during which the energy needed is provided without the need to use inspired oxygen. Examples include weightlifting and the 100-meter sprint.

androgenic effect—The masculinizing properties of a substance.

assume—To get into a stable body position before performing an exercise.

atrophy—A decrease in the cross-sectional size of a muscle fiber due to lack of use, disease, or starvation.

barbell—A piece of free-weight equipment that is used in two-arm exercises; a long bar on which weight plates may be placed on both ends.

basal metabolic rate (BMR)—The amount of energy, expressed in calories, that the body requires to carry on its normal functions at rest.

bench press bench—A bench with uprights where a barbell is racked or held.

bodybuilding—A sport that involves weight training to develop muscle hypertrophy.

body composition—The quantification of the body's components, especially fat and muscle. It can be measured by various methods, such as skinfold calipers, girth measurement, impedance, or underwater (hydrostatic) weighing.

calorie—The measure of the amount of energy released from food or expended in metabolism.

cambered bar—A bar that has the same characteristics as a standard or an Olympic barbell except that its curves create natural places to grasp the bar to place an isolated training stress on certain muscle groups during an exercise; also called an *EZ-curl bar*.

carbohydrate (CHO)—A group of chemical compounds composed of carbon, hydrogen, and oxygen. Examples include sugars, starches, and cellulose. It is a basic foodstuff that contains approximately 4 calories per gram.

cardiac muscle—A type of striated (involuntary) muscle tissue located only in the heart.

cardiorespiratory fitness—The efficiency of the heart and lungs to deliver oxygen to the working muscles.

circuit training—A variation of interval training that uses some type of external resistance and timed work and rest periods.

closed grip—A grip in which the fingers and the thumbs are wrapped (closed) around the bar.

coefficient—A number that represents a certain percent of a lifter's body weight.

collar—The part of a barbell or dumbbell that keeps weight plates from sliding toward the hands.

common grip—A grip in which the hands are placed at roughly shoulder-width, equidistant from the weight plates.

compound set—A set in which two exercises that work the same muscle group are performed consecutively without resting between them. For example, a compound set for the chest would be a set of the bench press exercise followed immediately by a set of the dumbbell chest fly exercise; often misnamed as *superset*.

concentric muscular action—A type of muscular action characterized by tension being developed as the muscle is shortening (e.g., the upward phase of a biceps curl).

conditioning—A process of improving the capacity of the body to produce energy and do work.

cool-down—The period in which an individual performs light or mild exercise immediately after completing a training session. Its primary purpose is to gradually return to a resting state.

core—The central section of the body that includes the low back, torso, and abdominal muscles.

core exercise—An exercise that trains the low back, torso, or abdominal muscles.

delayed-onset muscle soreness—The effect of becoming sore 24 to 48 hours after a strenuous training session.

dumbbell—A piece of weight training equipment typically used to perform single-arm exercises, consisting of a short bar with weight plates on each end.

dynamic—Exercise involving movement; its opposite is *static*.

dynamic muscle action—Involves movement and consists of concentric, eccentric, or both types of muscle activity.

eccentric muscular action—A muscular action in which there is tension in the muscle, but the muscle lengthens rather than shortens. An example is the lowering phase of the biceps curl exercise where the biceps muscles lengthen even though there is tension in the muscle. Eccentric muscle actions are associated with the muscle soreness commonly experienced in weight training.

ergogenic aid—A substance used to enhance performance.

essential body fat—The fat stored in the bone marrow as well as in the heart, lungs, liver, spleen, kidneys, muscles, and lipid-rich tissues throughout the central nervous system. A minimum value of 3 percent for males and 12 percent in females is needed for normal physiological functioning.

exercise prescription—An exercise program based on present fitness levels and desired goals or outcomes.

extension—A movement occurring at a joint that increases its angle. The downward movement of the triceps pushdown is an example of elbow extension.

EZ-curl bar—A bar that has the same characteristics as a standard or an Olympic barbell except that its curves create natural places to grasp the bar to place an isolated training stress on certain muscle groups during an exercise; also called a *cambered bar*.

false grip—A grip on a bar in which the thumbs do not wrap around the bar; also called an *open grip*.

fast-twitch muscle fiber—A type of skeletal muscle fiber that is highly recruited during explosive muscular activities such as sprinting, shot putting, and competitive weightlifting.

fat—A basic foodstuff that contains approximately 9 calories per gram and should constitute 25 to 30 percent of the diet. In the body, it is essentially nonmetabolically active tissue.

fixed-resistance machine—A machine that features a pre-set pulley design often by pulling or pushing on a handle attached to a cable–pulley arrangement. Sometimes a chain or flat belt is used in place of the cable.

flat-back—An upper and lower position of the back (spine) that is not rounded or hunched over.

flexibility—The ability of a joint to move through its available range of motion.

flexion—A movement occurring at a joint that decreases its angle. The upward movement of the biceps curl is an example of elbow flexion.

free weight—A type of weight training equipment that allows nonrestrictive effect on joint movement (in contrast to a machine that creates a predetermined movement pattern).

frequency—The number of training sessions in a given time period; for example, three times a week.

gynecomastia—Male breast enlargement as a side effect of taking anabolic steroids.

handoff—An assist by a spotter to move a bar off its supports for the lifter.

hang—A body position where a barbell is hanging from the hands at a mid-thigh, partially-squatting position.

hormone—A chemical substance secreted by an endocrine gland that has a specific effect on activities of other cells, tissues, and organs.

hydrostatic weighing—A method of body composition assessment that uses underwater weighing to determine the density of the body so that the percentage of body fat can be calculated. Generally accepted as one of the most accurate methods of determining body composition; also called *underwater weighing*.

hyperplasia—An increase in muscle size due to muscle fibers splitting and forming separate fibers.

hypertension—High blood pressure.

hypertrophy—An increase in the cross-sectional area of the muscle. More simply stated, an increase in muscle size.

hyperventilation—Excessive ventilation of the lungs due to increased depth and frequency of breathing, usually resulting in the elimination of carbon dioxide. Accompanying symptoms include low blood pressure and dizziness.

intensity—The relative stress level that an exercise stimulus places on the body.

ischemia—A condition in which the supply of oxygen to working tissues is reduced.

isokinetic—A type of muscular activity in which movements occur at a constant velocity as controlled by an ergometer. The term describes only a concentric muscle action.

isometric contraction—A type of muscular activity in which there is tension in the muscle but it does not shorten (there is no movement); also called a *static contraction*.

isotonic—Implies a dynamic event in which the muscle generates the same amount of force through the entire movement. Such a condition occurs infrequently, if at all, in human performance; therefore, the word should not be employed to describe human exercise performance. In loose terms, however, it is used to describe dynamic free-weight exercises.

knurling—The rough area on a barbell that helps a lifter to keep a better grip on the bar.

lean body weight—Body weight minus fat weight; also called *nonfat* or *fat-free weight*.

ligament—Dense connective tissue that attaches the articulating surfaces of bones together.

light-to-heavy pyramid training—A training method in which each succeeding set in a group of sets becomes heavier.

linear—A periodization model where the intensity is consistently increased and the volume is reduced over time.

load—The amount of weight lifted.

lock—A mechanism placed on a bar outside of the weight plates to hold the plates on the bar.

macrocycle—A time period or cycle of training within a periodized training program that typically lasts from one month up to four years for Olympic athletes; the common length is one year.

mesocycle—A time period within a periodized training program that typically lasts several weeks to several months; the common length is one month. Two or more mesocycles make up one macrocycle.

metabolism—The sum total of the chemical changes or reactions occurring in the body.

microcycle—A time period or cycle of training within a periodized training program that is part of a mesocycle that typically lasts one to four weeks; the common length is one week. Two or more microcycles make up one mesocycle.

microtrauma—The result of muscle tissue becoming torn down from a strenuous training session.

mixed grip—A grip on a bar that involves having one hand in an underhand grip and the other in an overhand grip; also called an *alternated grip*.

motor unit—An individual motor nerve and all the muscle fibers it innervates (stimulates).

multijoint exercise (MJE)—An exercise that trains larger muscles and involves two or more joints changing angles as the exercise is performed. In this book, the advanced MJEs are the bench press, machine chest press, standing press, seated press, lunge, leg press, back squat, hang clean, and push press.

multiple sets—Performing more than one set of an exercise (after a rest period) before moving to a different exercise.

multiple sets–same load training—A training method in which each set in a group of sets uses the same load.

muscle-bound—A term that has been used to describe people who weight train as having limited joint flexibility, which can be due to a lack of muscle activity or to chronic use of poor lifting and stretching methods. The term is inappropriate to describe those who practice sound weight training techniques and proper stretching exercises.

muscle balance—Training a muscle group's opposing muscle group to create balanced strength and muscular symmetry.

muscle group—In this book, seven muscle groups are named: chest, shoulders, back, triceps, biceps, core, and legs.

muscular endurance—The capacity of a muscle to repeatedly contract over a period of time without undue fatigue.

muscular strength—The capacity of a muscle to exert maximally one time.

negative work—A form of exercise that is more appropriately called *eccentric exercise* in which a muscle lengthens rather than shortens when it is under tension.

neural-learning factor—Ability to recruit more fibers and select those that are most effective to lift a load or perform an exercise.

neural—Referring to the nervous system.

neuromuscular—Involving both the nervous and the muscular systems.

nutrition—The study of how carbohydrate, protein, fat, vitamins, minerals, and water provide the energy, substances, and nutrients required to function during rest and exercise conditions.

Olympic bar—A bar approximately seven feet (2.1 m) long that has rotating sleeves on the ends to hold the weights. The diameter of the bar is about 1 inch (2.5 cm) in the middle and 2 inches (5 cm) at the ends. It weighs 45 pounds (20.5 kg); with Olympic locks, typically 55 pounds (25 kg).

Olympic weightlifting—A form of competitive lifting that involves a contest of maximum strength levels in the clean and jerk exercise and the snatch exercise.

one-repetition maximum (1RM)—The resistance (load) with which a lifter can perform only one repetition using a maximum effort.

open grip—A grip on a bar in which the thumbs do not wrap around the bar; also called a *false grip*.

overhand grip—A grip on a bar in which the palms are pronated (face down) or away and with the knuckles up.

overload principle—Placing a stress on a muscle that is slightly greater than what the muscle is accustomed to so that, over time, the muscle adapts and then can tolerate that stress.

overtraining—A state of undue mental or physical fatigue (or both) brought about by excessive training that does not permit full recovery between training sessions.

oxygen uptake—The ability of the heart and lungs to take in and utilize oxygen that is commonly expressed in milliliters of oxygen per kilogram of body weight per minute (ml/kg/min).

percent body fat—The percentage of body weight that is comprised of fat. Recommended ranges are 14 to 18 percent for men and 22 to 26 percent for women.

periodization—A method of varying a training program that systematically schedules high-intensity and low-intensity training periods.

physical fitness—An ability to be physically actively that is determined by an individual's level of cardiorespiratory endurance, muscular strength, muscular endurance, flexibility, and body composition.

pivot point—The axle on which a cam of a variable-resistance machine rotates.

positive work—The action of a muscle during a concentric muscle action.

powerlifting—A competitive sport that involves demonstrating maximum strength levels in the back squat, bench press, and deadlift exercises.

power zone—The thigh and hip area of the body that include the largest muscles of the body: the quadriceps (front of the thigh), hamstrings (back of the thigh), and gluteals.

practice procedures—Activities that teach a lifter how to perform weight training exercises.

program design—The "workout recipe" of a well-conceived weight training program.

program design variables—The components of a well-conceived weight training program that include exercise selection, exercise arrangement, loads, repetitions, sets, rest period length, and training frequency.

progressive overload—Systematically applying overload over time.

pronated grip—Grasping a bar at mid-body height so that the palms face down and the thumbs face each other; also called an *overhand grip*.

prone—Lying face down; the opposite of *supine*.

protein—A food substance that contains approximately 4 calories per gram and provides amino acids that are essential for tissue growth and repair.

pyramid training—A method of multi-set training in which loads get progressively heavier (ascending pyramid) or lighter (descending pyramid).

quick-lift exercise—A weight training exercise characterized by explosive movements; examples include the power clean, snatch, and hang clean exercises.

range of motion (ROM)—The available movement range through which a body part rotates about a joint.

recruit—To use or call into action a muscle during or for an exercise.

recruitment—The activation of motor units by the neuromuscular system during muscular activity.

relative strength—A comparative measure of strength based on a variable such as total body weight or lean body weight.

repetition—Performing the movement phases of an exercise one time; often abbreviated as *rep*.

repetition maximum (RM)—The maximum load that can be lifted over a given number of repetitions before fatiguing. For example, a 10RM load is the maximum weight that can be lifted for 10 repetitions.

resistance training—Any method or form of exercise that requires a lifter to exert force against resistance.

rest period—The amount of time between two sets or two exercises.

selectorized—Machines that allow a lifter to choose or select a load on the weight stack by using an inserted pin or key.

set—The number of repetitions consecutively performed in an exercise without resting.

single-joint exercise (SJE)—An exercise that isolates one muscle and involves movement at only one joint as the exercise is performed. Examples include the biceps curl, triceps extension, and standing heel raise.

skeletal muscle—A type of muscle tissue that attaches to bone via tendons and responds to voluntary stimulation from the brain.

slow-twitch muscle fiber—A type of skeletal muscle fiber that has the ability to repeatedly work without undue fatigue. This type of muscle fiber is highly recruited for long distance running, swimming, and cycling events.

smooth muscle—A type of involuntary muscle tissue located in the eyes and in the walls of the stomach, intestines, bladder, uterus, and blood vessels.

specificity concept—Training the body in a specific manner for a specific outcome.

split program—A weight training program characterized by scheduling certain exercises (for example, upper-body or lower-body exercises) on separate, alternate days.

squat rack—Supports (sometimes called *standards*) that hold a barbell at shoulder height; typically used so that a lifter can position a bar on his or her back in preparation for the back squat exercise.

standard barbell—A bar that is 1 inch (2.5 cm) in diameter and typically weighs approximately 5 pounds (2.3 kg) per foot.

static stretch—Involves holding a static position by passively placing the muscles and connective tissues on stretch.

sticking point—The point in the range of motion of an exercise at which moving the weight or resistance is the most difficult.

strength plateau—A temporary leveling off of progress in a strength training program.

strength training—The use of resistance training to increase one's ability to exert or resist force for the purpose of improving strength, athletic performance, or both. The training may use free weights, the lifter's own body weight, machines, or other devices to attain this goal.

striated muscle—Skeletal muscle that possesses alternate light and dark bands, or striations. Except for the cardiac muscle, all striated muscles are voluntary.

superset set—A set in which two exercises that work opposing muscle groups are performed consecutively without resting between them. For example, a superset for the arms would be a set of the biceps curl exercise followed immediately by a set of the triceps pushdown exercise.

supinated grip—A grip on a bar in which the palms face upward and thumbs point in opposite directions; also called an *underhand grip*.

supine—Lying on the back, facing upward; the opposite of *prone*.

tendon—Dense connective tissue that attaches a muscle to a bone.

testosterone—The principal male hormone that is produced by the testes and is responsible for male sex characteristics.

therapeutic index—The ratio between a steroid's anabolic effects and its androgenic effects.

three-days-a-week program—Training on Monday, Wednesday, and Friday; Tuesday, Thursday, and Saturday; or Sunday, Tuesday, and Thursday. In a three-days-a-week program, all exercises are performed each training day.

trial load—A load that is used to determine if the load is acceptable or correct to use in the actual training program.

two-for-two rule—A guideline indicating sufficient improvement in muscular fitness is achieved when a lifter is able to perform two or more repetitions above the intended or goal number in the last set on two consecutive training days.

underhand grip—A grip on a bar in which the palms face upward (supinated) while the thumbs face away from each other.

underwater weighing—A method of body composition assessment that weighs a person underwater to determine the density of the body so that the percentage of body fat can be calculated. Generally accepted as one of the most accurate methods of determining body composition; also called *hydrostatic weighing*.

undulating—A periodization model where the intensity and volume is varied day to day and from workout to workout; also called *nonlinear*.

Universal—A brand of resistance equipment.

variable-resistance machine—A weight machine that has a kidney-shaped wheel or cam that creates a more even stress on the muscles.

variation—Manipulating the frequency, intensity, duration, or mode of an exercise program to promote maximal improvements with minimal opportunities for overtraining, either mentally or physically.

vitamin—An organic material that acts as a catalyst for vital chemical (metabolic) reactions.

volume—The total work performed per exercise, session, or week. Volume is calculated as the total number of repetitions times the total amount of weight lifted or as the number of sets times the number of repetitions.

warm-up—A period in which an individual performs light or mild exercise immediately before a training session. Its primary purpose is to prepare the body for more intense exercise.

weight training—The use of resistance training to increase one's ability to exert or resist force for the purpose of improving strength, muscular endurance, hypertrophy, athletic performance, or a combination of these goals. The training may use free weights, the lifter's own body weight, machines, or other devices to attain this goal. In more recent years, this term has been replaced by *strength training*.

work in—Sharing a piece of equipment with other people by letting them use the equipment during the rest period between sets.

Conversion Chart

To convert pounds to kilograms, multiply pounds by 0.453593. For an estimate, use 0.45. In this chart, numbers are rounded down to the nearest quarter. For example, 185 multiplied by 0.453593 equals 83.9147. The kilograms are given here as 83.75 rather than 84.00. To convert kilograms to pounds, multiply kilograms by 2.2046. For a quick estimate, use 2.2.

POUNDS TO KILOGRAMS				KILOGRAMS TO POUNDS			
Pounds	Kg	Pounds	Kg	Kg	Pounds	Kg	Pounds
2.50	1.00	205.00	92.75	2.50	5.50	95.00	209.25
5.00	2.25	210.00	95.25	5.00	11.00	97.50	214.75
10.00	4.50	215.00	97.50	7.50	16.50	100.00	220.25
15.00	6.75	220.00	99.75	10.00	22.00	102.50	225.75
20.00	9.00	225.00	102.00	12.50	27.50	105.00	231.25
25.00	11.25	230.00	104.25	15.00	33.00	107.50	236.75
30.00	13.50	235.00	106.50	17.50	38.50	110.00	242.50
35.00	15.75	240.00	108.75	20.00	44.00	112.50	248.00
40.00	18.00	245.00	111.00	22.50	49.50	115.00	253.50
45.00	20.25	250.00	113.25	25.00	55.00	117.50	259.00
50.00	22.50	255.00	115.50	27.50	60.50	120.00	264.50
55.00	24.75	260.00	117.75	30.00	66.00	122.50	270.00
60.00	27.00	265.00	120.00	32.50	71.50	125.00	275.50
65.00	29.25	270.00	122.25	35.00	77.00	127.50	281.00
70.00	31.75	275.00	124.50	37.50	82.50	130.00	286.50
75.00	34.00	280.00	127.00	40.00	88.00	132.50	292.00
80.00	36.25	285.00	129.25	42.50	93.50	135.00	297.50
85.00	38.50	290.00	131.50	45.00	99.00	137.50	303.00
90.00	40.75	295.00	133.75	47.50	104.50	140.00	308.50
95.00	43.00	300.00	136.00	50.00	110.00	142.50	314.00
100.00	45.25	305.00	138.25	52.50	115.50	145.00	319.50
105.00	47.50	310.00	140.50	55.00	121.25	147.50	325.00
110.00	49.75	315.00	142.75	57.50	126.75	150.00	330.50
115.00	52.00	320.00	145.00	60.00	132.25	152.50	336.00

POUNDS TO KILOGRAMS				KILOGRAMS TO POUNDS			
Pounds	Kg	Pounds	Kg	Kg	Pounds	Kg	Pounds
120.00	54.25	325.00	147.25	62.50	137.75	155.00	341.50
125.00	56.50	330.00	149.50	65.00	143.25	157.50	347.00
130.00	58.75	335.00	151.75	67.50	148.75	160.00	352.50
135.00	61.00	340.00	154.00	70.00	154.25	162.50	358.00
140.00	63.50	345.00	156.25	72.50	159.75	165.00	363.75
145.00	65.75	350.00	158.75	75.00	165.25	167.50	369.25
150.00	68.00	355.00	161.00	77.50	170.75	170.00	374.75
155.00	70.25	360.00	163.25	80.00	176.25	172.50	380.25
160.00	72.50	365.00	165.50	82.50	181.75	175.00	385.75
165.00	74.75	370.00	167.75	85.00	187.25	177.50	391.25
170.00	77.00	375.00	170.00	87.50	192.75	180.00	396.75
175.00	79.25	380.00	172.25	90.00	198.25	182.50	402.25
180.00	81.50	385.00	174.50	92.50	203.75		
185.00	83.75	390.00	176.75				
190.00	86.00	395.00	179.00				
195.00	88.25	400.00	181.25				
200.00	90.50						

References

Baechle, T.R., and B.P. Conroy. 1996. Preseason strength training. In *Team Physician's Handbook.* 2nd ed. M. Mellion, M. Walsh, and G. Shelton (eds.). New York, NY: Hanley and Belfus.

Baechle, T.R., and R.W. Earle. 2005. *Fitness Weight Training.* 2nd ed. Champaign, IL: Human Kinetics.

Baechle, T.R., and R.W. Earle. 2008. *Essentials of Strength Training and Conditioning.* 3rd ed. National Strength and Conditioning Association. Champaign, IL: Human Kinetics.

Baechle, T.R., and W.L. Westcott. 2010. *Fitness Professional's Guide to Strength Training Older Adults.* 2nd ed. Champaign, IL: Human Kinetics.

Clark, N. 2008. *Nancy Clark's Sports Nutrition Guidebook.* 4th ed. Champaign, IL: Human Kinetics.

Earle, R.W., and T.R. Baechle. 2004. *NSCA's Essentials of Personal Training.* National Strength and Conditioning Association. Champaign, IL: Human Kinetics.

Evans, N. 2011. *Men's Body Sculpting.* 2nd ed. Champaign, IL: Human Kinetics.

Faigenbaum, A., and W.L. Westcott. 2009. *Strength and Power for Young Athletes.* Champaign, IL: Human Kinetics.

Hoeger, W.K. 1995. *Lifetime Fitness, Physical Fitness, and Wellness.* 4th ed. Englewood, CO: Morton.

Hoffman, J.R., W.J. Kraemer, S. Bhasin, T. Storer, N.A. Ratamess, G.G. Haff, D.S. Willoughby, and A.D. Rogol. 2009. Position stand on androgen and human growth hormone use. *Journal of Strength and Conditioning Research* 23(5): S1–S59.

Katz, J.N. 2006. Lumbar disc disorder and low-back pain: Socioeconomic factors and consequences. *Journal of Bone and Joint Surgery.* (Am) 88 Suppl. 2:21-24.

Komi, P.V. 2002. *Strength and Power in Sport (Encyclopedia of Sports Medicine Series).* Champaign, IL: Human Kinetics.

Lombardi, V.P. 1989. *Beginning Weight Training: The Safe and Effective Way.* Dubuque, IA: Brown.

McAtee, R., and J. Charland. 2007. *Facilitated Stretching.* 3rd ed. Champaign, IL: Human Kinetics.

Westcott, W.L. 2003. *Building Strength and Stamina.* 2nd ed. Champaign, IL: Human Kinetics.

Westcott, W.L., and T.R. Baechle. 2007. *Strength Training Past 50.* 2nd. ed. Champaign, IL: Human Kinetics.

About the Authors

Thomas R. Baechle, EdD, CSCS,*D-R, NSCA-CPT,*D-R, competed in Olympic-style weightlifting and powerlifting and was a weight training instructor and a strength and conditioning coach for 20 years. Currently he is a professor and chair of the exercise science department at Creighton University, where he directed phase III cardiac rehabilitation for 16 years. He is a cofounder and past president of the National Strength and Conditioning Association (NSCA), and for 20 years he was the executive director of the NSCA Certification Commission.

Baechle has been recognized as the force behind the creation of the Certified Strength and Conditioning Specialist and NSCA-Certified Personal Trainer examination programs. He has received awards for outstanding teaching and service from Creighton University, the NSCA's most coveted awards (Strength and Conditioning Professional of the Year and the Lifetime Achievement Award), and other honors from international associations and organizations. Baechle also served on state and regional boards associated with the American Alliance for Health, Physical Education, Recreation and Dance (AAHPERD); as president of the National Organization of Competency Assurance (now called the Institute for Credentialing Excellence); and as a member of various other regional, national, and international boards. Baechle has authored, coauthored, or edited 13 other books, including the popular *Fitness Weight Training*.

Roger W. Earle, MA, CSCS,*D, NSCA-CPT,*D, is the Higher Education and Professional (HEP) Division director for Human Kinetics. In this role, he oversees the content and the process of acquiring books and online courses in the physical activity field. He is also the head sport training coach for Threshold Sports Training, a comprehensive performance training business.

Previously, Earle worked with coauthor Thomas Baechle as the associate executive director for the NSCA Certification Commission, where he was responsible for promoting the Certified Strength and Conditioning Specialist and NSCA-Certified Personal Trainer examination programs. He also served as the head strength and conditioning coach and was a faculty member of the exercise science and athletic training department at Creighton University in Omaha. Earle has over 25 years of experience as a personal fitness trainer, competitive sport conditioning coach, and behavior modification facilitator for people of all ages and fitness levels. He has extensively lectured at national and international conferences about designing personalized exercise and training programs, weight management, and exercise motivation. Earle coauthored the first and second editions of *Fitness Weight Training* and coedited both the *NSCA's Essentials of Personal Training* and the second and third editions of *Essentials of Strength Training and Conditioning*.

You'll find other outstanding strength training resources at

www.HumanKinetics.com/strengthtraining

In the U.S. call 1-800-747-4457

Australia 08 8372 0999 • Canada 1-800-465-7301
Europe +44 (0) 113 255 5665 • New Zealand 0800 222 062

 **HUMAN KINETICS**
The Premier Publisher for Sports & Fitness
P.O. Box 5076 • Champaign, IL 61825-5076 USA